AFTERWAR

OTHER BOOKS BY NANCY SHERMAN

The Untold War:
Inside the Hearts, Minds, and Souls of our Soldiers

Stoic Warriors:
The Ancient Philosophy Behind the Military Mind

Making a Necessity of Virtue:
Aristotle and Kant on Virtue

The Fabric of Character:
Aristotle's Theory of Virtue

Aristotle's Ethics: Critical Essays
editor

AFTERWAR

HEALING THE MORAL WOUNDS
OF OUR SOLDIERS

NANCY SHERMAN

OXFORD
UNIVERSITY PRESS

OXFORD
UNIVERSITY PRESS

Oxford University Press is a department of the University of
Oxford. It furthers the University's objective of excellence in research,
scholarship, and education by publishing worldwide.

Oxford   New York
Auckland   Cape Town   Dar es Salaam   Hong Kong   Karachi
Kuala Lumpur   Madrid   Melbourne   Mexico City   Nairobi
New Delhi   Shanghai   Taipei   Toronto

With offices in
Argentina   Austria   Brazil   Chile   Czech Republic   France   Greece
Guatemala   Hungary   Italy   Japan   Poland   Portugal   Singapore
South Korea   Switzerland   Thailand   Turkey   Ukraine   Vietnam

Oxford is a registered trademark of Oxford University Press
in the UK and certain other countries.

Published in the United States of America by
Oxford University Press
198 Madison Avenue, New York, NY 10016

Library of Congress Cataloging-in-Publication Data
Sherman, Nancy, 1951–
Afterwar : healing the moral wounds of our soldiers / Nancy Sherman.
pages cm
Includes bibliographical references and index.
ISBN 978-0-19-932527-6 (cloth : alk. paper)   1. Soldiers—United States—Psychology.
2. Veterans—Mental health services—United States.   3. Soldiers—Mental health
services—United States.   4. Combat—Psychological aspects.   5. Guilt and culture—United
States.   I. Title.
U22.3.S439 2015
616.85'21206—dc23
2014034743

1 3 5 7 9 8 6 4 2
Printed in the United States of America
on acid-free paper

To Marshall, Kala, and Jonathan
The Loves of My Life

Yes. A man will talk about how he'd like to escape from living folks. But it's the dead folks that do him the damage. It's the dead ones that lay quiet in one place and dont try to hold him, that he cant escape from.

—William Faulkner,
Light in August

Contents

FOREWORD

Expanding Our Understanding of the Moral Dimension of War

America may be tired of war, but from all indications, war is not yet tired of America. The United States is entering its 15th year of war. Those being recruited and trained by our armed forces were 4, 5, and 6 years old at the time of the September 11, 2001 attacks. Yet with Al Qaeda affiliates spreading in North, West, and East Africa; the continued conflict in Yemen; the Taliban's intent to control Afghanistan; and ISIS, formerly Al Qaeda in Iraq, erasing the border between Syria and Iraq and solidifying its control over a self-declared Islamic State, more war is on the horizon. A renewed interest in the moral aspects of war, therefore, is only natural; for war inherently risks, uses, ends, and changes lives—of the innocent, of citizens-who-become-soldiers, and sometimes of the political community itself.

I want to claim a relatively unique perspective on war's moral dimension. I was a field commander—retiring from the Army as a Lieutenant General in 2008 after over 37 years of active service—and I am a moral philosopher.

I am an infantryman, a paratrooper, and a Ranger. I led units as small as a platoon of about 40 soldiers to a corps of over 46,000. I've worked and trained with the Armies of many nations: British, French, German, Polish, Italian, Korean, Japanese, Thai, Iraqi, and Afghan. And I've commanded U.S. and multi-national troops during operations in Haiti, 1994; Bosnia, 1999; and Iraq, 2007–2008. During "the surge" in Iraq I was responsible for accelerating the growth of the Iraqi Security Forces in size, capacity, and confidence. As a moral philosopher, I taught philosophy and just war theory at West Point, 1982–1985; just war theory at Dickinson College, Penn State Law School, and the Army War College, 2012–2013 as the Omar Bradley Chair in Strategic Leadership; and received a doctorate in Philosophy from Johns Hopkins University in 2014. I have both studied and lived war's moral dimension.

Traditional just war theory—*jus ad bellum*, the justifications for going to war, and *jus in bello*, right actions in the conduct of war—has been the way moral philosophers and others have categorized war's moral dimension. It is also the way soldiers and commanders learn about the moral aspects of their profession. Traditional just war theory categories, however, have been found wanting. *Jus ad bellum*, for example, assumes that war is primarily between nation states. Non nation-state entities were treated as sub cases, usually in the form of a nation's internal rebellion or civil war. Now, not only have they risen from a "sub case," but they are also waging war in the space between crime and war. In the face of the post-9/11 wars, traditional just war theorists, whether philosophers or lawyers, are rethinking the principles of *jus ad bellum* to account for non-nation-state entities like Al Qaeda and the kind of wars they are waging. One need only google "*jus ad bellum* and the war against terrorism" to see the breadth of this rethinking.

The principles governing traditional *jus in bello* are also being challenged. Previously, the principles of *jus in bello* were focused narrowly on right conduct during combat. The principle describing a legitimate act of war, the combatant/noncombatant distinction, the principles of proportionality, double effect and double intent, and due care/due risk—all address the moral responsibilities of those fighting a war. Traditional *jus in bello* principles arise from the tension between winning and fighting well. This account has been the framework, for example, used to discuss the moral and legal use of drones. This traditional account is necessary but insufficient, for it leaves out the moral responsibilities of those sending citizens-who-become-soldiers to war in the first place.

War-waging responsibilities are the *jus in bello* responsibilities of senior political and military leaders at the strategic level. These leaders decide and act far from the battlefield, yet have a direct effect on how the war is fought, whether the war is prolonged unnecessarily, and whether the lives used are used in war are used well or wasted. These strategic, war-waging responsibilities arise from three interlocked and shared responsibilities of the senior political and military leaders who wage a war: (1) set and achieve war aims by making strategy, policy, and military campaign decisions that increase the probability of being right, or at least less wrong than one's enemy; (2) translate those decisions into action to achieve war aims at the least cost—in lives and resources—and least risk to one's political community, then adapt decisions and actions as the war unfold; and (3) do all of the foregoing while observing the war convention and maintaining legitimacy, along with public support of the war effort.

Waging war justly is connected to the following question: "What does the nation owe its citizens-who-become-soldiers?" This question grabs media attention in that it concerns the availability and quality of post-war treatment of soldiers who are wounded—physically, emotionally, or psychologically. This attention is both necessary and welcome, for it reminds all citizens that institutional and fiscal support will be required beyond a war's end. The question, however, begs a deeper answer.

One such answer comes from expanding the traditional focus of *jus in bello*. That is, in recognizing that the conduct of war involves both fighting a war and waging a war and that war waging responsibilities and principles must be included to provide a complete account of *jus in bello*.

Nancy Sherman's *Afterwar: Healing the Moral Wounds of our Soldiers* provides a second, deeper answer; one that involves just war theory's still-developing *jus post bellum*. Thus far, the *jus post bellum* discussion has been primarily about how warring parties end war justly. But *Afterwar* takes a much more interesting and innovative approach by looking at war's enduring mark on the souls of those who fight. Professor Sherman goes to the very heart of the question, "What does the nation owe its citizens-who-become-soldiers?" She pulls back the curtain of war and exposes us, the political community on whose behalf soldiers fight, to the moral injuries war necessarily produces. Then she reminds us of our communal responsibility to those we send to fight for us.

She does not diminish the importance of identifying *jus post bellum* principles that apply to states or other warring entities; rather, she takes on much more profound tasks: understanding the injuries war inherently causes to a person's moral sense, and the implications of those injuries. *Afterwar* gains its significant credibility from extended and probing discussions Professor Sherman has had with many veterans and their families. In giving voice to the moral dimensions of these discussions the book brings to the fore topics previously left either unsaid, or spoken of only among veterans and a small handful of others. In doing so, Professor Sherman reminds those of us who sent others to do our fighting of our responsibilities in their coming home.

War changes lives. War is the realm of the paradoxical: the morally repugnant *is* the morally permissible, and even the morally necessary. Killing, even enemy combatants; destroying, even legitimate wartime targets; and razing or properties and lands, even when using proportional force—all involve taking away the most sacred and essential element of a human being—his or her life, his or her livelihood. War justifies—more importantly, demands—what, in peacetime, would be unjustifiable: the destruction of the lives and happiness of others. Those who fight live this paradox day in and day out. In a very real way, war is the abnormal turned normal. Such a life begs important questions, questions that often don't arise until years after a war: "What kind of person am I to have done this?" "How do I square my sense of self with what I had to do?" "How can I lead a good life, given what I did—even if what I did was justified?" Reconciling war's paradoxes, without dismissing the humanity of those whose lives were taken or whose livelihood destroyed, involves dealing with moral injury.

In war, even when everything goes well, people die or are seriously wounded. Unfortunately, war is the realm of error, mistake, and wrong judgments. War is, therefore, also the realm of guilt. But sometimes this guilt is misplaced: "Why didn't I do more?" "Why wasn't I there with them?" "Why did

I survive?" "Why did I fail my buddies?" Or, "Why did I fail those I led?" War often creates a gap between the ideals of self image and the realities of wartime behavior, between how things "should be" and how things "are."

The questions above reveal the internal struggle that is associated with the limits of responsibility, leadership, and vigilance; and the moral angst that comes with living in the gap between. War guilt often extends beyond the limits of reason. War often causes soldiers and leaders to transform omissions or commissions for which they are not culpable into transgressions worthy of blame. This is not just a psychological slight-of-hand. It is an injury to one's sense of self and of one's sense of obligation to others. It is a sort of moral dissonance between what soldiers or leaders expected of themselves and what they actually did or could do given the realities of combat. Addressing this dissonance means treating a moral injury.

War sometimes involves sacrifices made in vain. Losing a battle or engagement, fighting a battle that is unconnected to a larger purpose, being killed or maimed in an unjust, or imprudent, or unnecessary battle or war—any one of these can give rise to the sense of betrayal. From any one can emerge a sense of having one's life used for no good purpose. Any one of these can give birth to a sense of being suckered into losing or risking the most precious thing a human being has—his or her life—or worse: being suckered into ending someone else's life for no good reason. This kind of smoldering resentment illuminates a deep moral truth: each of us—even our enemies—is a human being, not an object. As human beings, each of us has moral worth beyond our instrumental utility to a task or to society. Demanding that a soldier risks his or her life for no good reason is to treat that soldier as an object, not a human being. This is, perhaps, the ultimate moral injury, another manifestation of war's hellishness.

All of us are instruments to one degree or another, and when citizens become soldiers they certainly understand that their lives can be used in ways that, quite simply, would be wrong in civilian life. But no soldier is a mere instrument. Even in war, soldiers remain human beings and their lives retain worth. Coming to grips with being used means healing a moral injury.

War alienates and separates. Much of what those who fight wars experience or do is simply alien to any sense of "normality." Those left behind, soldiers often say, "have no clue." This feeling is not just an experiential difference, it is a moral dislocation. It is a separation of individuals from the important and necessary ties with friends, spouses, families, and communities. None of us is the fully autonomous individual that stereotypes like to project. Each of us is part of multiple important networks of relationships and communities. War separates soldiers from these networks, not only physically because they leave, but morally because of the alien territory war creates. Disengagement upon return from war widens the separation, expands the moral dislocation, and thereby increases the moral injury already present.

These four examples of moral injury are merely illustrative of *Afterwar*'s depth. The book contains much more. Fighting a war on behalf of a political community necessarily involves being in situations where moral injury will result. Sending people to fight necessarily sends them into situations where moral injury will result.

Not only does Sherman dive deep to describe the moral heart of war, but she also resurfaces to discuss ways to heal moral injuries. Sherman could be called the "Jacques Cousteau of *jus post bellum*."

Injury opens the door to recovery, and Sherman combines her training in both psychology and philosophy to describe approaches to moral healing. Self empathy, self-forgiveness, re-experiencing, and re-envisioning moral frameworks are several of the ways she describes the moral reparative work that has to be done. She examines trust, resentment, betrayal, hope, meaning, and purpose and their roles in healing the soldier's soul. In each she introduces the role the network of relationships—the very network that is injured by alienation and separateness—plays in healing. Significantly, *Afterwar* highlights the role of the community in moral healing. "Thank you for your service" simply does not meet the community's obligation to those it sent to fight on its behalf. Members of the community and the community as a whole: both are obliged to learn more of what those who fought have gone through on their behalf, to understand them, to engage them, and to help them live well. It's not a matter of gratitude; it's a matter of reciprocity. *Jus post bellum*, Sherman is reminding us all, includes a very personal and very communal dimension.

Flourishing after war is also connected to how well those who fight on our behalf are prepared for the moral ambiguity, the havoc on the conscience, and the torments that come to even the most conscientious soldier. Preparing soldiers for war is not just a matter of technical and tactical training, not just a matter of building confidence and cohesion in units. Preparing soldiers for war also includes—or should include—helping soldiers figure out what war will do to them morally, and thereby to the network of relationships and communities within which each of them lives. This dimension of *jus post bellum* is—or should be—as much a subject of professional military education and training for combat as any other.

The moral philosopher in me is drawn to *Afterwar*'s creative analysis of this personal and communal aspect of war's moral dimension. The commander in me is drawn to Sherman's use of this analysis. Whether describing the injury or the treatment, Sherman introduces, and sometimes invents, concepts and language to guide the reader through the interior aspects of war's moral dimension. This is something traditional just war theory leaves unattended. *Afterwar* gives voice to the remarkable men and women who have fought on our behalf, who bring home enormous competencies, who possess unbelievable grit, and whose potential to contribute to America has no bounds. It also gives voice to what we, the political community who sent them to war, truly owe them.

James M. Dubik, Ph.D.
Lieutenant General
U.S. Army, Retired
Senior Fellow, the Institute for the Study of War

AFTERWAR

PROLOGUE

This book is about homecomings from the wars in Iraq and Afghanistan and the struggle to find inner peace afterward. It is an intimate look at a handful of the 2.6 million women and men who have served in these longest wars in American history, and what it feels like to return to a country that hasn't really felt war. There has been no war tax and little economic pain. As some soldiers put it to me, "We've been at war while the country has been at the mall." In the United States, less than half a percent of the population has served. This has consequences *now* for all of us, on a personal level. For many of us don't know how to begin a conversation with a veteran, how to ask where she's been and what she's been through, and how things are for her now. Each side feels the distance. This book is not a plea for national service. I am not prepared to make that case. What I am prepared to argue for is the moral necessity for each of us to be personally engaged in the largest reintegration of American service members into civilian society since Vietnam. The mil/civ walls have to come down. It is critical for the moral healing of soldiers.

We have heard much about institutional failures in services for military families and veterans, from unconscionable waiting lists to get medical appointments at Veterans Administration (VA) hospitals to military hospital malfeasance, to homelessness, joblessness, and inequities in the adjudications of military and civilian law. But what we have not heard enough about is our own inner struggles as civilians with what we mean when we say, "Thank you for your service," and why we can't say much beyond that. We have learned that we are supposed to separate the war from the warrior, but we are stuck there, not getting beyond that and haven't really explored why. The upshot is that we don't feel comfortable talking substantively with veterans about their wars, despite the fact that we teach veterans, work with them, sit next to them on flights, greet them at airports, and so on. War talk still seems taboo. And this is so even for those of us who are good with words, accustomed to meeting new people, whether as lawyers, negotiators, realtors, businessmen and women, high-tech managers and engineers, educators, doctors, architects, scientists, artists, and more. This is my world, and most of those I know, ranging from age eighteen through ninety-five, tell me routinely that they don't know how to talk about war with those who are coming home. Most worry about broaching subjects that are private, crossing lines, opening floodgates that will leave each side morally and emotionally vulnerable and unprepared.

And yet almost all the service members I speak with are eager to talk, so that they can begin to bring their wars home and normalize, somehow, in civilian society. These recent wars are not my dad's war, World War II, for which the distance of a faraway war mixed with etiquette about polite talk at home and in society meant that war wasn't a fit subject of discussion for those who didn't see it. That was my experience as a child of a WWII Army medic, the niece of a Marine who fought *mano a mano* in Okinawa, and the niece of an Army enlisted man who fought in Italy and the Pacific. And there were other service members in my childhood life, some who even came to visit in uniform. But we didn't talk about war then. It wasn't a fit subject for family evenings. But we are not living in the 1950s, and the current generation of veterans is not my father's. Even the toughest, stoic military types I know, among them Special Forces guys I teach, often want to share parts of their wars—so long as they can feel a sense of safety and trust. Many other veterans want the same. Let us figure out how to make this happen.

This book is my own journey in figuring out how to do this. It is not a how-to book. It is an exploration of the kinds of reactions that underlie what we say and don't say. It is about the emotions that bind us and that tear us apart, whether they be guilt, shame, resentment, rage, trust, wariness, hope, forgiveness, or empathy. These emotional attitudes are the subtext for our sense of alienation or connection, whether we to veterans and veterans to us; or veterans to each other and to their commanders, troops, veteran health-care providers, and civilian leaders; or to each of us, in uniform or not, to ourselves. Relationships, both interpersonal and intrapersonal, are built on emotional reactions and attitudes, many of them morally weighted and reflecting our views of whether we can count on each other and be viewed as worthy—respect-worthy and responsible. And so recovery is a matter of shared moral engagement. The afterwar belongs to us all.

We have a sacred moral obligation to those who serve, whether or not we agree with the causes of those wars and whether or not those who serve agree with them. Those moral obligations are institutional, both governmental and nongovernmental: veterans are morally owed the best possible resources across the widest swath of medical, psychiatric, social, legal, and technical services. But the obligations and expectations are also interpersonal, one-on-one. We have duties to each other for care and concern: normative expectations and aspirations that we can count on each other, we can trust and hope in each other, and we can be lifted by each other's support.

I have embedded, in a manner of speaking, with most of the service members you will meet in this book. That is, I have embedded for a time in their communities (and mine) stateside, in classrooms with veterans, in seminars with active service members, at think tanks where military and civilians work and research together, at service academies and postgraduate military schools, at military hospitals and rehab gyms where limbless veterans recreate themselves with unimaginable resilience, in behavioral health programs where that same resilience paired with a sense of safety and trust enables a soldier or Marine or sailor or wingman to keep going for another day, and at suicide review boards, where the light has gone out.

I share this world from my perch as a philosopher trained in Aristotle and the Stoics, in Kant, and in moral psychology and the emotions. And

I bring to bear research training in psychoanalysis and a longstanding professional affiliation with the mental health community. I am not a therapist and I have never had patients. But I know well the need for empathy in relationships and how sorely many soldiers and veterans, some barely eighteen or nineteen years old, long to be understood so that they can understand themselves. Telling your story is about processing the hard-to-touch moral wounds of war. For most, the wounds that come with holding oneself and others to account for the ravages of war will be wounds that last for a lifetime. Anyone who knows veterans, or has visited the Vietnam Wall or the beaches of Normandy, knows that the moral psyche does not easily erase loss that is tinged with the nag of "Did I do enough?" "Was the cause worth it?" "Did we fight for each other to fill the moral vacuum of not having a just cause for war?" For among those for whom the band of brothers and sisters *is* the cause, stricter rules of engagement ("courageous restraint," as General Stanley McChrystal called his counterinsurgency directive in Afghanistan) can seem harsh and hard to justify or accept. And what now of the unraveling of Iraq and the political instability in Afghanistan? As I write, thousands of soldiers and Marines who fought in the Sunni Triangle, in Baghdad, Fallujah, and Tikrit, and in outposts farther north, in Talafar and Mosul, are talking to each other online, in disbelief as they watch the undoing of their hardest won and bloodiest battles. Whatever our politics, we are in this together, civilian and soldier, as we go forward and recover from over a decade of war. There are broader lessons here. Constructive moral engagement, it's worth remembering, is not just for after war and at home. It is for always, as wide as we can expand our circles, over borders and checkpoints and differences, supporting each other in our shared humanity to live good and decent lives.

Josh Mantz (in cammies) with children outside Baghdad

CHAPTER 1

————— ★ —————

REBORN
BUT DEAD

NUMB

On April 21, 2007, Captain Josh Mantz died in Baghdad and came back to life after flatlining for fifteen minutes—long past the time doctors routinely mark as the cutoff point for lifesaving measures, given the likely damage to the brain without vital signs. Not only did Josh survive, but he returned to his unit five months later to resume his platoon command. Yet despite the remarkable revival and media tour as the resilience poster boy for the Department of Defense, Josh emotionally crashed four years later. "It's the moral injury over time that really kills people," he said. "Soldiers lose their identity. They don't understand who they are anymore." And he added, "Most people don't appreciate the awful weight of that moral injury."

What specifically weighs on him is that he survived, but his Staff Sergeant Marlon Harper did not. The details are wrenching: Mantz was guiding his troops near the Shiite rebel stronghold of Sadr City when a sniper fired a round of bullets that penetrated Harper's left arm, severing his aorta. The hot molten round fused with Harper's armor plate, forming a projectile the size of a human fist that ricocheted into Josh's upper right thigh, severing his femoral artery. Injured and dazed, Mantz administered first aid on Harper as he waited for medical assistance. A young medic arrived and immediately went to work on Mantz, not Harper, probably because an aortal wound is less viable than a femoral wound. Having died and returned "didn't bring me closer to God," Mantz says. "'Ah, He must have great plans for you,' people say. But what about Staff Sergeant Harper? I ask."

Josh Mantz struggles with survivor guilt, of having luck, miraculous luck and state-of-the-art medical interventions on his side, and yet experiencing that good luck as an awful betrayal of his buddy. It is one type of "luck guilt," as I call it in *The Untold War*. There are other kinds, like that of John Prior whom I write about there and here, who suffers from the bad luck on his watch of a turret gun misfiring and taking the life of one of his privates; though Prior was fully exonerated, like guilt a parent feels for the accidental death of her child, it wouldn't abate.

Other service members whom we will meet in the coming pages struggle to understand their own idiosyncratic experiences of war and the moral injuries they endured. The notion of an injury that is moral is at least as old as the preaching of Bishop Joseph Butler in early eighteenth-century England. The term has been revived in clinical circles, and though not exclusive to veteran populations, it is gaining currency in the military behavioral health arena. Roughly speaking, it refers to experiences of serious inner conflict arising from what one takes to be grievous moral transgressions that can overwhelm one's sense of goodness and humanity. The sense of transgression can arise from (real or apparent) transgressive commissions and omissions perpetrated by oneself or others, or from bearing witness to the intense human suffering and detritus that is a part of the grotesquerie of war and its aftermath. In some cases, the moral injury has less to do with specific (real or apparent) transgressive acts than with a generalized sense of falling short of moral and normative standards befitting good persons and good soldiers.

No single moral injury fits all. There is no easy diagnosis and code number. Scientific research models can belie both the variety of suffering felt and the centrality of a sense of responsibility that underlies much of the suffering. For the individual soldier, acknowledging moral injury often requires coming to feel the fine grain of the emotions and conceptualizing the moral implications for honor and dignity—and a sense of one's own accountability and that of others. It is not easy for those committed to lives of action and combat readiness to explore the interior of the self. It can feel narcissistic, indulgent, a way of dodging real work, a kind of malingering. But those I talk to are ready, more than ready, to understand how war has changed their lives—morally and psychologically, as well as, often, physically.

So we shall meet T. M. Gibbons-Neff, a Marine now at Georgetown University, who in the early days, having just returned from Marja fresh with losses of his buddies, felt waves of resentment surge when students would banter lightly about military interventions without much thought about who goes to war and who doesn't come back. For Lalo Panyagua, another Marine who served in Marja, what wracks him is the constant thought that he should have done more to save three of his troops. And it is his spouse, Donna Hernandez, through her remarkable vision and spunky wit, who has seen him through and found a way to rekindle his hope in himself in his new civilian life, shorn of both uniform and the sense of dignified purpose and identity it offered him. In the case of Jeff Hall, the overwhelming moral wound he feels pounds through in shame, and a sense of betrayal, that he was so hamstrung by an incompetent command that he couldn't properly help the Iraqi family he was charged with assisting in the burial of their dead. "Sally," who served in Iraq in the Air Force, worries about betraying the cause and mission if she reports that she is being stalked and sexually harassed to the point of feeling threatened in the mess hall. For Tom Fiebrandt, an intelligence officer who severed near Mosul, Iraq, the overwhelming relief from the hounding guilt of not being there for his buddy killed by an IED comes in the form of a moral epiphany—that he can't be there all the time for everyone in his command. This leads to profound self-empathy and self-compassion. Alysha Haran, a mid-level naval officer brought to captain's mast (a disciplinary hearing aboard ship) on a trumped-up charge, finds a reprieve from crippling self-doubt when her new senior commander, an admiral with compassion and a willingness to mentor, recognizes that an important part of her identity, as a former dancer and actress, is not a detriment to the Navy but a strong asset that can breathe life into a stodgy organization. In the case of Dan Berschinski, a West Pointer who lost the bottom half of his body in Afghanistan, the key to his postwar adaptation hangs on determination tethered to hope, and a remarkably upbeat disposition.

What emerges in these brief snapshots is the variety of moral injuries suffered and the variety of repair. Just as there is no one type of moral injury, so too there is no one-size-fits-all model of a soldier. Each experiences war differently, with a panoply of factors playing a role: individual family and childhood histories, life experiences before and during war, age, education, physical and psychological training, moral reflectiveness, relationships on the battlefield and at home, nature and number of deployments, risk levels and exposure, command climate, mission preparedness, and so on. There is no cookie-cutter story to tell. There is no "universal soldier."

Moral wounds demand moral healing. Experts in military and veteran mental health are now trying to articulate just what that healing would look like and how treatments overlap or are critically different from those routinely used in treating posttraumatic stress. But the general issue of moral healing from moral combat injury is not just for experts or clinicians. It is something we all need to understand as part of the reentry of the largest number of service members into society since Vietnam.

With 2.6 million service members having gone to war in the last thirteen years to Iraq and Afghanistan, and most of them now home with the drawdown of those wars, moral injuries are a part of that homecoming. Unlike lost legs and missing eyes, these wounds can often go unnoticed. And soldiers may keep them that way. For one year, for two, with stone silence. In some cases, for forty or fifty years, buried deep inside, untouchable, until perhaps another group of vets come home from war and they see themselves, now at sixty or seventy, in the faces of those twenty-year-olds. They may talk, some of them, to therapists who have earned their trust, and sometimes in healing centers in group therapy with those young vets. Sometimes they talk at "The Wall"—at the Vietnam Memorial—where Vietnam vets, like business executive Paul Baffico, fly in from across the country, monthly, to be docents at The Wall, to heal old but festering wounds as they reach out to those struggling with fresh ones. For some, The Wall is a meeting place for unofficial counseling, a place to bring a mother or sister or brother who hasn't served, a place where a new vet collapses in the arms of an older vet and shares an inward war he's never spoken about before and his family has never heard until now.

But whether they talk or not, many vets replay the horrors of their wars in traumas, feeling and tasting and touching their dying buddies' blood or seeing a child's exploding head in a collateral killing, and reissuing the same self-blame. Some, like the Vietnam veteran whose case a psychiatrist presented at a war trauma conference I participated in, retreat to treasure boxes in safe places where a trove of memorabilia are part of reenactment rituals that transport them back to Vietnam and its pain and maybe its openings for healing. Some, just home from war, feel too much guilt to visit the graves of their best buddies and then pile shame on top of the guilt. Some will self-medicate with alcohol or drugs, or recapture a bit of the high of war and thrill of arms through hunting trips with fellow warriors. Others may just go numb, and stay numb, until something snaps and stops the numbness from being protective.

In Josh Mantz's case, the real psychological recovery began only after he realized that he was physically alive but emotionally dead. The emotional withdrawal was killing him. Downrange, a version of it made for survival—it allowed him to operate with fearlessness, with a stoic indifference to whether he lived or died. He didn't become reckless, but simply was freed from unproductive worry about whether he would make it home. "The moment you stop caring about living, there is a great sense of freedom," he tells me. It's that liberation, "operating as above life and death" that allows you to "operate in and control chaos." You have two options, he said, when patrolling streets in East Baghdad "lined with cinderblocks of trash as far as the eye can see," each a potential hiding place for a homemade bomb. "You either stop at every rock and call EOD [Explosive Ordinance Disposal] and wait for four hours until they go and check it out, which is infeasible. Or you just say, 'screw it,' and you drive forward and you accomplish your mission. That's what we all end up doing—all the good units, anyway." But that same indifference to life and death is also indifference to social connection. "That restriction that comes with caring is no longer upon you anymore," says Mantz. "But it is also the point where emotional contact is severed."

For Mantz, numbness to fear became numbness to life. He lost zest, passion, commitment, connection, hope, and trust—the elements of "embrace" necessary for finding meaning in life. Finding meaning in life involves both *feeling* engaged and *believing* one's activities are worthwhile and worthy of one's esteem. Or, if not confidently believing, at least *hoping* they are in a way that anchors and gives the cognitive resolve needed to go forward. But for some service members, this requires reconciling a messy past and the realization that their war activities may lead to little lasting good—that they wasted lives or engaged in flawed and futile efforts. Futility is essentially meaninglessness, and without some resolution it bleeds into the present and can leave little taste for living. It drains away hope, hope in the goodness of self and others and hope for what one can bring about with due effort. And it drains away trust, that there is a point in turning to others and their turning to you. It eats away at any kind of self-compassion.

RESILIENCE

It is tempting to think about moral repair in terms of renewals, fresh starts, a fix for what's broken that looks forward more than backward. Moral repair should involve positive thinking and feeling—hope and trust, empathy and connection, as I've been putting it, without getting stuck in the negative. It should look to the possible and positive, and nudge and coach and persuade. It should be about bouncing back.

Resilience is a buzzword in the current military. Early on in the wars in Afghanistan and Iraq, with service members surviving their physical injuries at rates unparalleled in the history of warfare, it became all too clear at the highest echelons of the Pentagon that minds and not just bodies had to endure. Schooling in mental toughness and the ability to face cumulative psychological stresses needed to be a formal component of predeployment training. Alarming peaks in suicide within the military made the issue all the more urgent. Under the directive of Army Chief of Staff George Casey, the Army brought on board Martin Seligman, the pioneer in positive psychology at the University of Pennsylvania, to help design a predeployment resiliency program. Positive psychology, with its starting point not pathology or the treatment of posttraumatic stress but, rather, "the study of strength and virtue," attracted the Army's leadership. And so a $145 million Army-wide Comprehensive Soldier and Family Fitness program was unrolled in 2009, with an Army surgeon, Brigadier General Rhonda Cornum, (herself a poster woman for resilience as a former POW shot down during a medical rescue mission in the first Gulf War and a survivor of breast cancer), helping on the Army side to stand the program. Its focus, as Cornum and her deputy described it to me, is not "post-adversity," but "preventive," "to teach everyone to better thrive."

Cornum, who was retiring from the Army the week we spoke, had emptied her desk and shelves in her Crystal City office in preparation for its next occupant. But on the walls still hung the pictures of the Penn monthly graduating classes from the Master Resilience Training program, the Comprehensive Soldier Fitness core course. It's a "train the trainer" course in which groups of 180 combat vets (typically Army captains and staff sergeants) gather at Penn (or in mobile units at military facilities) for a ten-day immersion in "active constructive" attitudes that are alternatives to the kinds of "passive destructive" attitudes Seligman and his colleagues warn against, such as "ruminating misery" and "catastrophizing." The Master Resilience Trainers (MRTs) bring the coping skills to their units in informal problem solving that's the stuff of conversation and counseling, and more formally, to troops not yet deployed, in mandatory two-hour teaching slots four times a year. All troops take a required, anonymous, online psychological assessment test annually—the Global Assessment Tool, or GAT—ambitiously aimed at testing the psychological fitness of the force as a whole.

The program has been severely criticized from many camps as a quick and very expensive fix, not adequately tested with pilot programs on a combat troop population. Seligman's resilience work has been primarily with middle school children and their adjustment to school, not with troops facing day in and day out the war's detritus, where the exposure to killing in a death-saturated environment can affect vulnerability to posttraumatic stress and moral injury.

Others have implied that while the program is often promoted as asset-based, focused on fitness, wellness, thriving, and flourishing, the real impetus and urgency for crafting such an expensive program had to be from the start the prevention of negative outcomes, such as posttraumatic stress, depression, anxiety, substance abuse, and suicide. But if that were the case, then risk factors should have been more clearly articulated and targeted in order to empirically assess the efficacy of the interventions. Equally, some clinicians worry that the program may only worsen the stigma attached to seeking mental health treatment within the military. For if an individual goes through the program and returns from war with posttraumatic stress (PTS), then it may just exacerbate the sense, already prevalent in the military, that PTS has to do with one's own deficits and weaknesses rather than the war's stressors. Moreover, failure to screen for posttraumatic stress in the program, on the grounds that it might be suggestive and draw attention to the symptoms, plays into a deeper view some hold within the military that posttraumatic stress is only a psychological phenomenon with no neurobiological basis, and so easily fabricated. That view can betray mixed messaging within the Army about its mental health mission.

Around the same time Comprehensive Soldier Fitness was unrolled, the Army Vice Chief of Staff General Peter Chiarelli began to convene a monthly review board at the Pentagon to review fatalities due to suicide. The board was a part of the massive campaign to stem the suicide epidemic in the Army and to destigmatize the seeking of mental health treatment. Chiarelli, an infantry commander who headed coalition forces during the Iraq War, took on a new battlefield of brain research, biomarkers, and mental health advocacy. I met with Chiarelli's staff several times and attended some of those two-hour late-afternoon meetings. The meetings were brutally depressing, filled with harrowing details. Colonels and generals on "whose watch" a recent suicide occurred sat at a massive conference table in high-backed leather chairs or, in many cases, were video-teleconferenced in on large screens from bases in Iraq, Afghanistan, Fort Bragg, Fort Hood, Korea, and beyond. Each commander, flanked by a team, reviewed the known facts of the case, the risky behavior, the proximate causes—prescription painkillers, family disputes, troubles with mortgage payments, infidelities, a spouse's health problems, the death of an uncle, tensions with command, disappointment in being passed over for promotion, a parole—a raft of real-life issues, some with little to do with war. At moments it was easy to think that intervention here or there at a key juncture, or that a well-placed buddy, might have made all the difference. As Chiarelli listened to the cases, first one, and then another, and another, and another—a litany of details without clear patterns—his impatience at times flashed through as he demanded of his commanders after each review, "What are the lessons learned?" In truth, there were few unifying factors other than humiliation, hopelessness, or alienation, at home or on base, and too many weapons or drugs to carry out the deed.

Resilience techniques are not new. There are venerable ancient models. Greek and Roman Stoicism is preeminent. Epictetus and Seneca are radical exhorters and tough moral trainers. They are persuaders who urge their tutees to move on by unloosing debilitating, false beliefs about loss and injury. They argue that the only real evil is internal vice and the only real good is virtue. Uprooting false beliefs about external goods and evils is the path to self-mastery and liberation. And it is the path to emotions that are positive and uplifting. A sage feels only the slightest scar of the old hurts. There is no room in his emotional economy for anguish or distress, vengeance or rage. He moves on and leaves the perturbations of the past behind.

But from the scores of interviews I have had with returning service members while researching this book, it is clear to me that war does not move on easily. And the research data suggest the same. Figures from the recent wars suggest that 20 to 30 percent have come home with some form of traumatic stress. For some it is very mild; for others, it is paralyzing. In addition, from 2000 to 2013, as reported by the Congressional Research Service, there have been approximately 300,000 medical diagnoses of traumatic brain injury (TBI) across the services, and among those classifiable, they range from mild and moderate, to severe or penetrating. Another study suggests a rate of TBI as high as 23 percent in military personnel assessed after returning from deployments. Early on these were called the "signature injuries" of the wars, endured from explosive blasts or rocket-fast propulsions of the body that rattle the brain hard against the cranium, causing contusions, brain lacerations, hemorrhaging, sheared nerve fibers, and more. Unsurprisingly,

recent national attention to concussive injuries in football and other contact sports has coincided with the mounting evidence service members bring
home. Some of the symptoms of TBI overlap with those of PTS reactions, in
particular forms of emotional numbing and social withdrawal. Other symptoms of TBI, and especially severe TBI, involve cognitive impairments that
can look like the signs of premature aging: memory loss, difficulty focusing,
deficits in hearing and visual acuity, slurring, and aphasia.

Many soldiers, the majority, come home healthy and thrive from the
experience of war. Many whom I know, and have worked closely with over
the years, grow from war and go on to flourish in magisterial ways. They are
high functioners, elite performers, able to take on more than a full plate and
excel at what they do. The challenges of war that require astute leadership,
split-second assessments and decisions, endurance, selfless care, and deep
reserves of energy can grow individuals of simply remarkable virtue and wisdom. In courses I have taught on ethics and war, the presence of veterans in
a class who are willing to share their experiences can lift a classroom to new
heights. Typically, these are veterans in their mid-twenties, who have been
in the thick of complicated counterinsurgency and intelligence-gathering
operations, piloting and reconnaissance missions in insurgent villages, or
interrogation and detention operations when rage could easily get the better
of calm, strategic judgment. The demands placed on these young people are
staggering and the achievements of character and leadership, in the face of
those demands, often spellbinding.

But still, there is sometimes a wariness I see in some of the military men
and women I know. They don't want the occasional startle or nightmare to
trip them up. They don't want the fact that some have broken to mean that
all will. And so they are on guard and work hard at their own toughness; they
train for Ironman Triathlons days after they get home, sublimate their sense
of disconnect by retreating from family or friends or immersing themselves
in work. In the case of some women I know, they feel they need to "outbro the
bros." Many are on guard *for* themselves. But they also are on guard *against* a
public image. They don't want to feed the stereotype of a warrior who comes
home broken. And so they walk a careful line, helping their troops and buddies get treatment, being on alert for signs of risky and suicidal behavior,

taking seriously the massive campaigns led by the Pentagon and VA this past decade and more to destigmatize mental health treatment within the military and its families. And, they stay tough.

But control can't reach all mental recesses. The sight of your friend's skin dangling from a tree, its burning acrid smell, the feel of his torn-off calf muscle blasted fifty feet away from his foot, the dead weight of carrying his upper torso in your arms until the breath leaves—these imprints don't get more visceral or the sensed duty to not forget more acute. The latter, I suspect, is something of a decision; the former, perhaps not. Still, some traumatic stressors that make those deep imprints more likely might be minimized or avoided, such as collecting the body parts of those who are your closest buddies after a bomb blast. But to even consider ceding that task is for many a profound breach in solidarity and honor. Who else would do it? Who else is there to do it? How could you not? Put yourself into a service member's shoes: a second earlier your best buddy was in the Humvee next to you, cracking some awful joke, and now he is blown up; you both were on a rooftop taking fire from the same sniper and he stood up the second you decided to crouch down. From full throttle to full decimation doesn't take long. You're not even sure you are alive at this moment. Or if alive, intact: *Where is my foot? Is it still in my boot? Is the boot on my leg attached to me? Do I still have my member?* I hear these remarks all the time. *If I am not sure I'm alive, well, maybe my buddy is in the same boat.* How could you not hope against hope? Or, if there is no hope, then risk your own life to preserve his remains.

The work of control and passivity always collaborates and colludes in life. In taking in war and the afterwar, it is the same. Unproductive patterns of thought and feeling intrude, some from exposures that might have been avoided, but only at the cost of one's honor and sense of duty. The moments for moral injury, for a sense of grievous transgression and falling short, are all too abundant in war.

The challenge is to move on in ways that stay alive to feeling, including the residue of profound hurts, without being retraumatized. But war's hurts linger, and there is no easy way to understand healing without taking seriously the moral wounds that need healing and that can crack soldiers wide open.

A CALL FOR ENGAGEMENT

This is what I have tried to do as a philosopher—listen to those service members I have come to know, through hours and days and, in many cases, years of conversation, as they articulate just how their war lingers and in what emotions it lingers and what those emotions have to do with a sense of holding themselves or others to account. Philosophers call emotions such as guilt, shame, and resentment "reactive attitudes" that *call* self or others to account and that demand an appropriate *response*. Some philosophers, including myself, argue for the important role of positive, reactive attitudes such as hope and trust, gratitude, and perhaps empathy.

Josh Mantz experiences *moral* anguish, in part, because he feels he transgressed and fell short. He wasn't all he thought he should be as a commander. He let his soldier go without help while he was saved. Lalo Panyagua digs into himself: "You shouldn't have let him leave the vehicle without reminding him to secure the area. You lost your Marine." Implicit in that moral "shout out" is that he is holding himself to account. He is blaming and shaming. Whether he, in fact, says it out loud or just feels it, he's sanctioning himself, and hard. And he is demanding that he respond by accepting the rebuke, or proving to himself that he was somehow mistaken and doesn't deserve it.

The calls, themselves, needn't all be negative. They can enliven and encourage and invoke responsibility in positive ways. Donna will call out in so many words and gestures to Lalo that she has hope in him. She is investing in him, expecting him to try to meet the tough challenges ahead of seeing therapists, going to school, laying down his weapons and rage. The calls can be positive, and so can the responses. Resentment can be assuaged by assurance, by trust, by forging the bonds that overcome contempt and resentment. Trust is what so many alienated soldiers yearn for, but can't find in broken military judicial systems that make sexual harassment cases near impossible to prosecute fairly, veteran hospitals with unconscionable waiting lists, civilians saying "Thank you for your service" that can ring hollow, or shield a gaping disconnect between those who wear the uniform and those who don't.

This book examines that disconnect. It aims at forging a stronger moral community that involves both soldiers and civilians. The calls *invoke* response and they *convoke* (call together) community. Service members returning from the longest wars in our history are calling out (often *to us*) to share the burden, to advocate on their behalf, to take up responsibility for sending them to war and for bringing them home, to bring military justice in line with equitable judicial standards, to get members of Congress and a commander-in-chief to take seriously their constitutional roles as overseers of the military and its top brass and institutions. The lives and well-being of service members are in the hands of a military hierarchy and a complex bureaucracy when they deploy and when they return. And they are in the hands, too, of armies of military contractors, in and out of uniform, who work in sprawling bureaucracies that push paper slowly and in byzantine ways. Military service can ennoble in thousands of ways, but it also can wound; and its sprawling networks of institutions, civilian and military, when understaffed or rigidly bureaucratic or mismanaged or silo-ed off from one another, can retraumatize those wounds.

This book is not a manifesto for institutional change. Advocacy groups and the media are better suited for that. Still, this book is its own kind of manifesto. It is a manifesto for how to engage in moral repair, one on one, with individual service members and veterans so that we can begin to build a new kind of integrated community. Once we appreciate the reactive attitudes as emotions that call for a response (often *from us*), we can see what it might take to forge such a community.

Within the military community, *engage* can sound sinister—with *enemy* as its object, as in "Engage and destroy the enemy." A military engagement is, of course, a call to arms. But I have in mind a rather different kind of call for engagement—a call to be engaged with service members and to share the burden of sending them to war and bringing them home injured and needy. When my father returned from three and a half years of Army service in the European front of World War II, he was stamped a "veteran," proudly so, who in quick order became part of the workforce, a husband, a father, a neighbor, an active member of his religious community, and a lifelong user of the VA and its healthcare system until his death at eighty-nine. He kept much of his war to himself, far too much, but never that he was a GI and that once home he had a profound sense of belonging there and finding meaning in civilian life.

There is a lesson here for all of us as we share the current homecomings. We *are* a part of the homecoming—we are implicated in their wars. They may feel guilt toward themselves and resentment at commanders for betrayals, but also, more than we are willing to acknowledge, they feel resentment toward us for our indifference toward their wars and afterwars, and for not even having to bear the burden of a war tax for over a decade of war. Reactive emotions, like resentment or trust, presume some kind of community—or at least are invocations to reinvoke one or convoke one anew. Guilt is a call to self, resentment to another. They are a part of the reintegration of a self and a community after war. This book is an exercise in that moral engagement.

The Philosophical Perspective

Before resuming that engagement, a few words about my philosophical perspective are in order. My subject matter is not a traditional one for philosophers of war, whose primary focus is and remains the justification of norms of war—of going to war, fighting in war, using discriminate weapons in war, leaving war, creating conditions for stability and peace after war. The *inner* psychic moral war and afterwar of those who deploy are not typically part of this agenda. But they should be, and philosophers have much to offer. For the work of moral philosophy and its subbranch of moral psychology, from Plato and Aristotle onward, involve articulating what it means to live well, to have moral obligations and sometimes transgress, to set moral expectations and promote ideals of character, to experience emotions expressive of a sense of responsibility that hold persons to account. All these concepts are involved in making sense of the experience of going to war and returning home. Returning soldiers struggle with questions and doubts day in and day out, sometimes in paralyzing flashbacks and night traumas that touch precisely on issues of accountability, trust, betrayal, obligations to friends and buddies, and helpless victims; they worry about what it takes to be a good commander and a person who is good enough. Many are engaged in Socratic *elenchus*, a cross-examination of the self to know if one has served honorably and with excellence. In processing their war, they are doing philosophy. Philosophers can play a role, humbly so, in helping to make the moral terrain a little less murky. In my own case, philosophy melds with a research background in psychoanalysis. I do not practice, and have never seen patients. But I have been part of a community whose work is dedicated to listening empathically. My hope is that I have learned to listen empathically to the military members and their families I have interviewed, catching what nags and lifts in the residue of their wars, and building bridges to their world.

What do we mean when we say "Thank you for your
service"?

CHAPTER 2

———— ✯ ————

DON'T JUST TELL ME "THANK YOU"

MIL/CIV STRAINS

At a civilian-veteran gathering in D.C. in early summer of 2012, a young vet came forward, turned to a civilian he hadn't met before, and said: "Don't just tell me 'Thank you for your service.' First say, 'Please.'" The remark was polemical and just what was meant was vague. But the resentment expressed was unmistakable. You couldn't be a civilian in that room and not feel the sting. The remark broke the ice and the dialogue began.

I brought a Marine vet with me that evening who had just finished his freshman year at Georgetown. He wasn't the vet who spoke those words, but he shared some of the anger.

At twenty-two years of age, T. M. ("TM") Gibbons-Neff served as a rifleman in charge of an eight-man team in a second deployment to Afghanistan. His unit was among the first to arrive in Afghanistan in December 2009 as part of President Obama's surge that would send 30,000 additional U.S. troops to try to turn around the course of the eight-year-old stagnating war. Like many of those troops, TM was posted to the southwest of the country, to the violent southern Helmand Province.

On the evening of day one of the first mission, on the edge of a Taliban-held village, TM and two other teammates were crouched down on the highest rooftop they could find, surveying the nooks and crannies where the insurgents could hide and arm. They had their scopes on several who looked suspicious, but they drew no fire and so just kept to their lookouts. Then, it got "sporty," says TM, in his measured way, with lightning rounds and pops coming in from three different directions. Two rounds hit the arms of his buddy, Matt Tooker, just as he stood up to launch a grenade; another ricocheted off the body armor of his light gunner, Matt Bostrom, leaving severe chest wounds. Less than 24 hours into the mission, and TM was already down two out of his eight men. The game plan had totally shifted: he had been the observer and now he was the primary shooter, and needed to find another observer. By the end of the day he was squarely in the role of "strategic corporal," the apt term coined by retired Marine Commandant General Charles Krulak for a low guy on the noncommissioned totem pole, typically in a remote and dangerous outpost, away from direct supervision, having to implement quick tactical and moral decisions with far-reaching strategic implications. For TM, resuscitating the mission all-consumed him. Even the thought that he had two friends who had just got badly wounded barely surfaced. He was operating in "code red." Not even the most subliminal, sweet thoughts of home and his girlfriend darted through his mind.

In due course the losses sunk in. And more losses piled on. A year and a half later, Matt Tooker, shot that night, was killed in a motorcycle crash back home. TM is pretty sure it was the culmination of risky, suicidal behavior: with a maimed arm, he could no longer hold the sniper role that had come to define him. Two other close friends were killed in action in Afghanistan in May 2010. TM's Marine career had begun with his father's death (a Vietnam War Navy veteran), just days after TM had arrived at boot camp. "I'm no stranger to people I know getting ripped out of my life pretty quickly," he says, at twenty-four, with a war weariness that doesn't easily match his boyish looks and small frame. The names of his three fallen best buddies are engraved on a black bracelet he wears on his right wrist. It is his own memorial, a place to remember his buddies by touch, the way visitors run their fingers over the names on the Vietnam Wall.

TM has done his share of grieving and visiting team members at Walter Reed Hospital who weren't as lucky as he. Still, the grief and the visits fuel a deep sadness about what he thinks of as the futility of some of his missions in Afghanistan. When he first got to Georgetown University, the loose political banter on the social media sites about the need to intervene in various conflict areas around the world—Libya, Iran, Syria—riled him. It was hard to watch his peers beating the war drums while fully insulated from the consequences of deployments. The media- and philanthropy-backed campaign against the Ugandan warlord Joseph Kony and his abduction of children as soldiers in his Lord's Resistance Army (launched through the popular YouTube video "Kony 2012") made him especially resentful of his classmates' sense of comfortable entitlement. His own losses were still fresh. He didn't want to see more: "You know, a thing like Kony ..., and all these people saying, 'We should do more. What are we going to do about it?' You're not going to go over there! ... That will be our job, and then more of my friends will get buried, and then you guys can talk about it on Facebook. That's what upsets me.... The politics. The policy. The rant.... Oh, you want to go over there and stop Kony. Hey, you YouTube watcher: Is this going to be you?..."

> I am not saying don't support that political agenda. Or don't think about those little kids who are dying out there. But what about our kids who are dying out there!

TM did not hit the Send button on any of the Facebook replies he composed. Instead, he went on to write about his war experience—for the *New York Times* war blog, the *Washington Post, Time,* the *Atlantic,* the *Nation,* and other war blogs. He has served as executive editor of Georgetown's student newspaper, *The Hoya.* A year or so after we met, he took a seminar I taught on war ethics, and helped create in that class a remarkable civilian–veteran dialogue. And he has done that on campus, too, serving as the head of the campus student veteran association. He is processing his war publicly and reflectively in writing and community outreach. But his early feelings of resentment, like those of the veteran who turned to the civilian that night, are important to hear and important to try to understand. Those feelings are, in part, resentment at too easy a beating of the war drums by civilians safe from battle, infused with militarism at a distance.

Resentment toward civilians is, I suspect, an emotion felt by many who have recently served, even if the feeling is often kept under wraps. It is a way of holding another to account, of demanding respect, of calling out another for due attention and recognition as part of a shared moral community. It is a way of saying another is responsible *to you*. Sometimes it morphs into feelings of alienation and disengagement. For some veterans, the tipping point is being publicly glorified as a war hero while privately disdained (or not at all understood) for having heeded the call of military service.

Jonathan Wong, a former Marine from University of California, San Diego, who later came to Georgetown for a master's degree in security studies, spoke to just this point. He told me that when he came home from Iraq in the early days of the war, he would go out to dinner with his friends and there would be "excess adulation." With a few too many drinks, his buddies would boast to his date that he "saved Jessica Lynch. That's all they knew." They knew little about his war or what Marines like him were doing in Iraq. As civilians they were uninterested in his real military life. All they wanted to do was turn him into a war hero. "That really brought it home to me. Nobody really understands. And after that, I started really withdrawing." He took up surfing. He would go out alone often: "The ocean really doesn't care that you went to Iraq," he told me. "It's just going to dunk you to the bottom anyway." The sea couldn't praise, blame, glorify, or judge. Turning to the sea was Jonathan Wong's way of disengaging from civilian disengagement. It wasn't just the interpersonal reality that felt alien. It was the visual environment too, and especially the assault of "vibrant colors" on the San Diego campus. "Even after three months of coming home, the amount of colors in the clothes, in the buildings, even the sky was colorful," compared to Iraq, "a beige kind of place, covered in dust." That Kodachrome world, Wong said, could "either disconcert and unsettle you, or it could make you excited about the possibilities for the future."

Others come home alienated in ways that don't so clearly involve resentment or disappointment or visual dislocation. What they feel is profound moral dislocation and a consequent slipping sense of connectedness with family they love. Some turn to work as their drug of choice. This was the experience of Air Force Colonel Erik Goepner upon returning home as Commander of Provincial Reconstruction Team Zabul in southern Afghanistan (2010). During Goepner's time Taliban fighters poured into Zabul Province, trying to gain a stronghold over its patchwork of 2,500 remote villages. His forces partnered with local government officials to stabilize institutions rife with corruption and incompetency: "The stories you hear about corruption, at least for Zabul, probably understated it, to be honest with you. I mean the corruption was that bad," he said. "Governance is bad, corruption's high, and there's not a lot of government guys that are capable."

Goepner has gone on to write scholarly articles about the "mission-ineffective" environment of counterinsurgency operations with failed and weak states. He argues that the prevalence of PTS in a war-torn population like that in the Zabul Province both exacerbates vulnerability to insurgency and makes effective counterinsurgency intractable. His was a mission you couldn't accomplish in the time frame allotted, with U.S. "touch-and-go" security and the fragility of the host institutions. The corrosive environment and futility of the operations hit him personally: "Anyone who comes close to that environment is going to come away maybe not ruined but tarnished, dirtied, sullied," he said as we talked. But he wasn't prepared for what those sullied feelings led to at home: "I'm fairly introverted anyway—but I became *hugely* introverted. I had a very strong desire to disengage from most everything. Work went fine. I was still doing a grade-A job there. And I think in a sense that became its own little cathartic area, if you will. But in terms of my wife, in particular, I was *very disengaging*. And I became highly insecure as I related to her, for no reason whatsoever. And not any reason you might think, like, "You're separated, and so maybe someone was unfaithful." It wasn't that type of insecurity. Just very bizarre.... And it was fairly persistent. And so my response was instead of ever getting angry or yelling at anybody, I just disengaged. I didn't want to spend time with them, I'd read a book, I'd do some writing or something like that.... I'd say I now have a higher need for privacy and alone-time than I used to."

The disengagement may have seemed unfamiliar and "bizarre," but Goepner had been exposed to this kind of afterwar during much of his childhood. He told me about his beloved and much admired grandfather, a German soldier who served for six years during World War II and then emigrated to the United States. War left its mark on his "Opa's" soul and bearing: There was always a "steady tension" in his face, he said, and "no ability to cry anymore." But what Goepner remembered most was how his grandfather had retreated: "There would be a week that would go by and he would literally not say two words to my grandmother. She endured quite a bit of pain as a result of his pain." If times had been different, she confided to Goepner one day, she would have definitely left his Opa. "It was just too hard" to live with someone so emotionally disengaged. Goepner doesn't want to relive that part of a soldier's life.

Steady tension and disengagement may keep in check the display of anger and resentment, but the feelings can still brew. In the example in the beginning of this chapter—of the vet who turns to the civilian and says, "Don't just tell me 'Thank you for your service'; first say, 'please'"—the display of resentment comes to the surface, and the moral invocation to another, in second-personal address, is overt. Still, the "you" who is addressed is not really the civilian whom the veteran happens to be talking to but, rather, a generic civilian, a "personation" for a group, a stand-in for civilians who haven't served or who are not part of military families that have recently served or who haven't felt the pinch of war through war rationing or lifestyle changes. ("They've been shopping at the mall while we've been at war," as some have said to me.) It is a heterogeneous group of U.S. citizens who may include one-time war supporters or dissenters, politically active or inactive citizens, and those with varying degrees of engagement in veteran outreach efforts.

Assigning responsibility in light of group membership is messy here, and messy in general. Philosophically, the topic touches on a host of extremely thorny issues some to do with complicity and group identification. Focus on these issues would distract and take us down too many winding roads. Still, I mention the point to underscore that reactive attitudes can have a wide address, with the appropriate target not just persons, but persons whose relevant status is as members of specific groups and, in the case at hand, non-serving fellow citizens. This is important for understanding the military–civilian exchange. It's second-personal address, but also at times impersonal. And the fact that it can be impersonal, addressed to *you* as the civilian from *you* as the service member, puts each of us in a box that can alienate and further complicate and strain any reconciliation. The work of emotional communication becomes all the more critical, as we shall soon see.

We are beginning with tensions, rifts, feelings of being misunderstood and not given one's due, as a soldier or as a veteran, as one who has served honorably or, in some cases, less than honorably. In those latter cases brought to attention of late, bad conduct caused by the strain of war can result in carrying "bad paper" (a dishonorable discharge), which cuts one out of the benefits, jobs, education, housing, or medical and mental health care due a veteran. The punishment can be severe, deeply inequitable, and cause the bitterest sort of resentment.

But before we probe veteran resentment and the conciliatory work of a civilian "Thank you for your service," a few general remarks about the current military–civilian gap are in order.

The gap is, no doubt, exacerbated by the fact that we are not in an era of conscription. Less than 1 percent of the population served in the armed forces during the recent wars. And we don't have general requirements for universal national service; examples of selfless service to causes larger than oneself don't abound. I am not advocating for universal national service, nor do I have good ideas about how it could be instituted in a way that doesn't replicate the Vietnam era inequities of conscription, or that doesn't undermine national labor markets and employment growth. Thankfully, that is not my task. But the absence of a generalized obligation to serve one's nation does isolate, and at times over-idealize, the military as a special group that serves and sacrifices. And it contributes to a sense of us vs. them moral tribalism. That isolation is no doubt exacerbated by the fact that not only do the military typically deploy to remote places, but once they are back stateside, they often live in isolated bases, away from major metropolitan hubs and civilian networks. Remote bases are, in a way, "inside the wire," in places like Fort Hood, Fort Bragg, Camp LeJeune, Fort Lewis-McChord, and so on. These are not destinations for civilians who don't already have military connections. And so the encamped mentality persists, with little mingling and with an entrenched sense of distance.

Congress is also disengaged in its own way, with a historic underrepresentation of veterans within its ranks. As I write, only 20 percent of Congress's members are veterans, compared to more than 75 percent in the post Vietnam era. This may help explain the absence of a sense of camaraderie within the halls of Congress, but it also mirrors, at an institutional level, a public distance and disengagement from the veteran experience. These are impressionistic remarks, but they indicate the gap many of us see and feel, as well as the desire to narrow it and the belief that we ought to do that.

There is a further element in the moral background that is never far from us, and that is the legacy of Vietnam. "Thank you for your service" is a national reaction to a past negative reaction. Speak to many Vietnam vets to this day and they will tell you how demeaned they felt when they got off planes and how reluctant they were to wear uniforms in public places, especially near academic campuses. Take Paul Baffico, whom we met earlier. He was an ROTC graduate, class of 1968, the University of San Francisco, who couldn't bring himself to burn his draft card, and so he headed to Vietnam without believing in the war or its conduct. Over the course of six months, as a communications platoon leader, changing out equipment and personnel every three or four days, he faced 206 combat assaults and lost five of his men. Some of his assignments were "suicide" missions, he said, dropping off one kid, and then another, and another by helicopter in firebases (essentially artillery bases) that were entrenched enemy encampments. In one case, Baffico dropped Ken Luttle, Dennis Borhman, and Bob Woodall, "at 4 o'clock in the afternoon, and four o'clock in the morning Ken and Dennis were dead, and Bob was seriously wounded. The place was overrun with the enemy."

"Why did I pick them for the mission? Why didn't I have the courage to stay with them? That haunts me. Forever." Paul carried that guilt off the plane when he came back from Vietnam on a commercial flight to Travis Airport, just south of Sacramento. When they landed, a crewmember gave him specific disembarkation orders: "When you get off the plane, there will be a yellow stripe on the ground down the stairs and on the tarmac. Stay on the yellow stripe. *Do not deviate. Do not engage anybody.* That stripe is going to lead you through a cyclone fence tunnel, and it will put you into the terminal. Your family will be waiting for you on the other side of the terminal."

"Sure enough, through the tunnel all the protesters [were] there, and they were jeering and booing, paint thrown on you, spitting water." Paul Baffico was in his tropical weight khakis. That was his welcome home. "My defense mechanism was, "It don't mean nothing. I'm going to stay encased, and I'm going to keep all that. And I'm going to move on. My drug of choice? It was work."

From my conversations with many Vietnam veterans and dissidents of my generation, this homecoming was not atypical. Public dishonor was thrown onto many who already felt profound private moral ambivalence. Resistance to a war turned into antipathy toward its warriors. The homecoming left abiding scars on both sides. The residue within us is "Thank you for your service."

RESENTMENT AND GRATITUDE

We've been probing the feelings of resentment and grievance that underlie the sort of remark that opened the chapter: "Don't just tell me 'Thank you for my service.' First say, 'Please.'" Philosophers, since at least the time of Bishop Butler's famous sermons in the Rolls Chapel in London in the 1720s, have reflected on the ubiquity of resentment and how, in particular, *moral* resentment (of the sort felt when one suffers a moral injury) can have warrant, even if the feeling puts one at odds, as Butler worried, with a Christian command to love our enemies. The warrant has to do with the importance of voicing moral outrage and of bringing a community together in that outrage, where moral protest and the demand for justice are distinct from vengeance and acts of payback and revenge. Given the strength and prevalence of feelings of resentment in many veterans who are transitioning home, it's worth pausing for a moment to explore the structure and content of that resentment and examine how attempts to allay it in explicit expressions of gratitude, such as "Thank you for your service," might be appropriate responses.

Resentment is a reactive anger grounded in a belief, thought, or perception of being wrongly injured by another. The emotion is *about* objects and states of affairs in the world. In this way, it is different from a mental state like anxiety or edginess, where we do not know what we are anxious or edgy about, and we may not be anxious or edgy *about* anything at all. Put otherwise, anger *represents* something: that someone unjustly wronged us. In the cases we are interested in, there is the implicit complaint that civilian fellow citizens, or some subset of them, fail to assume an adequate degree of moral responsibility for the wars that they (indirectly and directly) help wage, and for the afterwar—the arduous veteran recovery that follows in the wake of going to war. How one assumes and accepts moral responsibility is often a vague and varied matter. But at very least, it seems to have to do with *backward-looking responsibility*, or accepting some accountability for action taken, and *forward-looking responsibility*, or accepting some accountability to another for future restoration or repair.

What is the specific grievance being aired in the veteran vignette with which this chapter began? I am pretty sure that the veteran who says "Don't just tell me 'Thank you.' First say 'Please'" is not reproaching the civilian for bad manners, like picking her nose in public or using a dessert fork for the entrée instead of a dinner fork. The demand for "Please" here is not about etiquette, any more than is the expectation for what is conveyed in a "Thank you for your service."

Expressed gratitude in the form of a "Thank you" is due another because she has benefitted or served you in some way or, more paradigmatically, because she has gone above and beyond the minimal requirements due you. I suspect that this latter idea comes closer to the work of gratitude. In saying "Thank you" to a service member, we are recognizing another for service to the community that involves considerable risk-taking and sacrifice at its vocational core. Of course, soldiers have a contractual obligation to accept a certain amount of risk. "It's a job," as an officer friend is fond of reminding me—"for which there is compensation," he adds. But I suspect that accepting risk is often motivated by professional honor and not just consent to a role; and it is, in part, that *motivation* that we in principle are crediting in our expressions of gratitude. We are recognizing character—courage tied to public service—even if somewhat abstractly. We see the combat fatigues in an airport, and we honor an individual as a group member, with some notion in mind about where she has been or will return to. Civilians and service members both wear their group identities in the interaction. They represent their groups and they engage in a ritual that each tacitly recognizes, whether or not they fully endorse it.

The eighteenth-century German Enlightenment philosopher Immanuel Kant can help here. Gratitude, he insists, is more a matter of morals than of manners. Specifically, it is an expression of respect toward another person and the reciprocation of the goodwill that the person has shown, either directly or indirectly, through some deed. In showing gratitude, we are letting another know that we are not taking for granted her assistance, even when it is due; or, as in the present case, when it involves great risk or hardship that was accepted willingly. The reciprocity may not be especially robust in the sense of trading places, in fact or fancy. A civilian may say "Thank you" sincerely, yet with an unspoken sense of relief—*I am glad it's not my child returning from war*—or without much empathic energy going into imagining what it would it be like to wear full-body armor in 110 degree weather, carrying an eighty-pound pack through booby-trapped terrain.

Still, Kant emphasizes the "appreciativeness" that pre-exists the giving of gratitude or that comes to be cultivated through it. The gratitude is itself a moment in gift giving: one is "to accept the occasion for gratitude" as itself an occasion for giving "a moral kindness"; it is "an opportunity...to combine *sensitivity* to others' benevolence with the *cordiality* of a benevolent attitude of will, and so to cultivate one's love of man." Put otherwise, gratitude is part of a mutual transaction of service and benefaction that builds community and fosters mutual respect and a sense of humanity. All this is critical for soldiers and civilians as they work to convoke a community and morally re-enage with one another at home. Kant wisely warns that genuine gratitude does not manipulate indebtedness for future service: gratitude "is not a mere *prudential* maxim of encouraging another to show me *further* beneficence by attesting my indebtedness to him for a past kindness...; for in such a maxim I use him merely as a means to my further purposes."

Again, there is a crucial lesson here for us. Soldiers can rightly feel "used," sacrificial, exploited by their nation-states or leaders, when gratitude is merely instrumental, for the sake of getting them to renew their service, or takes for granted their participation. Here I hear the words of Fitzroy

Newsum, a Tuskegee Airman who served in World War II and received the Congressional Medal of Honor. He recalled an exchange at a speaking tour: "A young white man came up to me and thanked me for serving our country. 'Are you including me when you say, "our country?" ' I asked."

Worries about morally dubious or thin gratitude are background to the polemical "Please" in our opening vignette: Don't take for granted my service. Don't be cavalier in a call to arms. Take greater responsibility for the wars that our country wages. You, as a citizen, through public debate and an electoral process, through taxes and lobbying, through your military contracts and civilian defense work, are partially responsible for sending me to war, keeping me at war, and integrating me into the workforce when I come home. You are morally obligated to assume some ownership for that participation, even if not for my particular conduct within a war.

The imagined dialogue I've just given vividly captures the notion I will appeal to often in this book; it expresses the reactive attitudes, such as resentment, that call another to account with the implicit expectation or demand of a reply to that call: "Hey, there, you owe me an RSVP." The presumption is of a shared moral community with expectations of mutual recognition and goodwill. To show resentment is to call out to another in response to some perceived wronging and hold him to account. In the case of returning veterans, the wronging that is the object of resentment may be more a passive than an active wronging: a perceived denial or failure to accept responsibility for one's facilitating and participatory role in the country's war activities. What hurts is that civilians appear to be free-riding, enjoying and having enjoyed for more than a decade the benefits of peace at home—economic, emotional, and material well-being—without taking on the costs of a nation at war.

SHARED MORAL RESPONSIBILITY AND LIABILITY

I have framed the question of civilian moral responsibility for war in terms of civilian participation and contribution to a war effort. That way of framing the issue embraces larger ongoing policy and includes just war theory debates being carried out within the halls of academe and outside. A key question is: Who can be held responsible and liable for intentional harm in war? Relatedly, are there just and unjust combatants (and noncombatants) in war, where the distinction hangs on whether or not the cause of their war is just? The conceptual terrain here is fine-grained, but the discourse has engaged many young soldier-philosophers with whom I work, who have been to war in Iraq and Afghanistan, and have led troops in thickly populated civilian environments in morally trying partnerships with civilians, tribal and national soldiers, and warlords. They worry often about who the players are in war, who is liable for its harms, and to what degree. For them, these are not abstract questions any more than is the question of civilian responsibility at home for a war effort. Many of those same mid-level officers—Army and Marine and Air Force majors and Navy lieutenant commanders—are now teaching young cadets and midshipmen at West Point, the Naval Academy, and the Air Force Academy. Those students, too, especially the better ones, reflect hard on their moral responsibilities as they contemplate following orders someday to go to war and prosecute it, and to leave behind a better peace for locals. For those who teach, the lessons are still being worked out, especially in light of the massive reversals in regions where there has been so much bloodshed. In short, the issues are very much on the minds of some of the best mid-grade officers, as well as those who will follow them. In light of this, it is appropriate for us to dip a bit into the philosophical issues ourselves here.

The most prominent strand in the recent philosophical discussion is a critique of traditional just war theory, a theory championed by Michael Walzer in his famous *Just and Unjust Wars* (written in the wake of the Vietnam War). Just war theory has roots in early theological doctrine, dating back to Augustine (fourth century) and Thomas Aquinas (thirteenth century), and concerns the central questions of what counts as a just cause for going to war and what counts as just conduct in its prosecution. In the past two decades, the philosopher Jeff McMahan has spearheaded a wide critique of Walzer, attacking the central assumption that, in just war doctrine, there is moral equality on the battlefield, irrespective of a combatant's cause. As Walzer puts the claim, all combatants have "an equal right to kill." McMahan's view, however, is that moral justification for self-defense on the battlefield is far more restrictive and is inseparable from cause. In this regard, the permissions and justifications for killing people in war become like those in other contexts of individual self-defense. The proposal is radical, and a full examination of the issues would take us far afield. But one small aspect of the debate sheds important light on the issue of returning soldiers' resentment at civilians for not taking more seriously their own accountability for war. And it is worth turning to that briefly.

One way to enter the debate, as one philosopher has, is to think about different degrees of moral responsibility. Someone is morally responsible in the *weak* sense if he or she causes a wrongful harm, but is not, strictly speaking, culpable for it (perhaps he or she caused this harm without meaning to). Someone is morally responsible in the *strong* sense, by contrast, if he or she causes a wrongful harm and is culpable for it, such that he or she deserves praise or blame. To be culpable, one must typically, though not necessarily, understand that the action is right or wrong and perform it freely.

Suppose that a military operation goes awry and that several noncombatants are caught in the crossfire. Who is responsible for their deaths? In the strong sense of moral responsibility, it may be that no one is responsible. Even the soldiers who pulled the trigger did not knowingly and intentionally kill these noncombatants, and thus they arguably lack culpability. In the weak sense of moral responsibility, on the other hand, it may be that many, many people are responsible—even the taxpayers who financed the military operation are linked in the causal chain leading up to this harm.

Thus, weak moral responsibility—being enablers and causers and facilitators of wrongful harm without being strictly culpable—characterizes many combatants and noncombatants alike. It is not a salient moral marker that distinguishes combatant from noncombatant. So, some combatants may not fire their arms out of reluctance to kill, yet their very presence on the battlefield, armed as they are and standing as a part of the forces, may contribute to the war effort by detracting an enemy from taking out a more lethal threat. Similarly, noncombatants may make causal contributions to the course of a war in a multitude of individually unnecessary ways. If weak moral responsibility is all it takes to become liable for war's killing, then too many noncombatants would become permissible targets in an all-out total war. They'd be sucked into the "liability net": "Many noncombatants ... make small, individually unnecessary contributions to their side's ability to wage the war, both directly and indirectly. Direct contributions include paying taxes that fund the war, supplying military necessities, voting, supporting the war, giving it legitimacy, so attracting further support from others, and bringing up and motivating the sons and daughters who do the fighting. Indirect contributions include the ways they have built the state's capacity over previous years, giving it the strength and support to concentrate on war, and contributions they have made to the fighting capacities of specific combatants: the math teacher, for example, who imparts skills to a student, later necessary to his role as a gunner; the mother who brings up a strong, lethal son.... In the modern state, almost everyone contributes to the capacity of our government to act—all the more so in democracies. Though our contributions are individually small and unnecessary, that does nothing to distinguish us from ... [some] combatants.... If their causal contributions cross the liability threshold, then so do ours."

The point is highly relevant to the sort of resentment soldiers express in the cases we've been considering. When soldiers suggest that their fellow civilians aren't shouldering their share of the moral burdens of war, I doubt most mean that, in general, civilians' moral responsibility is such that civilians should fall within the liability net of war's intentional or collateral harms—that they should have skin in the game in that way. Moreover, as a background point, I strongly doubt most would even view liability to attack in war as itself based on moral responsibility for cause, whether minimal or maximal. Most soldiers implicitly hold the traditional view (which Walzer articulates) of the moral equality of combatants on the battlefield—that combatants are liable for military attack, irrespective of their cause. What they are morally responsible for is their individual conduct, and specifically for fighting in ways that are discriminate and that minimize collateral damage to noncombatants.

Some version of this traditional view seems reasonable, and I shall assume that here for reasons others have argued for well: the hurdles for determining justice in the cause for war are extremely high, given the contentiousness of academic theories of just war, the interpretive complexities of international war conventions, and the obscurity and unavailability of many nonmoral facts relevant to the battlefield. Moreover, the justification for wars may simply not be available when soldiers are deployed and required to serve. For it is only after the fact that knowledge affecting the justification of a war, such as the proportionality of violence to good accomplished, can be assessed. Predictions are limited and often wrong. And even if we could predict fairly accurately the future outcomes, proportionality typically involves weighing incommensurable goods. It is unreasonable to expect ordinary soldiers to have knowledge that simply may not be determinate or available. The same, it might be argued, holds for the ordinary citizenry.

Still this line of reasoning won't assuage many soldiers who feel that civilians can and should take greater responsibility than they often do for both indirect and direct support of wars that are botched, imprudent, or only dubiously just. And they may reasonably and implicitly feel that, however difficult it is to determine the justness of a cause, civilians are often better situated to investigate the cause, and are morally and politically able to protest appropriately. Furthermore, civilians are not subject to the constraints that service members face—the punitive consequences of selective conscientious refusal, the shame of abandoning fellow service members who have come to be family, the guilt of vacating national defense when an investment has been made in their training at great taxpayer's expense. Civilians are proxies for service members in important ways, and their position gives them certain advantages and responsibilities, as well as incurs costs. Those expanded responsibilities may not be an argument for pulling civilians into the battlefield and incurring its liabilities, but it does suggest the need to look for other ways of accepting responsibility that are both backward looking and, more important, forward looking—and that may better represent the nature of our *shared* moral responsibility. To put the point differently, civilians may not be *liable for* the harms combatants face, but they are nonetheless *responsible to* combatants for the harms they suffer in defending the nation.

There is an additional worry in thinking about causal contributions to war that would pull civilians into the liabilities of the battlefield. And that is that it is just too individualistic a measure for understanding the real nature of owning and accepting shared moral responsibility in a country's collective projects, such as its military interventions. The point about *shared* moral responsibility doesn't have to rely on abstract notions of collective agents or psychologized notions of group identity that suggest strongly felt nationalistic and tribalistic feelings. One philosopher and legal scholar has argued in important recent work that the very nature of certain kinds of group membership, including that of nation-state citizen, may itself ground certain normative expectations of shared responsibility and obligation. And that sense of shared responsibility may hold even when citizens do not directly participate in an activity—in our case, go to war, or support it, or materially contribute to its prosecution.

I leave it to others to develop that philosophical argument. For now I want to embrace the conclusion: civilian gratitude expressed toward service members is a token acceptance of that shared responsibility and accountability for sending fellow citizens to war, independent of specific causal contributions to war activity or to its support. Saying "Thank you" is a way we civilians acknowledge and accept some responsibility for sending our sons and daughters to war and a way of acknowledging our responsibility for taking care of them when they come home.

But there is a question that nags us: How can gratitude be substantive when its expression is so trivialized in a pat, easy-to-say "Thank you"? How can that reentry ritual contribute to any kind of genuine reintegration?

Before answering, it is worth remembering the primary aim of this book: understanding the one-on-one obligations and expectations that are part of bringing soldiers home. The work is woven in the microfibers of moral communication and address—the subtle texture of individual engagements, in words and emotional tone and in body language and conduct, that convey our moral regard for each other and our responsibilities as members of a shared community. These engagements, right down to the feel and quality of the exchange, are a critical part of moral healing and moral repair. And so we need to understand the kinds of engagements that go into recognizing service through gratitude, placing hope in others and in ourselves; counting on ourselves and others through overtures of trust and returned assurances; and letting go of paralyzing shame and guilt by addressing the accused self with empathy, compassion, and imagination for a brighter future. All this takes place in interpersonal and intrapersonal moral (or, more broadly, normative) space. It is part of our sacred obligation to those who serve.

Of course, healing after war is a nation's work, driven by enlightened institutions and policies, tax dollars and allocations, governmental and nongovernmental agencies. A veteran's embrace of life after war—in some cases, choosing life—is impossible without state-of-the-art medical and mental healthcare and research, expanded veterans education and training opportunities, nonpredatory housing loans, and meaningful work. And, too, there has to be adequate care, education, and job opportunities for military spouses, who have vicariously gone to war for over a decade by struggling to keep up the home front. And there are the special needs of many military children who have been strained by years of separation from one or both military parents, and the stress of living with fear and uncertainty. All this is part of reintegration and repair at the macro (and, we might say, mezzo or mid-) level. It would be hard to imagine effective one-on-one engagement without robust institutional programs at all levels, as well as careful monitoring of their efficacy.

I don't take any of this for granted. But I also don't underestimate the power of one-on-one interactions in invoking and convoking a sense of community that supports and is supported by enlightened policy.

THE MANAGED "THANK YOU"

We hear "Thank you for your service" in airports and planes, on Veterans Day and Memorial Day. The practice can seem hollow, mechanical, and rote. Whether service member or civilian, it's easy to be cynical. But the distinctions here are too coarse, and the idea that emotional expression should show exactly what is felt is too simple.

We manage our emotional expressions in all sorts of ways—we suppress tears, coax a smile, prevent a face of disgust from taking over our demeanor. In short, we are used to exerting "emotional labor." But the military case is fraught precisely because of the resentment (and reciprocally, the guilt) that can be an undercurrent in the exchange. Even if we are used to illusion in our emotion performances, when there is a perception of inequity or entitlement, the illusion grates and we beg for some emotional honesty. In cases of consequence—namely, a nation's regard for its soldiers—there is little honor in the illusion if neither side moves beyond a ritualistic volley of pat phrases. This volley resets the rift and likely widens the misunderstandings.

Consider the case of Phil Carter, the National Veterans Director in the first Obama presidential campaign and now counsel at the Washington think tank Center for New American Security (CNAS), focusing on the reintegration of veterans. Carter served nine years as an Army military police and civil affairs officer, including a year in Iraq, where he advised the provincial police, judiciary, and prisons in Diyala Province. In an opinion piece that appeared on Veterans Day in the *Washington Post*, Carter spoke candidly about the resentment he felt toward civilians upon coming home from Iraq in the spring of 2006. The "Thank you's" and "hero" labels rang hollow in light of what he had left behind: "Thousands of Iraqis … dying each month in a hellish civil war. If we were really heroes, why was the war in Iraq going so badly?" He was alienated and withdrew from civilians: "I … resented the strangers who thanked me. I suspected that they were just trying to ease their guilt for not serving. Instead of thanking me, I wanted them … to make some sacrifice greater than the amount of lung effort necessary to utter a few words." Words were cheap and action was dear, especially the sort of action he valued as a military person.

He pushed away his family, tightening his web of trust to a near exclusive circle of veterans. There he found mutual trustworthiness rooted, likely, in the mechanisms that often inspire trusting attitudes: a sense of shared loyalty, a presumption of virtue or goodness in those one trusts, and a belief that trust is to everyone's mutual advantage. With veterans, he didn't need to take much of a gamble: trust was easy. Many veterans feel similarly. And the assumption that those trust mechanisms will always be in place is at the heart of many support groups, formal and informal, as well as the drinks that veterans have shared with each other over the years. (I know veterans who will go out for a beer almost exclusively with fellow veterans because they know that, if one drink too many should lead to a flashback, another veteran will be there who understands.)

I explore trust in a later chapter, in addition to the challenges of expanding trust circles. But for now, we note the messy and unspoken emotional subterrain that can underlie a perfunctory "Thank you." There is the nagging sense, often private but felt by both sides, that more needs to be said—just not here and just not now. There is the worry on the part of the "Thank You-er" that she might seem meddlesome if she asks more, or cold if she keeps the exchange formal, or superficial if she utters a pat expression that doesn't convey her true feelings; that she may feel upset about the hardships of the tours, doubtful about whether the sacrifices have been worth it, skeptical about whether twelve years of war have reduced the threat of either radical Islamism or terrorism, or given real hope to failed states or the means for reversing new insurgencies. The worry is not whether civilians will go back to receiving veterans the way they did after the Vietnam War. It is whether the gratitude ritual can ever be more than just a "thin crust of display." Can it function as overture to a more satisfying form of moral address and recognition? Can it do substantive work to bring the sides closer?

The provocative remark that opened this chapter expresses these demands or, more loosely, the normative expectations. I presume in this case the veteran was not only expressing resentment but also feeling it. His remarks *announced* his angry feelings. They were evidence of it; in a loose sense, his resentment became perceptible through his words. Emotional expressions often reveal underlying, corresponding emotional states; they don't always, but when they do, they do far more than that. They are pieces of conduct, emotional interactions that can be untethered from their matching inner states. When the drill sergeant screams at his recruits, he may not really be angry; he may be using anger behavior to motivate and achieve specific ends. The point is one Cicero and Seneca routinely make in discussing motivational techniques in oratory. The orator may need to show "the guise of doing harm," says Seneca, in order to inspire fear in his audience. Real anger is never to be encouraged, on Seneca's Stoic view, for it disarms control; but it can be *performed* strategically: "Anger can never be permitted though it may sometimes be simulated if the sluggish minds of the audience are to be aroused."

Emotional posturing, demeanor, and mien are critical aspects of oratory, and more generally, of "interaction rituals" in daily life, as the great sociologist Erving Goffman famously taught in a similar vein. We are emotional performers, on stage and off. We have audiences, real and implicit, including ourselves. Verbal intonation, dynamics, facial and body gestures, open and closed body positions toward those we address, and body distance all are constitutive elements of emotional communication: of signaling anger, delight, annoyance, and interest, as well as resentment, blame, guilt, trust, gratitude, hope, disappointment, shame, and empathy—the emotions of moral engagement, injury, and repair.

But communication involves signaling *and* receiving. And while there is some evidence that the expressive behavior for basic emotions, like anger, fear, disgust, or sadness, are the same across cultures, more nuanced emotional expressions will vary considerably across gender, cultural, ethnic, national, and linguistic groups, with some also idiosyncratic to individuals or families. And different emotional styles can pose obvious interpretive challenges. "Emotional communities" can challenge broad, inter-group communication. Yet even if we have to work sometimes to successfully convey and recognize others' messages, we do so all the time. There are attunements and misattunements, communications and miscommunications, signalings and resignalings, receivings and re-receivings. "Thank you for your service" and "You're welcome" represents just one emotional performance among thousands that we engage in and decode.

So, in what sense is this ritual more than a "thin crust of display"? What kind of richer content might it have? What are some of the possibilities implicit in our performance?

When a civilian says "Thank you for your service," he may be addressing his remark *to* a service member, but it's made before a larger real or imagined audience of which he is a part and before whom he is modeling his behavior. He's signaling a norm and conveying a shared (or what he thinks should be a shared) response. The basic idea borrows from early developmental literature on *social referencing* and on observations of how young children assess target objects: Should they be scared or comforted by the new person who walks into the room? Children look, or "refer," to their parents (or caregivers) to read their faces and see how they comport themselves before the stranger. They then regulate their emotions by reference to the parents' reactions. We adults continue with this practice, checking others' faces and emotional behaviors to gauge how we should react, looking for cues from others about the norms of engagement. As addresser, we can intentionally send messages to third parties, both by what we say and how we say it or behave; other times, that is not our direct intent, though we are aware that we are signaling and do little to make the display private.

I think some of this is going on in civilian "Thank you's" to military members. We civilians are addressing our gratitude *to* the military, but we are also modeling *before* the fellow civilians whom we stand for or with. We are saying "Thank you" on their behalf. The display is a public enactment and recommendation of a norm. Again, the parenting model has some purchase. For instance, I may indirectly signal to my husband through my emotional reaction how I think *he* should be reacting to our children's behavior at the table. I'm modeling what I think "we" should do, and I'm hoping he shows solidarity. This is a way of thinking about a *shared* reactive attitude: it is addressed *to* another but *for* others (and *on behalf of* others) whom we regard as teammates and partners committed to underlying group values. We are doing some of this when we thank soldiers for their service. Our show of gratitude shows *others* how to respond. That's one substantive role of the ritual.

But a second role is that in *showing* gratitude, we ourselves come to *feel* gratitude. The idea is again familiar: we nurse our hearts from outside in. Kant urges us not to be put off by these enactments: "Men are, one and all, actors—the more so the more civilized they are. They put on a show of affection, respect for others, modesty and disinterest without deceiving anyone, since it is generally understood that they are not sincere about it. And it a very good thing that this happens in the world. For if men keep on playing these roles, the real virtues whose semblance they have merely been affecting for a long time are gradually aroused and pass into their attitude of will."

The remarks shed light on Kant's Pietism and his concern with what's inner—in this case, inner feeling promoted through outer "aesthetic." Charges of inauthenticity, of faking it, get dispelled once one appreciates that display can be constitutive of character formation. We take on the benevolent feel of a smile by practicing smiling, Kant reminds us (we now know that there is some physiological evidence for this in the notion of efferent bio-feedback loops): "Affability, sociability, courtesy, hospitality, and gentleness" may be "small change," he concedes. "Yet they promote the feeling for virtue itself by [arousing] a striving to bring this illusion as near as possible to the truth."

It may well be that at times surface acting leads only to more convincing acting. But it seems plausible that it can also lead to deeper acting that involves deeper engagement, vulnerability, and authenticity. The managed "thank you" becomes an occasion for stabilizing genuine and reliable gratitude. And if Kant is right, we don't necessarily undermine the aimed-for uptake of our remarks when those who are targeted recognize we are engaged in a performance ritual: we all know we role-play at times and that a way of *becoming* is by *doing*. There is tacit acceptance of the point. Goffman gives a contemporary gloss to Kant's point: "Regard is something" an individual "knows enough about what to feign on occasion"; in turn, the recipient of that regard knows not "to steal information" that goes too deeply behind the façade.

So far we've indicated two ways even a routinized "Thank you for your service" can do substantive moral work: First, through a ritual display of gratitude, we *model behavior* and *instate a norm* in a public way. Second, the performance is a way to *manage* our hearts and at the same time *teach it* how to feel differently.

A third function of the ritual is more straightforward and basic to both of the above cases. In thanking you, I am engaging you in *second-personal address*, as philosophers put it. I am calling out to you that you have met expectations or exceeded them. I show approval or recognition through my gratitude. And that address can itself take two forms. The performance may be disclosive: I am *showing* what I now feel. I *avow* my heart and its truth. But my expression may also be a sign for something else—that I am expressing interest and opening a door for future interaction.

All this has relevance to the "Thank you" rituals we civilians find ourselves engaged in with veterans. The address may be emotional performance, but the performance does moral work—that we lock eyes, show interest, listen, and, in the best case, take the outreach and connect to the next step.

In all this, the basic worry really is: How do we impose costs on civilian "Thank you's"? That was Phil Carter's worry. It seems too cheap. I'm suggesting that we go beyond a cheap aesthetic when we willingly engage in an ongoing dialogue with a veteran and that we recommend and model that commitment for others. Moreover, it's likely that if we incur that cost, we do so because we truly feel gratitude, whatever else we may believe about a war and its cause. But we also are likely to deepen our gratitude and make more concrete our appreciation through the engagement. Emotional attitudes are rarely pristine, well-formed states that we simply turn inside out; even when we do *show* our heart, it's through nuanced conduct that shapes our mental state in the very outing.

PEACE GIFTS OF WEAPONS

Resentment, as has been said in this chapter, is about past injury, holding someone to account for a past harm, whether apparent or intentional. You step on my toe; I hold you to account. There is no point in my demanding that you undo that step; it's done. It is a fantasy of sorts to replay the tape differently, even if that is often how we satisfy our wishes for respect and redress. Resentment gets answered, constructively, in part, through assurances about the future, about one's own future treatment but also treatment of others like oneself. Indeed, for many soldiers, the assurance wanted most is that future generations of soldiers will not be subject to the same sense of betrayal when fighting imprudent, unjust, or unnecessary wars. But, of course, that is an abstract aspiration, addressed at an indeterminate group of political and civilian leaders who may or may not be able to shape political will, now or in the future. Moreover, the kinds of assurance wanted—that wars will be justified on moral or even prudential grounds—may simply not be available when troops are deployed. As a result, deep resentments may fester, and veterans may become re-traumatized as they live through new wars that they believe are unjustified or unnecessary, and they watch a new generation of veterans—some their own sons and daughters—come home, or not come home. The sense of anger, helplessness, and futility gets refueled: new afterwars rekindle old ones. Not surprisingly, the kind of trust and assurance that can often salve deep disillusionment may come not top-down—from the promises of civilian and military leaders—but, rather, from the bottom up, in one-on-one engagements that build interpersonal connections and develop a sense of being understood.

In this vein, consider a case that a psychiatrist friend, Sam Goodman, shared with me, involving a Vietnam veteran he saw some forty years ago. Sam served during the Vietnam War as an Army psychiatrist, although he treated this patient after he was out of service. He was reminded of him as we talked about a new generation of soldiers transitioning home.

The soldier, call him "Bill," entered Vietnam early at the encouragement of his father, who regarded it a patriotic act. Bill rose fast to become a sergeant and an exemplary leader who cared deeply for the lives of his troops. "This guy won my heart," said Sam. "He was a wonderful man."

Bill later became a Green Beret, slipping through enemy lines as part of President Nixon's secret war in Cambodia. In the stealth of the night, Bill would leave his lethal mark on many an enemy sentinel, slitting the guard's throat while others were asleep, as a calling card of what might come. In one intimate, deadly encounter, Bill was pinned down, but managed to pull out a concealed knife and stab the enemy fatally in the chest. The corpse fell on him, with Bill remaining perfectly still so as not to awake others, himself corpse-like under its dead weight for over an hour. In that hour, Sam said, Bill savored "the sense of peace" in knowing how close he was to the enemy and almost dead, yet alive, the victor in this battle.

But that sense of peace or victory wasn't to last. Bill came home profoundly disillusioned, regretting his war, feeling suckered by the Army, and angry that he was fooled into thinking that his service was patriotic. After a violent car accident, frequent panic attacks, self-medication with alcohol, and a search for redemptive meaning through religion and pacifism, Bill came to Sam, whom he saw for four years, twice a week, in face-to-face psychotherapy, in conjunction with anti-depressant drug therapy: "I'd say he responded very deeply to the therapy, but his depression remained."

What marked the therapy is that for four years, "Bill was so very, very engaged in telling his story and having his story understood" by Sam, as a proxy for others. In the final session of their time together, in deep gratitude, Bill bequeathed Sam a peace gift of weapons—a bazooka and a gun that had been disarmed and were no longer utilizable: "Give them to your children," he said, "and tell them never to use them." The sadness, said Sam, is that in Bill's own eyes, "he was a murderer," whose deeds in war were ultimately unjustified. The depression was, in part, his unrelieved guilt and grief at being caught in that untenable position.

Bill's self-loathing mixed with raging resentment toward those whom he believed aided and abetted his becoming a murderer. Sam, himself, often feared for his life: "I was always very cautious about making him too angry, and at times my blood ran cold when I realized that he could kill me without a weapon at any time—a completely foreign idea under any other of my life circumstances. The work involved this fear that he had at all times that he could, if made angry, kill again or he could kill those responsible for his being in the war."

This is an extreme story of resentment, indeed vengeance, but not an unfamiliar legacy of the war in Vietnam. The story of the most recent two wars is still being written, though views of them are taking shape. The war in Iraq is now considered by many to have been fought for an unjust cause and based on false information and faulty reasoning. Even if not viewed as unjust, many see it as an unnecessary and optional war. And it is a war that has not left a better peace; rather, it has reignited war in a failed state. And the war in Afghanistan, while widely viewed at its inception as "the good war" and a just defense in response to domestic attack, has, over twelve years later, left many soldiers wondering whether their efforts were ultimately worth it; whether their mission of wooing tribal populations away from the Taliban and establishing a stable, U.S.-supported government, with its own economic and political infrastructure, was any way achievable or laudable, versus the kind of end that demands a traditional ground war where we "defeat" an enemy. This is the political backdrop for individual soldiers' resentment, even when those soldiers are volunteers who often feel great pride in their service, loyalty to their comrades, and have identities and personal ideals tightly wrapped up with their service in the military.

RESENTMENT'S BID FOR RESPECT

In light of Sam's vignette about Bill, it is all too tempting to think of resentment as essentially defensive anger, a "brandishing of emotional arms." Sam feels fear, he's "cautious," often on guard. Bill's resentment is murderous; it feels that he could still kill, with or without weapons. The resentment is displaced, in this case, on a near-to-hand object. Sam is the replacement target for some ill-defined generic, a fellow citizen-injurer.

In his *Fifteen Sermons*, Bishop Butler articulates this notion of resentment as defensive anger in his classic sermon on resentment, mentioned earlier: resentment is "a weapon against injury, injustice, and cruelty." It is retaliation against "one who has been in a moral sense injurious" to ourselves. Nietzsche, in a similar spirit, roots the morality system for compensation and blame in what he famously names the revenge impulse to *ressentiment*—a "reactive *pathos*," "a yearning … to anaesthetize pain" through vengeful emotion. Nietzschean *ressentiment* is perhaps better thought of as a perversion of resentment, a "squint" and grudge, malice and spite that last too long. It is the morality of the enslaved and inferior, he tells us, and it needs to be overcome. The point echoes Seneca's views in *On Anger,* in which he paints a graphic picture of the depravity of revenge feelings.

But resentment in general, and the practice its expression mediates of holding another to account, is often too narrowly conceived as essentially retaliatory—a return of disrespect with disrespect, a retributive tit for tat. That is one manifestation, but the underlying notion is broader and not, at its core, belligerence or bullying. Resentment, at its most basic, is a bid for respect, a demand of the person who caused the injury, or who contributed significantly, to acknowledge one's standing. One prominent contemporary philosopher reconstructs a version of the sentiment in just this way: "These circumstances can give rise, in the victim or in someone else on behalf of the victim, to a very special fantasy of retrospective prevention. As victim, I have a fantasy of inserting into the agent an acknowledgement of me, to take the place of exactly the act that harmed me. I want to think that he might have acknowledged me, that he might have been prevented from harming me."

Blame (or more precisely, as this writer puts it, "focused blame" for culpability, and not simply causal agency) "asks for acknowledgement." In general, it takes seriously the other's person's deliberative process in something of the way that offering advice does, but in retrospect, not prospect: It "involves treating the person who is blamed like someone who had a reason to do the right thing but did not do it." So although resentment cannot *demand* that the other undo the past, the retrospective fantasy is more than just a wishful imagining of an alternative past. Its focus is on an *alternative deliberation*—that someone had a reason to do the right thing and didn't. And that is future-oriented; it's about how one normatively expects to be acknowledged in another's deliberations, in general and in future dealings, where there is forward-looking responsibility. We are calling attention to another's regard for us (or lack of regard) and asking for receipt and recognition of that review in a way that may have some influence on future behavior. As such, blaming, on this view, is neither moralistic disdain nor manipulation by coercion or force. The point is not to shame or threaten another with your will—you are not brandishing your will, to bully or dominate; rather, your aim is to engage with another whom you take to have the authority and competence to *understand* your complaint, to acknowledge it, and to be guided by it in future interactions with you or others like you.

The point is one the Scottish Enlightenment philosopher Adam Smith long ago recognized: "The object ... which resentment is chiefly intent upon, is not so much to make our enemy feel pain in his turn, as to ... make him sensible that the person whom he injured did not deserve to be treated in that manner." What really enrages us, he continues, "is the little account which he seems to make of us ... that absurd self-love, by which he seems to imagine that other people may be sacrificed at any time, to his conveniency or his humor."

This is important background to further understand the resentment some veterans feel. The resentment is typically not a demand for pity or sympathy.

("Don't pity us," one four-star Army general invoked repeatedly in a keynote speech to civilians and veterans at a Georgetown Veterans Day celebration.) Nor is it necessarily a demand for empathic sharing of feeling, at least if that means access to the horrors and gore of war through vicarious arousal; many who go to war want to protect civilians from just that kind of exposure. Rather, at the core of the resentment is "a bidding to recognize ... a kind of relationship ... in which parties are responsible to each other."

That accountability of civilian to soldier is ongoing. The soldier wants assurance from civilian and military leaders and, collectively, from a nation, that they are *never just forces*, never just an asset to be used (or preserved) instrumentally as a part of military necessity in achieving missions (and continuing the fight). They are fellow citizens, with rights to life and liberty, not alienated even in fighting. And they are fellow citizens with rights to protection, not just in battling the enemy outside but also in battling the enemy within—all too vividly illustrated in the case of sexual assault within the military, which we take up in a later chapter.

And as military veterans, they have rights to live *good* lives—to the degree that is possible, given severe impairments and disability. The needs here are profound. If past wars are an indicator, the numbers with mental health issues will likely rise, with deferred onsets and delayed seeking of treatment peaking some ten to twenty years after a war ends. Recent spikes in suicide rates speak to the desperation already. And there are the staggering physical wounds, the legacy of advanced battlefield medicine that keeps soldiers alive at rates unheard of in history, but who are profoundly altered in face and limb (and altered by surgery too, as in facial cases, where forty to fifty operations may be required to keep reversing the fresh scarring that closes up orifices and makes impossible basic functioning.) The "transitioning" of soldiers after more than a decade of war is an antiseptic term that barely touches the ravages of war on those bodies and souls.

All this is to point to the hard work of building concrete moral respect for veterans in the complex and interconnected arrays of institutions public and private, at federal, state, and local levels, and combinations thereof, regarding healthcare, housing, employment, education, transportation, recreation, extended family assistance, and more. The nation's obligations to provide veterans with the best care and the greatest means for social reintegration are strict. Foundation work and private influence, however critical, can never replace public institutions and the democratic obligations to fund them.

But building concrete moral respect also takes place at the micro level, in the fine texture of moral interactions and engagements through which we acknowledge and accept moral responsibility for each other, both within and outside larger institutional networks. Those practices of recognition constitute a critical level of social and informal institutional reality.

UNSHAKEABLE RESENTMENT

Some examples of moral injuries and reactions I have been discussing (and will go on to discuss in the pages that follow) may strike readers as not grave, however much they represent genuine tears in service members' psyches and communities. Reconciliation after mass atrocity may be a different matter. And here, letting go of grudges may be a pernicious form of "cheap grace." In such cases, resentment, and particularly Nietzsche's version of it, *ressentiment,* with its enduring "squint" of grudge, may strike us less as a perversion and more as an essential way of holding onto humanity, as the moral protest required for retaining membership in a moral community. It is what is left for moral survival when repair is not possible.

This is the view of Jean Améry, an Austrian (whose father was an assimilated Jew and mother was a Roman Catholic) who, after the Nuremberg Laws of 1935 marking his Jewish ancestry, fled to Belgium. After Belgium's occupation by the Germans, Améry was expelled as an enemy alien, interned in France, and then escaped and joined the Belgian Resistance Movement. Soon after, Améry was captured by the Nazis and tortured during his two years of internment in the camps. His memoirs, which he began writing in the mid-sixties, are a remarkable rehabilitation of *ressentiment.* They pose an argument worth considering: that reconciliation, in the case of some moral injuries, risks undoing the humanity of the victim.

I cannot take up the case here in any detail, except to consider that, when trust in a world has been so thoroughly shattered by the barbarism of other humans, letting go of the grudge may seem a nullification of the unspeakable atrocities suffered.

After twenty years of silence, Améry began writing his essays—some of which he read on South German Radio (now a part of Southwest Broadcasting)—just after the Frankfurt Auschwitz Trials and during a move within Germany, in the wake of those trials, for reconciliation. The essays, on the state of one who has been "overcome," lost, robbed of dignity and trust, are meant as a correction to policies of forgiveness and neutralization of the past from the perspective of one who cannot give up the grudge. I don't pretend competence in German history of this period, but I call attention to Améry's work simply to claim that there may be moral injuries that can't be healed and reconciliations that defy preservation of humanity.

Améry writes in the essay "Ressentiments," with explicit allusion to Nietzsche: "My personal task is to justify a psychic condition that has been condemned by moralists and psychologists alike. The former regard it as a taint, the latter as a kind of sickness. I must acknowledge it, bear the social taint, and first accept the sickness as an integrating part of my personality and then legitimize it." Améry is well aware of the cost of his resentments and its inconsistencies: "It nails everyone of us onto the cross of his ruined past." And "absurdly, it demands that the irreversible be turned around. . . . It desires two impossible things: regression into the past and nullification of what happened." It leans backward and forward, with the fantasy, as we might put it, that in going back, the agent of moral injury could be trusted to have acted differently, that he could have inserted into his agency "an acknowledgment of me, to take the place of exactly the act that harmed me." But Améry's humanity cannot trust this fantasy for long, in the face of the more pressing moral reality that torture imprinted on him: "The Flemish SS-man Wajs, who—inspired by his German masters—beat me on the head with a shovel handle whenever I didn't work fast enough, felt the tool to be an extension of his hand and the blows to be emanations of his psycho-physical dynamics. Only I possessed, and still possess the moral truth of the blows that even today roar in my skull, and for that reason I am entitled to judge, not only more than the culprit but also more than society—which thinks only about its continued existence. The social body ... at the very best ... looks forward, so that such things don't happen again. But my resentments are there in order that the crime become a moral reality for the criminal, in order that he be swept into the truth of his atrocity."

Améry's point is that forward-looking healing and forgiveness may restore the *social* body and politic, but it cannot restore the body *corporel* and soul of the tortured innocent. Day and night the "moral truth of the blows" still "roar in [his] skull." Améry can't forget or forgive or move forward. He must bear witness, lest he undo the moral reality of the crime for the criminal. The passage is stunningly powerful and gives pause to the work of moral reconciliation in places where there have been genocides and systematic atrocity—in South Africa, Rwanda, Bosnia, Syria, and possibly others. I turn to Améry to remind us of limiting cases for relieving moral resentment, where there can be no possibility of moral healing, whether in the work of self-empathy, hope, or trust. The assaults of unmitigated evil erase any reasonable hope for redemption. In many of the cases we take up in this book, there are openings for hope and rapprochement. Still, the healing doesn't come easy.

OUR OWN MOVING FORWARD

We have covered much ground in this chapter, much pivoting on a phrase that symbolizes homecoming—"Thank you for your service." The phrase is unanalyzed for most of us, but said and heard, often with a sense of shrinking and denial. Do we really mean it? What are we *not* saying when we utter the words? What are our underlying obligations in sending troops to war and bringing them home? Why are we, as fellow citizens in a shared project of nation at war, not liable for war's harms? If we aren't liable for battlefield harms, then what responsibilities can be expected of us as we bring troops home? I have argued that personal, supportive engagement is critical at the fine-textured level of one-on-one emotional communication and rapport. That engagement is part of healing and recovery from war. It is part of our shared responsibility toward those who fight our wars.

I began with resentment and gratitude because they are often the starting points for our mutual interactions—or the points of blockage, the unspoken resentment and the ritualistic "Thank you." We need to get beyond that, together. And one way to begin is by exposing the practice and its implications. In what follows, I move to other emotional impasses that need relief if the healing of moral injury from war is to take place. Among them are the pounding guilt of not being able to save a buddy and the self-indictment of falling so short of what one thinks a good soldier, sailor, Marine, or wingman ought to be able to do. Here, the moral call and response are internal, but the healing depends in part on being able to tell others about the inner struggle, and in the telling others, allowing them to empathize and share some of the journey together. In that sense, *we* also are being asked to listen.

Lalo Panyagua in Marja mud hut, preparing for the surge in December 2009

CHAPTER 3

————— ★ —————

THEY'RE MY BABY BIRDS

I'M THE GUY IN CHARGE

Eduardo "Lalo" Panyagua is one of those Marines who looks just fine on the outside, just a bit rounder in his face and waist than the Marine he was eight years ago, at seventeen and a half when he enlisted. He survived the most dangerous and demanding engagements the Marines have been put through in twelve years of fighting—in Fallujah, Iraq, and in Marja, Afghanistan. And he's received his fair share of medals and honors for his service. He'll tell you that the first two deployments in Iraq were easy. He was a "new kid," spit-polished with no command responsibility. Third time round, "I'm the guy in charge." His lieutenant, a recent ROTC graduate, had not yet cut his teeth on war. He was happy to swap rank for experience. Lalo recalls their first encounter:

"Look, I know I'm in charge," the lieutenant told him. "But this is my first rodeo. You know how to get this shit done." At twenty, Lalo, war-tested and eager, found himself de facto in charge of a platoon of thirty-five Marines, plus fifteen Afghani National Army soldiers partnered with the unit. He was a corporal filling a sergeant's billet in a mixed armory/infantry battalion, shaping the battlefield for the surge in the Helmand Province to be unleashed in January 2010.

Lalo joined the Marines as a way out of tough gang life in the L.A. barrios that enmeshed his family and pals, and was beginning to entrap him. A scuffle at Dorsey High School landed him with a revenge threat and an after-school meeting for the deed to be delivered. He skipped out of school before day's end, and by the afternoon was enrolled in a new school. At Hollywood High, in his honors classes, he met Donna Hernandez, a dark-haired, dark-eyed, then Goth girl with street smarts and a bookish sensibility. She was an only child in a protective, traditional Mexican household, with her dad no stranger to gangs. Lalo and Donna fell in love and worked hard to hide the relationship from her parents, and from the extended family who lived across the street. But they all knew.

During his senior year, Lalo enlisted. A year later, in 2008, he headed to Iraq and the following year, Donna went to Georgetown University's School of Foreign Service. On September 21, 2009, three weeks into her first semester, Lalo drove up to Washington, D.C. from Camp Lejeune, North Carolina, where he was stationed after his two back-to-back tours in Iraq. He took Donna by surprise when he told her about an imminent third deployment. "On an impulse, we eloped."

"To my parents' joy," says Donna, "I did not get married to validate a pregnancy or receive military benefits." But they still weren't pleased, nor were some of her mentors at Georgetown who thought that she might be giving up her education. (I did not know Donna at this point. I met her in the fall of 2012.) A month later, Lalo was on his way to Afghanistan. And Donna was immersed in her studies and busy with a job; in her spare moments, she was tracking any news she could find about a firebase called "Fiddler's Green" in the Helmand Province.

For Lalo, the Marines almost instantly became his core and, along with Donna, his chosen family. After seven and a half years in the Corps, he will leave on medical disability with benefits that match those of someone who served for twenty years. Seven years, in and out of war, speed up the time.

As with many of the walking-wounded veterans of these wars, the injuries Lalo suffers can be hard to see, but they pile onto each other and disable. And there are psychological and moral rewoundings. He has skeletal injuries: upper and lower spine bulgings and herniated disks and nerve damage that shoot pain down his arms and legs and that alternates with numbness. He suffers from traumatic brain injury: his short-term memory is sketchy and he has trouble remembering people's names. He gets disoriented easily, and his hearing and vision aren't what they used to be. "I'll be driving, and five minutes later I'm like, "How the hell did I get this far?" He is still amazed that the barrage of explosives he endured most days could wreak so much havoc on his body and soul when at the time everything seemed so intact: "I had no idea that would come from getting rocked, you know?"

He has been diagnosed with severe and chronic posttraumatic stress. He tells me he struggles with "nightmares, hypervigilance, daydreams ... flashbacks, outbursts of anger, aggressiveness, fatigue all the time. I'm tired all the time ... I daze out throughout the day." Once when Donna was traveling out of the country with a state department internship, he took to the bottle and near destroyed his liver. He's given that up. But now, under extensive care and therapy, he pops a pill per symptom and hates it, but hates going without out his meds even more.

The full onset of all the symptoms, especially the PTS and TBI, was slow. Like Josh Mantz, he felt nothing for months after returning from war. He was home on a routine cycling from Afghanistan to the Marine base at Quantico, Virginia. Life was good: he was enjoying, as he said, a "new honeymoon stage" with Donna, and was ready to leave the Marines and start his marriage for real. But he had done well in the Marines, and an offer of staying stateside at Quantico, only an hour from Georgetown, with a likely option for officer training, was too good to turn down. And so he re-upped.

The adjustment was rocky and the challenges Lalo faced in moving from battlefield to stateside base give some insight into what a homecoming can look like for hundreds of other service members. Two weeks after being in charge of nearly fifty troops in a high-risk, op-tempo, kinetic environment, Lalo found himself hunkered over a computer for eight hours a day, surrounded by both military and civilians, most of whom had not deployed. He felt out of place, unskilled and untrained, with equipment that seemed alien; all of a sudden "my primary weapon became a keyboard, and my handgun ... a mouse." He wasn't ready for the transition. And he wasn't ready for all the time on his hands, for thoughts and memories to crowd in, and for the chance in idle moments to go back to Afghanistan and follow troop movements vicariously on the web: "Even though it was hell, I still freakin' miss it." "It's like ... home, you know."

At home, the anxiety mounted, the flare-ups started to come, and after a full two years out of Afghanistan and a frightening episode of hurling Donna half way across the bedroom when she tried to calm him down during a night trauma, he agreed to get help.

Lalo takes care of his "baby birds," as he puts it with tenderness. To hurt Donna was the ultimate wake-up call: "I woke up to her crying. And I noticed that I had hurt her. And at that moment, I'm like, 'I'll do anything to make sure I get better, even if it means I've got to go talk to the wizard.'... That's what we Marines call the psychologist. So I told her, 'Look, I'm going to go get assessed. I'll go do an assessment. And we'll see; we'll go from there.' I went, and they're like, 'Sir, you have severe PTSD. You need help.' And that's when the treatment started. And even then, I'm still like, 'Look, I'm fine.'"

It is tempting to think of Lalo's posttraumatic stress, and that of many service members like him, as primarily physiologic or autonomic. He reacts on a dime, as he would in a war zone, hypervigilant and hyperreactive. He revisits his war in nighttime traumas; he disconnects from those who don't understand his war. Exquisitely honed reflexes and observational skills highly adaptive in war become maladaptive at home. As Charles Hoge, a leading Army psychiatrist, has put it, "under prolonged stress, the stress 'thermostat' is reset." Recalibrating the thermostat to what is conducive to healthy living in a peaceful civilian environment can be, for some, no small challenge—even if for many the transition is without trauma.

Still, the metaphor of resetting thermostats is limiting, as Hoge himself, a veteran of war and expert in combat trauma, knows well. In Lalo's case, what anguishes the most are not the conditioned fear responses that can unleash real and lethal aggression. For help with that, he now has Max, a black lab-spaniel therapy dog. "Max covers my back and takes the first hit," he tells me when I first met Max. And Donna has also taken away Lalo's knife that has gotten him too close to danger too many times. But what really torments Lalo is the relentless sense of guilt he feels. And appeasing that is not a job for Max, or fear deconditioning, or even anger management or weapons disarming.

Lalo can't let go of the guilt of not coming home with all his Marines. It near kills him: "To be honest, the thing I have dealt with the most [in my therapy] is guilt—survivor guilt. I would say the better part of the last year and a half, the better part of my therapy has been focused on survivor guilt.... I was in charge of guys, and my biggest fear out there was losing any one of them. They're all like little brothers who I trained. So, you know, I had guys that died because.... Before that [therapy] I never focused on myself, or the trauma that I went through. I mainly focused on the guys that died in my arms."

It is hard for Lalo to finish the "because." And even thinking of himself as the deserving subject of therapy and the focus of care seems a transgression, a way of letting up on his standing obligation to the others. "Before, in Fallujah, it was: I don't want to die. After that, I accepted that I might die. But I didn't want my Marines to. My biggest fear going into Afghanistan was losing a Marine."

He lost three Marines in Afghanistan. Two deaths haunt him, four years later, leaving him drenched in sweat at night as he rewatches the inner movie and relives the self-rebuke.

It was November 2009, the beginning of his command in Marja, and his platoon was preparing for the surge of 30,000 U.S. troops who would soon fan out in the southwest corner of Afghanistan, along the Helmand River, not far from Dasht-e Margo, literally, "the Desert of Death." Lalo was in charge of a unit emplacing remote ground sensors to gather early warning of enemy movements for target support. The area was riddled with insurgent bombs, and Lalo was wont to warn his Marines as they prepared to leave their armored vehicles to be sure to secure the area and take extra precautions in watching their steps.

On this day, he was one of four Marines in the second vehicle of the convoy. They were in their MRAPs, Mine Resistant Ambush Protected vehicles that could keep you more or less protected, at least if you stayed inside. Corporal Justin Wilson was a mile ahead in the lead vehicle. He had to go— "number 2," as Lalo put it delicately—when he first talked about the incident in an undergraduate ethics of war seminar I was teaching in which Donna was a student. She was eager to bring him to class, and he was psyched about coming.

"Wilson," Lalo said to the spellbound class, "really had to go." The driver of the MRAP stopped the vehicle. Wilson jumped out, found himself an empty hut for a bit of privacy, and got blown up.

Lalo heard the blast, called his corpsman, and rushed to the hut. The unit was under heavy mortar attack, and though a medevac helicopter was in the area, it couldn't land for close to ten minutes because of the barrage. Lalo made it to Justin and cradled him in his arms. "He was my Marine," Lalo later says to me, a year after this class, reliving the scene. "I was holding his hand, his body—his legs were somewhere else. And then it looked like he just faded away.... When he died, I finally put him on a bird ride." Some Marines were sobbing, he said. But there was no time to mourn. They were still getting shelled. Lalo gave the order: "Alright, he's on a bird. Move on."

He justifies to himself the "move on" tempo. "As someone in a position like that, I couldn't allow myself to be mad. I couldn't let emotions take over. I had to pick up the body parts." And Lalo did. He stayed behind, collected the strewn body fragments, and put them in the only bag he had in the vehicle, a black trash bag. A brief memorial would come later.

It is hard to hear this narrative without thinking that Lalo bears little or no culpable blame for his friend's death. The cause was an insurgent IED and the bad luck of stepping on it.

Lalo sees it differently: "The Marine had to take a shit. I could have said through the radio, 'Don't forget to reinforce the area.'" The wait to call in the medevac could have been shorter, he adds: "The sergeant who was on site didn't have frequency to call in medevac for five minutes. I could have pushed harder, found a way to make the call."

In his mind, luck—at least this manifestation of bad luck—doesn't mitigate the obligations of command responsibility. "I'm the guy in charge," he puts it. It's a father talking, a big brother. "They're my kids," he says, whether older or younger. "They're my baby birds. Ever since I was little, I didn't like people bullying other people. I would see people—like, five kids would get onto this one kid—and I would jump in, even though I don't know this kid.

You want to fight somebody, fight me. I loved fighting, but at the same time I didn't like people bullying other people. It was a rush to me. I loved it. I feel good helping out....In high school I always protected all of my friends."

Lalo is the protector, in the hood, of his Marines, and now of Donna. In his psychic reality, he sees only his missing causal agency—what he *let* happen on his watch. He doesn't see the inflated sense of control he *inserts* in constructing this picture of volitional and morally responsible agency. He doesn't see that he is making the blame fit by turning an omission, for which he isn't at all culpable, into a transgression that will hold him blameworthy.

But why should Lalo see that? At least, right away and without probing and time? Here we can be speculative for the moment and interpret, at a distance, psychoanalytically. I suspect that some of his aspirations to protect and be in charge are rooted in desires and fantasies of childhood about how "super parents" can rescue and save, and in his *real* childhood world about how *machismo* men *do* really protect and how gang leaders really *are* all powerful. Marine ideals reinforce that familial and childhood world: *semper fidelis*—never leave a comrade behind, protect your own, be in charge, bring your troops home. The socialized ideals of the profession resonate with a protector culture of honor: to take care of those in your orbit. It is not surprising that Lalo found a home for himself in the Marines.

The hyper-idealization of those Marine ideals is that the "guy in charge" doesn't lose troops. Or, that's how the superego takes up the ego ideal and punishes the self who is just a "good enough" commander who did his best with what he had. "His best was not enough," is the superego's devastating critique. "To settle for losing guys is shameful." *Guilt* is the anxiety of being punished; *shame* is the anxiety of having one's *persona* (the compromised and managed ego) exposed and laid bare as mere pretense. The pretense, the "thin crust of display"—to invoke the last chapter's theme—doesn't really convince Lalo. The failure of pretense to satisfy the fantasy of how it is all supposed to work out leaves a hole for crippling disappointment and despair to fill.

The fantasy, as I say, draws from different sources: from lofty norms and primordial pulls, both internalized in the psyche; from a moralized Marine ethos and from archaic longings about how grown-ups take care of those who are vulnerable. We tend to forget that Marines, like Lalo, go to war as child warriors, barely eighteen, with a mix of a child's needs and the self- and group-projected identities of how adults are supposed to take responsibility. The combination can be soul-destroying. Donna puts her finger on the point: "He gets so mad at me because I told him that when he got out of boot camp he had PTS [posttraumatic stress]. I told him that you can't be a young seventeen-, eighteen-year-old, go through three months of this people yelling in your face, stripping you of your identity, giving you a new identity, all in three months, and then spits you out into the world, without some sort of side effect."

The socialization is meant to be all-transforming, and for many it is experienced as a new, chosen identity.

There are other factors that likely contribute to Lalo's trauma and that have to do with the specific circumstances of Wilson's death, as well as another that we will turn to soon. First of these other factors is the open-endedness of the loss. There was a delay in the memorial service, which meant that the private and collective grieving had to be deferred, and with it, the honor giving and tribute, through religious or secular ritual, that can help dignify a loss: the rifle barrel in the boots, the helmet atop the rifle, the dog tags draped, each Marine, one after another, paying private respect to the one who is missing. Second is the prolonged immersion in detritus. "I slept with Justin for two nights next to me," Lalo said in passing, after telling me about his death. I wasn't following. Lalo had just told me he had put Justin on "the bird," and then joined his troops on the ground. "In a bag," he explained. "The remaining body parts were in a bag." Those were the remains Lalo had collected for two hours before rejoining his unit. It was two days before the remains were repatriated with the corpse that was in the medevac. All that time, Lalo kept vigil, protecting his Marine by his side. Third was the inglorious "black trash bag." That's all they had in the truck, Lalo tells me, when he was picking up the body parts. "A *trash bag!* I was putting my friend in a *trash bag*. I can't have black trash bags in my house because of that. Right, Donna?"

Lalo's moral injury is complex, with layers compounded on layers. At its core is a young person's self-imposition of oversized liability—liability for the destruction of a friend who has instantly become body shards that have to be gathered up in a shameful trash bag, with no time to properly mourn. The detritus alone leaves imprints that few of us, half a world away from the battlefield, can fully grasp. Lalo was seeing, smelling, and touching the charred and bloody flesh that had shot across a landscape, scrupulously picking up the tiniest of pieces so they wouldn't turn into enemy trophies. The most avid followers of war coverage these days rarely see what the combatants see; the public is protected, even when photojournalists are onsite. And that sensory overload—stored in the brain in ways that we now know are hard cognitively to mediate and process—can get stuck in repeating video loops, flashbacks that attach to a punishing narrative of moral accountability. The self-condemnation turns toxic through the imagery.

THE RIBBON CHASER

Corporal Justin Wilson's death is one moral wound. There is another loss that racks Lalo with guilt and smoldering resentment. In Arlington Cemetery, ten feet away from Wilson, lies Sergeant Christopher Herbeck. Herbeck commanded Lalo's sister platoon in Marja. In December 2009, Lalo headed up patrols in which he would locate IEDs and then debrief a unit intelligence officer on their coordinates, so the bombs could be defused and the area secured. Lalo reconstructs the events that led to Herbeck's death. The conversations, the tone of voices, the looks, the glances, the anger and disbelief—he's sifted through the scenes over and over to see if he missed something: "There was one [an IED] in southwestern Marja that I reported a month earlier, and it was supposed to be taken out. And this second lieutenant [the unit intelligence officer], because he had heard of all the battles we had gotten into there, wanted to go out and patrol there....I called him 'a freakin' ribbon-chaser.' He just wanted to go out there and get his combat action ribbon. So he gets a platoon to go there—gathers a bunch of guys that had never patrolled in the area....And he gets my friend, Sergeant Herbeck, to be the guy in charge of the patrol. I go and I brief them....'Look. My guys have been patrolling this for months.

This is here; this is here; this is here. You want to go here; you want to go here; you don't want to go there.'"

Lalo pressed the lieutenant on his motives for the patrol: "'What's your guys' mission?' The lieutenant looks at me, 'We're just going to go out there and poke.' What do you mean, you're just going to go out there and poke, sir?' He's like, 'Exactly that, corporal.' I'm like, 'Sir, if you guys are going to do some sort of mission, I understand that.' He's like, 'No, we're just going to go out there and poke and see what's going on and what to do about it.' At that moment I look at Herbeck, and I ask, 'Look, do you need me and part of my guys to be attached to your guys? We've been there; we know the area. We know what it's like.' And the lieutenant answers, 'We don't need you. You'll be our backup. In case we need you; just be on your radio.'"

Soon after, Lalo got the distress call: A Marine stepped on an IED. The caller read off the grid square coordinates. "I'm like, 'I know these coordinates.' Sure enough, those were the coordinates I gave the second lieutenant a month prior so they could have the IED blown up. And they didn't do it." Lalo rushed in with his unit to set up a cordon and secure the area. "Where's Herbeck?" he blurted out. A dazed Marine stared back. "Where's your platoon sergeant?" he demanded again. Then he heard what he feared: "Corporal, he's the one that stepped on the IED." There was no need for a medevac. The explosive had instantly pulverized Herbeck—an area, fifty square feet, "filled, spread out with body parts of my friend."

From the narrative so far, this is a tale of dereliction of duty by a superior officer, hungry for action and a medal for it, and cavalier about who will pay. Ask any young Marine or soldier: a superior's ribbon chasing turns them livid. But in Lalo's mind, there is blame enough to go round: "The IED never got cleared. And I never went back to check if it got cleared, either. I'm the guy patrolling the area. Why the hell didn't I go to check it out with my guys to make sure? You never know—especially, if I'm patrolling the area. You know? And here's one of my good friends, whose body parts I picked up for how many hours? Six hours. Because we didn't want to leave a single piece of him there for the enemy." The body remains, again, went into a black trash bag.

Protecting his and the Corps' ideals against a clear, professional betrayal turns the screw of subjective guilt a bit tighter. The counterfactuals, the "what ifs," pour out: "I feel like I *could have* done something else. I *could have* persuaded them to stick me with them and let me patrol. I *could have* gone and made sure that the IED was taken care of. In a big way I feel guilty that my friend died. And sometimes *I wish I could* just go and make sure that the IED wasn't there anymore. It's out of my power. It's out of my control now. But, shit, I was the guy in charge … of a whole combat area. I *could have* made sure that it got taken care of. But I trusted that second lieutenant to take care of it."

Philosophers and others who hear narratives like this are quick to tell me that guilt feelings of this sort are essentially irrational and inappropriate reactions. A Marine like Lalo must know that he can't control for these kinds of battlefield vagaries. His guilt is recalcitrant: the indictment that is at the basis of the guilt is in conflict with and lags behind a belief he endorses—that he did do what he could, without negligence or culpability. There is cognitive dissonance. Alternatively, if there isn't cognitive conflict, Lalo is just mistaken in his beliefs. Maybe he's naive about what he can control—maybe he's in the grip of wishful fantasies or has a sense of grandiosity.

Many in the military have similar views: "You can't go into war, command units, and think you are not going to lose lives." So insisted a West Point instructor to a group of cadets in a class I attended. Others I have spoken to view soldiering like doctoring: you know you are going to lose some lives. And you need to get calloused if you are going to do your job well. You need to be exposed not only to blood and guts, in both professions, but also to the limits of moral responsibility. Lalo has similar thoughts: "In war, is it expected to lose guys? Yeah. We had been trained to a point where combat is second nature. It's muscle memory. You get hit with a mortar attack. You get up, everything's attached, you keep going. You don't stop.… I mean I got blown up a couple of times in firefights. It was normal, it was expected."

But what is in muscle memory is how it feels for *him* to get hit and move on. How he feels when *others* he is in charge of get hit, and don't move on, is something different. A sense of command, a "strict liability" kicks in. "I don't look at the stuff I went through [as] traumatizing to me as it was to lose my guys," he says. "I trained these guys for a whole year, they deployed with me, and here they are dying in my arms, and here I am picking up their body parts for six hours at night. That's what hurts me the most.... And I haven't been able to figure it out."

Part of the ambiguity here is in what "normal" or "expected" means. In one sense, it is *predictive*—that there is a more than likely chance that, in war zones like Marja, a unit like Lalo's will take losses. "I'll lose some and I may get killed." What's in muscle memory is not so much that declarative thought but, rather, the procedure for what to do when you do get hit. You move on. You move your troops on. The ancient Roman Stoics talk about "pre-rehearsal of evils," or getting used to bad things happening. They invoke this kind of habituated, rehearsed response and something more—that you can learn to act habitually without fear or distress, in part, because you have come to believe that there *is* no real threat or loss to cause full-throated fear or distress in the first place. As long as you are holding on to your virtue, and it's rock solid, you have nothing to fear and have lost nothing. That recalibration of value takes the sting out of loss. The only loss that is real and stress-worthy, on the Stoic view, is your virtue.

But that's the rub for Lalo, and it's at the heart of a different meaning of what's "expected." Lalo has *normative* expectations of himself, both morally and in his role as a good leader. Whatever he expects to happen as probable outcomes, he has *idealized* expectations for himself, nourished by boyish fantasies and realities and by Marine affirmations of them. He judges himself by how well he meets those aspirations. And he has set the bar high, in abstraction from the very external challenges that figure into the probabilities about outcomes. With the bar set so high and so much psychic energy hanging in the balance, the inner challenges and outer challenges and constraints blur. He lost guys, he failed to meet what he views as a reasonable challenge: he failed to meet the normative expectation he set for himself and others set for him. And *that* failure and disappointment is not at all in his muscle memory. Moreover, in his own case, he reads normative expectation rigidly, as close to a demand. To fail to meet the demand as the "guy in charge" deserves stern self-punishment and guilt.

All this is an interpretation, as I said earlier. Away from treatment and a clinical setting, it is not therapy. In part, it is an attempt to understand if the conflict Lalo struggles with—and that so many other veterans face—is best understood as a kind of flat-footed irrationality, of believing p and *not-p* at the same time. Or, is it better thought of as a different kind of conflict, between what he reasonably expects out there, in specific circumstances, in light of enemy fire and the quirks of accident, and what he expects of himself? Strict self-demands push him into a preventive fantasy, with "could have's" and "should have's" of how he *might have* fulfilled his expectations while defying luck. I think it is the latter kind of ambivalence that is at play here. And as I will say in later chapters, erasing the irrationality in a way that obscures the demand on self and an idealized command role does a disservice to service members. It also veils the need to change professional development training so that the internalized normative expectations with which young military men and women go into war are more realistic. Grit, resolve, motivation, and reliability don't have to depend on models of zero-defect perfectionism.

Lalo holds himself responsible for losses caused by his acts or omissions, irrespective of culpability. At least in the case of his care for his troops, he subscribes to a version of strict liability. In tort law, *strict liability* is imposed without a finding of fault for the damages or proof of negligence. In his court, Lalo is, of course, plaintiff and defendant. And he is a fairly merciless plaintiff. He sees now what he couldn't fully see then, and holds himself to the retrospective assessment. Scottish Enlightenment philosopher Adam Smith offers a description of the dual stance we take in self-assessment: "When I endeavor to examine my own conduct, when I endeavor to pass sentence upon it, and either to approve or condemn it, it is evident that, in all such cases, I divide myself, as it were, into two persons; and that I, the examiner and judge, represent a different character from that other I, the person whose conduct is examined into and judged of. The first is the spectator, whose sentiments with regard to my own conduct I endeavor to enter into, by placing myself in his situation, and by considering how it would appear to me, when seen from that particular point of view. The second is the agent, the person whom I properly call myself, and of whose conduct, under the character of a spectator, I was endeavoring to form some opinion. The first is the judge; the second the person judged of."

The "spectator" that Smith famously has in mind is not an actual bystander but, rather, an imagined "impartial spectator"—or, as fellow Scottish philosopher, David Hume calls it, in modeling a related notion, a "judicious spectator." The "agent" judges himself by imagining what the impartial spectator would "approve or condemn" in his conduct. The emphasis on imagination in Smith's notion invokes a spectator who doesn't just mirror social praise and blame (or internalized versions of it), but who, free of actual bias and its limits, can assess praise*worthiness* and its opposite.

With this in mind, what if Lalo were to try to get to that fairer tribunal by bringing Herbeck into the room—at least, in imagination and fantasy? If he were present, would he be the plaintiff that Lalo now is? Would he accuse? Would he hold Lalo strictly liable for actions and omissions, independent of fault or proof of negligence? The idea of bringing an empty chair into a safe therapeutic setting, where the lost buddy or victim can return and perhaps absolve the patient who feels responsible for his death, is a technique being developed by some VA clinicians to supplement or replace more standard cognitive exposure techniques, commonly used in trauma treatment. Lalo's therapy has, in part, as he has explained it to me, involved more standard exposure techniques used in fear extinction. With a therapist, in a clinical context that feels safe, the traumatic scenes that are so often blocked and repressed are revisited; what happened is felt and experienced and narrated. In some cases, when recorded in journals or on audiotapes, those narratives are reread or replayed on one's own at night. The aim is to desensitize what one couldn't earlier touch. It is a de-conditioning exercise, on the model of deconditioning fear.

However, guilt is in many ways more complex than fear. On a *cognitivist* view of emotions, both emotions have cognitive content and are not just brute feelings. They are *about* something—fear about a real or apparent threat and guilt about a real or apparent transgression. Guilt, in addition, as an attitude of moral engagement, engages or addresses the person it is directed at and looks for some uptake. Lalo blames himself and demands, through his guilt, both payback of a kind and penitence.

Would the fantasized Herbeck do the same? Who knows? Even if resentment and guilt don't necessarily co-travel—one can feel resentment toward an individual without that individual feeling guilt, and vice versa—we are here talking about how Lalo would reconstruct Herbeck's reactions: Would he imagine Herbeck as a benevolent presence who could help construct a corrective emotional experience? I suspect that is what the "empty chair" therapy is banking on—revised or updated uptake through the mediation of benevolence.

This "transposition of disposition" is complicated, in general and here. But the first step is a willingness to hear oneself addressed by another—in this case, to make room for an imaginary conversation with someone who is not just a beloved buddy who covers your back, as you do his, but also who is now a "black trash bag" of "body parts." That may be in part why a conversation of this sort is so hard. The traumatic imagery is part of the causal narrative and part of the roadblock. The repetitive compulsion to undo what happened in part involves a wish to erase that horrible ending. The step forward requires keeping what's done done and lifting the misplaced and overwrought blame. This is the purported role of a benevolent empathizer. Herbeck may be that person, or at least as introject—that is, an internalized object—that Lalo can vividly imagine. But first he has to detoxify the image of Herbeck that he carries with him and that so torments him.

MORAL REWOUNDING

Lalo is trying to take care of himself these days, to turn his gaze inward and acknowledge that he's hurting. At first, compliance was to please Donna, but with more psychological and physical injuries showing up, it's been hard for him to deny the evidence. Treatment of all sorts has been required: a pile of pills, physical and psychological therapy, memory coaching for diagnostic and MRI workups, arm surgery, and more.

None of this went over easy with his immediate superiors at Quantico. And the moral rewoundings began. He was threatened with a disciplinary separation from the Marine Corps for the weight gain after he started taking some of his meds. Then, a staff sergeant grew tired of all the time he was taking off for medical and mental health appointments, and accused him, in so many words, of being a malingerer. "It's convenient that you have invisible injuries," Lalo reported him saying. "It got to the point," said Lalo, that he told that boss flat out, "Look, yeah, I'm a Marine....I'm used to getting my big-boy straw and sucking it up, but I need help." His psychiatrist—a civilian contractor on another base—intervened, reporting the staff sergeant's obstructive behavior up the chain of command and threatening to go higher, if there wasn't a quick remedy. Lalo's sergeant relented, but only after insisting that Lalo make up time by reporting to work at 5:00 A.M. daily. That was hardly viable, given Lalo's chronic insomnia and night traumas, and treatment for it, that make sleep regulation a challenge at the best of times. A confrontation ensued that brought Lalo right to the edge. The commander told Lalo he didn't have a choice in this matter: "Well, it looks like you're going to have to stop taking your sleep medication."

The tirade went on. Tempers boiled over. Lalo insisted that they go outside and talk about matters privately, but the sergeant persisted, in full view of Lalo's junior Marines. When "he got closer nose to nose," and "bucked up like he was going to do something," Lalo's hypervigilance kicked in and he brandished a knife (the knife that Donna has since removed).

It's easy to portray Lalo, and those like him, as a veteran with a short fuse, ready to snap and turn violent. Hyper-arousal and flashbacks to the battlefield are certainly part of his symptom set. But this exchange with his superior was also a full plate of moral reactions to moral abuse: he was made to feel weak, a fake, an impostor, a Marine who couldn't make it, a Marine who should be able to suck it up without medical or psychological help. Wounded was weak—at least, *this kind of wounded*. And he was told so to his face, and in front of his subordinates.

That shame and humiliation was piled on top of what Lalo already felt. Still, in the case of these shamings from outside, Lalo is able to create some distance, with Donna's help. Lalo knows the sergeant was out of line in denying him official Marine-approved appointments. And the appointments are ones he, in fact, needs; they are not an indulgence, and he is not a malingerer. And the sleep meds are also not optional, at least at this point, without an alternative sleep-treatment program. Lalo gets that psychological and moral injury is real. The sergeant doesn't, or at least it is convenient for him to deny it. But the shame for not being the Marine he thought he was, or thought he could be for his subordinates—*that* judgment is one he still takes to heart. He believes it. He can't wiggle out of it easily. And the moral despair it leads to can be paralyzing.

Three years after arriving home from Afghanistan, Lalo was selected for the Wounded Warrior Battalion at Walter Reed Military Medical Center in Bethesda, Maryland—a residential program for Marines with psychological and physical injuries, aimed at providing care coordination and recovery support. The commander at the Quantico base supported his application: Lalo's full-time job as a wounded Marine was to get better. That was his only job, the commander told the obstructive sergeant.

But there was a bureaucratic wrinkle that would injure again. Lalo showed up on campus with Max, the certified and trained therapy dog that was helping keep him calm and getting him out of the house regularly. But according to local base regulations, Max was not an official service dog, even though he was ADA (Americans with Disabilities Act) certified. From the point of local base rules, he was just a pet and wasn't allowed in the barracks. But Lalo wasn't going without his dog. There had been too many sudden changes in his life; he had just driven Donna up to New Haven, where she was starting a master's program. They were back to an every other weekend visiting schedule. He had just given up his therapist of one and a half years as part of the transfer of bases from Virginia to Maryland. He wasn't about to also give up the only constant at this point in his therapy. After some wrangling, an accommodation was found: he would live off campus, in a military retirement home in Virginia, with Max. And he would commute daily to the Bethesda hospital. A critical piece of the program—wounded warriors living together 24/7—was compromised from the start.

It's a glitch in huge, lumbering bureaucracy. As an Army colonel at West Point put it to me: "In my experience, you can't make it in the military unless you have a sense of the absurd." Lalo actually handles the "absurd" fairly well, with a little help from Donna's sass. Upon coming home, he was asked to pay the replacement cost for his Kevlar flak jacket because he returned it "damaged"—it was stained with blood! "Excuse me," Donna erupted, finishing the story for Lalo, "the vest did its job. They owe you for having gone through the injury." His commander wrote him a letter to get him out of the equipment fine: "The fact that the letter had to be written in the first place.... This is how I started becoming an advocate for these guys," says Donna.

Donna is Lalo's advocate. It would be hard to imagine his recovery without her, and without her sustained hope in him. I explore this in chapter 6. But for now, this story serves to give insight into the crushing guilt and humiliation many service members feel and the hard road they encounter in seeking help. Lalo's guilt may be overwrought, built on narratives constructed around fictitious missteps and impossible omniscience. But it is a guilt that needs to be understood and acknowledged by us at home because it is one way that service members can honorably bear the burden of taking young men and women into war. There are other less destructive ways to honorably carry that burden. And finding them is critical to resilience and recovery. But for those who do feel the guilt, a first step forward is having it recognized for what it is, with its moral pulls and aspirations, and its blurred vision.

The heavy weight of loss

CHAPTER 4

RECOVERING LOST GOODNESS

THE WOUNDS OF SHAME

Army Major Jeffrey Hall deployed to Iraq twice, commanding infantry and artillery units (at the time, at the rank of captain) near Baghdad and Fallujah. He signed up for the Army at seventeen, and at forty, despite having implemented versions of COIN (counterinsurgency operations) in those last deployments—serving as mayor of a local advisory council of elders, painting schools and laying sewers, outfitting scores of children with shoes (who never having worn them before had no clue that shoes, or their feet, had a right and a left), and risking life to bring food and medical care to families in need—he still thinks what he should do in armed conflict, and what he is good at and trained to do as a soldier, is to engage and destroy an enemy.

And yet that was not what his war in Iraq was about. Once Baghdad fell in 2003, he found himself deep into softer and more cultural methods of warfare, often inadequately supported, and unclear of the cause or mission. He often felt betrayed by his command, and as a result, he in turn was forced to betray those who counted on him. Stateside, he was diagnosed with severe, near suicidal posttraumatic stress (PTS), and with the support of his wife and his commander at home, sought treatment at Walter Reed Army Medical Center.

As he puts it, "You have to understand. My PTS had everything to do with moral injury. It was not from killing, or seeing bodies severed, or blown up. It was from betrayal, from moral betrayal."

One incident stands out. In his first deployment in 2003, a civilian family driving home from church in Bagdad's Mansour district crossed a cordon and got caught in the crossfire of a U.S. attack on a high-value target. Hall's unit didn't carry out the attack, but he was near the scene at the time. The mother and son were evacuated from the car, though died shortly thereafter. The father was instantly killed, his body parts strewn over the road. Hall and a buddy gathered up the fragments and rolled them up in a rug that they then loaded onto an ambulance. "It was collateral damage that happens and that is probably justified in war," Hall says philosophically. "The car just turned a corner at the wrong place at the wrong time." But in his mind what followed was not at all justified or unavoidable, and that is the aftermath that unravels him.

Shortly after the accident, Hall got orders from his battalion headquarters to find the surviving family members and begin to make amends. He found the home and a young daughter and elderly uncle, who had stepped in as guardian. Over Chai the family made it clear that what they wanted most was the return of the bodies for a prompt burial. Hall set to work, but his efforts were stymied at every turn. His battalion was partnered with the Coalition Provisional Agency (CPA)—Paul Bremer's American occupation administration set up to govern Iraq after the fall of Baghdad—and incompetence, by many accounts, ran deep. Hoping to cut through the bureaucracy, Hall drove to the morgue himself and located the bodies. But the CPA wouldn't release them without official paper work authorized and signed by the Iraqi Ministry of Health. So began the wait for over a month for the bodies.

In the meantime, Hall's commander called to inform him that the CPA had issued solace money for the family. With cautious excitement, Hall drove to battalion headquarters to pick up the money; finally, he'd have something positive to show the uncle and daughter. He was speechless when he opened the envelope and counted the bills. It was a piddling $750. He let his commander know how he felt: "Sir, they lost a father, a mother, and a son. And a car that is probably as important to them as the other losses." He handed the money back to the commander in disgust: "You go pay them with this!" The commander, cocooned for much of the war inside Saddam's former palace in the Green Zone, was unmoved. Hall had an unequivocal order to deliver the money.

And so he did. In silence, he handed the uncle the envelope and watched as he counted the bills, and then flung them to the ground. "I deserve whatever this man does," Hall recalls thinking. "If he slaps me in my face, I will take it. I will just take it." But the uncle just stood up, turned his back to Hall, and walked out of the room, the money still strewn on the floor. With the young girl's eyes glued on him, Hall put on his helmet, snapped his chinstrap, and left the house, covered in shame.

But the ordeal, and the shame, wouldn't end. The bodies were finally returned to the family, unembalmed and rotted beyond recognition by the scorching desert heat. The family had one last request of Hall. They needed death certificates to finalize the burial. And so Hall returned to the Ministry of Health and was given the certificates. On each was stamped in bold red letters: ENEMY. "Can't you give me something that doesn't have "enemy" stamped on it?" Hall beseeched. "No," the official curtly replied. "They are enemies. They are considered enemies."

The incompetence of Hall's superiors verges on the comedic, but the profound moral injury that Hall suffered verges on the tragic. Disarmed of much of his usual arsenal as a warrior, more than ever he needed to be able to trust his own basic goodness and have some assurance that he could compassionately help these noncombatants caught in war. However much a part of the just conduct of a soldier it is to minimize collateral damage in war and ameliorate its effects, for Hall the duty was more basic: it was an intimate duty to a family he had come to know and care for. He felt thoroughly impotent in the role. He felt profoundly betrayed by his command and coalition, and humiliated that their massive incompetence forced him to betray innocents who had suffered so grievously. When he says the injury was worse and more lasting than what he suffered from seeing the detritus of war for three years, what he means in part is that the betrayal by command put him in a position of feeling trapped and helpless, much more powerless and captive than he had ever felt in facing enemy fire. He was stripped and left defenseless, with nowhere to go. That shame haunted him until one day back home, on base at Fort Riley, Kansas, he simply couldn't put his combat boots on. Suicidal feelings and ideas took over. It was at that point that a new, far more benign commander than his previous one got him help. Empathy and self-empathy were a critical part of the healing.

The idea of self-empathy may strike some as odd. As an epistemic notion, empathy is typically directed at another and is a vehicle for understanding how to see the world from someone else's particular corner. As an affective mode, it is a way of being able to share someone's emotion and so have congruent feeling. But what work does empathy do when directed at the self? Even if we are never *fully* in sync with our own minds and emotions, for most of us there isn't the same gap within us as there is between people. The idea of empathizing with oneself, some might say, is redundant. I argue in this chapter that this is not so. Even if we are already in sync with many aspects of ourselves, there are still corners we don't peek into because their contents are too alien, so possibilities for change there are closed off. Self-empathy (or what I am interested in, therapeutic self-empathy) can play a role in peering into those corners and opening the doors. It can be an important part of recovering a sense of lost goodness. It can be a way of calling out to oneself that one is hurt and in need of attention and response.

Put this way, self-empathy can be construed as a kind of positive reactive attitude, alongside trust and certain forms of hope—in ourselves and in others. These emotions, each in their own way, and whether directed at the self or others, expose vulnerability and call out to others about one's needs, dependence, aspirations, normative expectations, and so on—*and* they seek a response. With trust, we call upon another to tend to our interests when we cannot. With hope, we call upon another to aspire to heights that we may not expect that person to reach without our setting the challenge. And with self-empathy, too, we call upon ourselves to re-evaluate our past actions, and to show mercy and understanding where we could not before. Sometimes we "grow" responsiveness in those we engage through our emotional calls. This is often true in the case of trust, where if we are a bit wise with regard to whom we trust for what and when, our very act of trusting may elicit and reinforce another's trustworthiness. Something similar may happen in the case of therapeutic self-empathy. We uncover our hurt to ourselves, and in that acknowledgment can sometimes elicit resources for responding to and ameliorating the suffering. In the case of punishing guilt, in empathetically reviewing the very evaluations that are at the core of our self-reproach, we may find room to hold ourselves to account in a more compassionate and equitable way. Rather than focusing on the fact that we have fallen short of some standard to which we hold ourselves, as we do when we take up the perspective of the accuser, we learn to empathize with our imperfect selves: we take up the perspective of the accused, of one who genuinely attempted to meet the endorsed standard, but who failed through no fault of her own.

We shall come to the various dimensions of self-empathy and their healing powers. But first I retell another story of shame, this one an ancient tale. And then I turn to a contemporary story of guilt with underlayers in shame.

In all this I come to moral repair slowly, as do the veterans I talk with, through the concrete challenges and anguish of real moral damage. For them, thriving or flourishing after war is rarely just about positive thinking. Healing requires a complex understanding of one's war—how to make sense of its detritus and profound losses. Those losses can seem, on the one hand, all too futile in the face of war's often dubious and grand political goals, and on the other, thoroughly avoidable if only one's own conduct were just a bit more perfect. Repairing selves involves a kind of inner moral dialogue, a kind of call and response. Soldiers often feel need and hurt, and seek help that acknowledges that hurt and helps to redress it. Healing starts, then, from recognition and empathy; self-healing starts with self-empathy. All this takes time, loving support, and intellectual honesty. For many in the military, it is still all too easy to soft-peddle the realities of mental and moral injury, and to believe that with just a little bit more positive thinking and stoic sucking it up, they can get the mission done. But healing after moral trauma is not that kind of mission. Thriving after war requires a different kind of resilience.

AJAX'S SHAME AND PRIOR'S GUILT

I first met Major Hall at a reading of Sophocles's *Ajax,* performed by the Theater of War before a mostly military audience at the 13th annual Force Health Protection Conference in Phoenix, Arizona, in August of

2010. The play is another story of shame, with disastrous outcome. Ajax is stripped of his *timē,* his honor and status, when the Greek chiefs vote to award Achilles's armor—a prize given to the best fighter—to Odysseus rather than to him, despite his legendary status. As Homer chronicles in the *Iliad,* Ajax was "the bulwark of the Achaeans" in their fight against Troy, "giant" in size, "powerful and well-built," "the giant god of battle," unrivaled as a fighter. In a famed duel with Hector, he is easily the victor. His own warrior mettle is storied, god-like, but so too is his father's. He is the son of Telamon, who battled the Trojans alongside Heracles and who, for his mettle, was awarded the Trojan king's daughter, Hesione, as a war bride.

In the play, Ajax's shock and shame of losing a prize comparable to his father's becomes part of a more generalized, psychological break. He has lost all face before those who matter: "I will return from Troy having earned nothing. How could he [my father, Telamon] stand to even look at me?" In a pique of blazing rage, he sets out to take revenge on Odysseus and his troops, and to prove once and for all his unmatched skill as a swordsman. But the goddess Athena blinds him and he flails his sword in the dark, mistaking barnyard animals for his rival: He "hacked at this chief and that chief," recounts Athena. And after tiring of the slaughter, he took the rest of the beasts captive and tortured them. Ajax "comes to" in a bloodbath of butchered carcasses and mutilated livestock. He mocks the sight of himself: "Look at the valiant man! The brave heart! The one who unflinchingly faced the enemy! You see the great deeds I have done to harmless beasts? Oh, the ridicule runs riot against me!"

There is ironic distance, but it fails to insulate. Ajax's self-evaluation couldn't be more unforgiving. He seems to look at himself as someone in the past. But his past is not *past.* It consumes him in the present. In an unparalleled moment in Greek tragedy, this great Greek general falls on his sword on stage. In this particular staging of the play, before a community that has come to know suicide all too intimately, the scene brought a hush like few moments I have known in theater. Ajax was in the room, in Major Hall and in many others, who felt they had lost their identity as warriors, and then their good name.

Here, the work of psychoanalyst Melvin Lansky is pertinent and well worth mentioning. Lansky, who has worked extensively with Vietnam War veterans, writes insightfully of stages that lead up to a violent, impulsive act, such as suicide, and the role of shame as a precipitant. Though Lansky's discussion is not focused on Sophocles's *Ajax*, the stages he describes have interesting correlates in the play and underscore the power of the play for understanding suicidal impulses and the role of shame as a causal factor:

(1) In the first stage, turbulence and shame erupt from a "narcissistic wound" that exposes one's own "limitations." In our play, Ajax is passed over for the all-critical prize, to which he believes he is entitled. This injury to his ego throws him into a narcissistic rage.

(2) Next, there is a "dissociative" break that may follow the upsurge of shame. As Lansky puts it, "In more protracted cases, the patient often reports a disorganized, fragile, paranoid state of mind." Similarly, for Ajax there is madness induced by a god: "Never in your right mind / Would you, Telamon's son, / Go so far as to slaughter livestock. / The gods must have driven him mad!" sing the Chorus. "I can darken the sharpest eyes," Athena boasts to Odysseus.

(3) The dissociative break is followed by an impulsive act, with the impulsive actor "oblivious" to its consequences. Ajax finds himself in a delusional state: "He thought he was bathing his hands in your blood," Athena tells Odysseus. Mad with rage, Ajax is unaware of his environment and the objects he acts on.

(4) The agent's consequent "reaction to the act," often "conscious remorse or guilt," can mask the shame of dissociating and of the impulsive act. Surveying the massacre he has executed, Ajax bemoans: "You see the great deeds I have done to harmless animals." So Ajax's wife, Tecmessa, reports: "He has been laid low by this evil. He won't eat or drink or say anything. He just sits in the midst of his butchery."

(5) Finally, there is a tenuous and manipulated reaching out to loved ones in response to the intimidation of self-harming. So Ajax demands that Tecmessa bring to him their son for a final encounter: "Lift him up to me here. The sight of fresh blood will not frighten him—Not if he is truly his father's son. Now he must begin to be broken in and hardened to the ways

of his father." In Ajax's case, shame piles on shame—the barnyard massacre piles on top of the loss of the coveted and anticipated prize—leading to the final, irrevocable act.

The experience of shame—as Ajax's and Hall's stories, ancient and contemporary, show—is about being seen and about having nowhere to hide. Greek etymology is a reminder. *Aidōs* is related to *aidoia*, genitals. To be ashamed is to be caught without your fig leaf. The audience can be real or imagined. When Aristotle says, "eyes are upon you," he should not be read literally. That is how shame *feels*.

In some cases, shame can be too toxic to be consciously experienced, screened as a more socially respectable and manageable feeling of guilt with its presumption of a discrete act of wrongdoing and its promise of redemption through moral repair. Indeed, perhaps one way to think of certain instances of epistemically ill-fitting (or irrational) guilt is as a substitute for shame, a sublimation of sort. So an Army commander who loses a private owing to an accidental blast of a turret gun on an army vehicle may not be culpably negligent, though he feels horrific and unabated guilt.

This is a case of what I call "accident guilt" in *The Untold War*. In the specific case I detail there, the commander, Captain John Prior, approved, with the advice of his team of engineers, the use of a Marine replacement battery for the Army's Bradley Fighting Vehicle in the early months of the Iraq War. What no one foresaw was that turning on the ignition would now cause the current to jump to the turret and automatically fire the gun. The blast scooped out the face of young private Joseph Mayek, who did not survive the ordeal. Prior tells me, several years later: "The aftermath of that was the guilt of the situation because I'm the one who placed the vehicles; I'm the one who set the security. Like most accidents, I'm not in jail right now. Clearly I wasn't egregiously responsible. Still, I dealt with and still deal with the guilt of having cost him his life essentially."

After a lengthy investigation, the mechanical cause of the misfire was pinpointed to the amperage of the replacement battery. Though the Marine battery had the same voltage as the original Army battery, the amperage was different and that turned out to be all-critical. In this case, the guilt Prior feels may be morally fitting and admirable, though not strictly speaking objectively fitting, given the actual facts of moral responsibility. That is, in feeling guilt (perhaps mixed with shame), he may be expressing the sense of falling short in his inability to save one of his men. He failed Mayek, in a way, and there is something admirable in that sense of taking seriously his obligation to his troops. But at the same time it is irrational to think that he really was at fault for failing to understand how the replacement battery would work, especially in light of having authorized its use only after expert consultation on the matter. Prior is well aware of this and so, in a way, his guilt is "recalcitrant." That is, the belief or appraisal that grounds the feeling is in conflict with another belief or appraisal he holds that he was not at fault in causing the accident.

What Prior feels is that he *should have* been able to take care of his soldiers better, or as philosophers might put it, that he less than perfectly fulfilled his imperfect duty of care. (As an imperfect duty, there is typically "room for play," as Immanuel Kant calls it, for how and how much one fulfills the duty, but Prior viewed the duty as having to be fulfilled perfectly.) So cast, the emotion may have more the color of shame than of guilt, the shame of falling short of an ideal that Prior set for himself and that captures his responsibilities of office and role. But given the context and the fact that a unit member was killed in a noncombat action, in "friendly fire" on his watch, for Prior and (for many like him, I suspect), the more ready-to-hand way to express that self-reproach is in holding oneself culpable for a negligent omission.

Guilt brings with it concrete opportunities for moral repair—to the mother of the dead soldier, to soldiers who lost their good buddy, to unit members who need reassurance that a similar accident will not be repeated. Shame may bring opportunities for moral repair, as well, in terms of reinstating oneself and reviewing one's commitments to ideals. In some cases that repair may be more self-regarding than other-regarding. In other cases, not. Hall feels diminished by his stymied efforts to aid the Iraqi family, and the discomfort of that shame may motivate him to redouble his efforts at aid. In his case, at least, it seems the urgency for action comes from a desire to right a grievous wrong to others that will derivatively help restore his own sense of goodness. One can imagine other cases in which the fall in self-standing and self-image itself pushes toward correction and a closing of the gap between reality and aspiration. In such cases, the push comes from the damage to the self more than the damage to others.

In pointing to the complex and camouflaged nature of this emotion, I am not suggesting that the feeling of guilt, here or in similar cases, is in any way manipulated—a contrivance that allows for a contrition that might not otherwise be possible. Rather, I am suggesting that feelings of guilt can easily eclipse feelings of shame; and when the shame isn't obvious or manifest, we may be too quick, both as self-judges and as judges of others, to think that what we feel is misplaced or epistemically irrational guilt. As shame, in contrast, the feeling is all too epistemically fitting, whether manifest or not—Prior *did* fall short of an implicit image of himself as a commander who takes care of his troops. Moreover, the idea of seeing oneself as a leader who should be able to avoid this kind of malfunction on his watch is not that far-fetched or grandiose; at least, it does not seem over-idealized to me, in the way that, say, thinking one can avoid enemy-inflicted combat death is. Epistemically fitting shame, in this regard, seems more permissive than epistemically fitting guilt and perhaps less "irrational." Still, shame of this sort can linger far too long. That is precisely why it is important to try to unmask the shame, differentiate it, and find ways to own and tolerate it. Self-empathy plays a role.

RECALCITRANT EMOTIONS AND UNCERTAINTY

We are nearly ready to turn to self-empathy and its role in helping to assuage the hounding (sometimes suicidal) recalcitrant shame and guilt feelings soldiers can experience after traumatic incidents in war. But to understand the reparative work of self-empathy, we need to understand better in what sense these emotional experiences are, in fact, recalcitrant. Consider one philosopher's view of recalcitrant fear: In a recalcitrant bout of fear, a person "is primed to act on and assent to her construal of her situation as dangerous, but does not act on or assent to this construal, believing instead that her situation is *not* dangerous." There is a waste of cognitive resources here. "Recalcitrant emotions therefore involve the mobilization of cognitive resources in the service of a question that has, by the subject's own lights, *already been answered*." The waste of resources means that attention is taken away from factors that *are* relevant to one's situation, and invested instead in an inclination to seek more confirmation of an evaluation one doesn't believe.

But sometimes—I suspect often, in difficult cases—feeling guilt involves an *open* question of one's moral responsibility. One simply may not have settled the matter as to whether one is fully off the hook. There is lingering doubt and enough harsh self-judgment to keep the question alive. It is not so much that one has an "incoherent evaluative profile," as this philosopher puts it, a conflict of evaluations about what one did and its potential wrongness. It is that one is genuinely uncertain, not sure what to believe about one's moral responsibility given one's causal involvement, whether one could have or should have known the consequences of one's actions (as in Prior's case, in replacing the battery) or could have or should have found a more graceful way out of complicity (as in Hall's case, in betraying the civilian family through the bureaucratic operations of his command chain). There are shadows of doubt, not a flat-out conflict of evaluations in the way there is, say, in the case of a knowing phobic who walks onto a plane and immediately becomes frightened, evaluating the upcoming flight as dangerous, though she in fact believes the situation poses no threats. Recalcitrance often comes in shades—it is a spectral notion, with unstable or ambivalent emotions occupying points on a continuum.

In the case of subjective guilt, to call it "irrational" or recalcitrant can be dismissive, encouraging us to overlook the genuine figuring out that is often part of the psychological process of healthy ownership of moral responsibility. That process may include an investigative sorting out of the facts of the matter: a psychological "working-through" (what Freud called *Durcharbeitung*) of the conflicts, investments, and losses; an acceptance of the limits of control that often are part of this kind of reflection; and an openness to feeling new emotions, such as grief, sorrow, and self-empathy, based on new evaluations once self-reproach lifts its grip. As such, subjective guilt may have deep connectivity to a range of epistemically appropriate feelings that we come to only indirectly, after first experiencing guilt and then surmounting it.

Consider the following case involving a student of mine. Again, the details are important for capturing the contours of the moral phenomenology—how it feels to experience this kind of guilt. Tom Fiebrandt served in Iraq between July 2001 and December 2005. At twenty-one he was a young sergeant and a team leader of a group of intelligence analysts attached to an Army cavalry squadron of 410 men in Tal Afar, a desert town not far from Mosul, about forty miles from the Syrian border. As cavalry, his unit served as the "eyes and ears" of the battalion, collecting and sorting intelligence critical for a dynamic picture of the current battlefield. The unit was a bridge between those inside and those outside the wire, with Fiebrandt himself spending much of his time outside, talking to troops and locals, and drawing and redrawing a visual, first-hand picture of the vicinity and its dangers. He knew how tall buildings were on different streets, where snipers could lurk, where you did and didn't want to be. He became the point guy who noncommissioned officers and officers alike sought to get their information. As he put it, with modesty but candor, his superiors "had confidence in his competence."

About three months before his deployment was up, he was ordered to take a few days of "R and R" (rest and relaxation) in Qatar before returning to the States for a longer two-week leave. Fiebrandt was reluctant to abandon the unit so close to the end of their deployment, but an order was an order and leave time was mandatory anyway. He was stressed of late, "bouncing inside and outside the wire," as he put it, and at some level, he knew that a break was probably a good idea.

En route to Qatar, he learned that his unit was about to run a cordon and search operation in the southeast corner of Tal Afar that had become a major smuggling hub, with weapons pouring in from unsecured border spots with Syria. It was now time to flush out the weapon caches and insurgents with a strong show of troop forces and a door-to-door raid. What Fiebrandt didn't know was that as part of the preparation, one of the platoons, headed by Lieutenant William Edens, a close friend, had been ordered to scout out a potential egress route at the backside of the city, where a wall of troops could be mounted to block insurgents fleeing the raid into the desert. It was during this preparatory drive-through that an IED struck Edens's vehicle, killing him and two others. Fiebrandt learned about the incident a few days after he arrived in Qatar. It hit him hard: "What bothered me was that it was in an area that I knew very well. It was in a part of the city that you really had to see in order to visualize. And I had this lurking suspicion that my soldiers, who had never actually, personally been there, didn't really have a grasp of all the information that I felt I did. In some way, I almost felt responsible for not being there to provide them with the information that may have potentially resulted in a different outcome. So it is rough. It is a difficult thing for me to process.... So here I was sitting by a pool, and I hear this. It was—I don't even know how to describe it. It was—devastating."

Had Fiebrandt been there, he is sure he would have recommended against Edens's taking that road. He knew that back area of the city was especially dangerous and that no unit vehicles had traveled down that road for good reason. He would have urged more reconnaissance on the routes and potential alternatives. "Whether or not I would have been successful in getting that to become the battle plan, I don't know." But given that he was relied on for this kind of information, he had a good chance of making the case. In his mind, he let down his command as well as a friend. What happened, as he puts it, "reflected poorly" on him. He "faults" himself for not being there, and though he is "frustrated" that his unit members "didn't have the same clout" as he did, and couldn't "pick up the slack" in his absence, he doesn't fault them for failing to make the call.

Significantly, it is just this sense of feeling that he is the only guy who can do the job and that it is a job that requires constant vigilance, without gaps and breaks, that both hounds him and ultimately opens the way for self-exculpation. The fact that he didn't *choose* to take the leave—that he was acting on an order—only gets him so far. The real exculpation comes some three to four months after the incident, when his deployment is over and he reflects on the incident in connection with whether he should re-enlist and return to Iraq after what would amount to a longer period away. He now sees, somehow, that the demand he put on himself to be quasi-omniscient, to keep constant vigil of the changing battlefield, as he puts it several times, without "gaps in his knowledge," is unsustainable. He reconstructs the thinking: "Well, god, I thought to myself, if I am not here in a two-week period of time and things go to hell in a hand basket ... what is the situation going to be like when I get back, having been away longer? I am going to be less equipped to handle any further situations, because now I have a real gap in my knowledge. So all of this was coalescing at the same time, and it took me a while to sort of realize that I couldn't be the person that was there all the time. I could only be in one spot at a time. I could reenlist and I could stay in the job. But ultimately I am never going to cover the whole country. I was never going to be the one-stop intel analyst for the whole Army. Maybe my role was actually very small."

Looking on from the outside, we might say, "Well, of course." However well Fiebrandt served in his role and however critical he was to the safety of his unit, he wasn't there that day, he wasn't at fault for not being there that day, and he wasn't at fault for not briefing in advance his unit about a mission that he didn't even know was going to take place. Yet for Fiebrandt, it was an epiphany to see that holding himself responsible was grandiose. It required too idealized a sense of his role responsibilities and duties, and too idealized a set of expectations and injunctions about how he was supposed to function. And yet the unreasonableness of the demands to which he held himself only dawned on him with time, when he realized their absurd implications—that he was expecting of himself something close to full omniscience and omnipresence, a constant vigil on the battlefield that could produce an accurate, automatically refreshed picture without gaps, breaks, and breaches. He chuckles as he thinks about the absurdity of it all and of the *reductio* that it took to get him to realize it. But, it is a tentative laugh. He still knows the pull of those expectations and what it is like to be in their grip. He may no longer endorse the evaluations so intimately related to the feelings, but when he says, "I kind of fault myself," or "I almost felt responsible for not being there," he still can put himself in the mindset of what it was like to endorse those evaluations and feel their tugs. He is now at a point where he has moved on. But he got there only through an honest moral struggle with what it means to be vigilant as an intel guy. There were limits to his knowledge and frailties that he had to accept, however they compromised his agency. Like many soldiers I have spoken to, Fiebrandt doesn't easily volunteer the word *guilt*. His words are *fault* and *responsibility*. But, it is clear that he is talking about self-blame.

I tell this story to illustrate the function of guilt, as a way of working out the boundaries of moral responsibility. There is genuine *intellectual* figuring out. The emotion of guilt is not just recalcitrant in this case, with Fiebrandt seeking confirmation of a construal "despite believing that there *are* no genuine reasons in favor of that construal." Fiebrandt is not sure what he believes, and he is not going to let himself off the hook until he is sure. The rub, of course, is that having "to be sure" quickly spirals into intellectualization and rationalization, an inventing of reasons. In short, it becomes primitive thinking that mixes rational processing with the illogicality of wishful/magical thinking and presumptions of omniscience. There are elements of this in Fiebrandt's thinking. Without any inkling of the planned raid, Fiebrandt had no reason to inform his commanders of potential dangers before he left for R and R. Yet, he repeatedly put himself back in the reporting chain as if he knew, or should have known, what would become relevant only later. Similarly, there was little reason for him to have pointed out that particular street to Edens; though projecting forward, he helps himself to what is now the salience of that piece of knowledge and faults himself for failing to share it earlier. He faults himself for an epistemic stance he couldn't easily have had then.

But my point is what Fiebrandt was going through wasn't *just* that. He was also thinking, as he put it: Was he like the homeowner who never quite got around to putting a fence around the backyard pool and then one day discovers a child has wandered into the pool and drowned? Or was he more like the cop who might have had helpful information but was legitimately off-duty at the moment and nowhere near the scene of danger? In the end, he seemed to think he was more like the cop than the homeowner, but accepting that required a lengthy psychological process of surmounting his self-reproach. It required accepting his limits and the bad luck of being up against them then. It required self-empathy.

SELF-EMPATHY

Much has been written on empathy in the past three decades, and so I will be brief in this prelude to self-empathy. "Empathy" is a term of fairly recent

academic coinage. It came into use at the turn of the twentieth century with
the translation by Titchner of the German word *Einfühlung*—"to enter into
a feeling"—a term itself first used by Robert Vischer in 1873 in the context
of the psychology of aesthetics and developed by Theodor Lipps in the context of how we know other minds. Two prominent models of empathy have
emerged in recent years as something of competitors in the psychological and
philosophical literature. The first is empathy as vicarious arousal or contagion. The key historical figure is David Hume and his notion of sympathy,
though what he means is what we would now call "empathy," a mechanism
that allows us to "catch" another person's affect. We know others' emotions
by coming to feel qualitatively similar or congruent emotions. Hume's metaphor is intuitive: We are attached, as if by a cord, with movement at one end
reverberating at the other, causing a fainter impression of the original feeling.
The second camp, led by Adam Smith, conceives of empathy in more robust,
cognitive terms. Empathy (again, "sympathy" is his term) is a process that
engages imagination, requiring simulation and the taking up of roles or perspectives. We come to know another's emotions by trading places "in fancy,"
as Smith puts it, and coming to "beat time" with their hearts. But Smith
insists that the swap is not only situational but also dispositional. We not
only stand in another's shoes, we try to become them in their shoes: to "enter,
as it were, into his body and become in some measure the same person with
him."

How do these models fare with respect to *self*-empathy, and in particular,
with its role in surmounting overly harsh self-reproach? One obvious worry
for the contagion model is that it suggests a picture of empathy as a repetition
of the same stuck, often intrusive feeling, and it risks re-traumatization as a
secondary effect of the repetition (even when the repetition is in the service
of mastery and self-understanding). The idea of emotional fixity or stubborn-
ness is part of a more general worry about the inbuilt biases of emotional
construals (or ways of "seeing as") that predispose us to judgments (in the way
perceptions do), but also, sometimes, predispose us to what we don't believe.
As one philosopher puts it, emotional subjects tend to confirm rather than
disconfirm their evaluative construals: "The feeling directed toward the
object of the emotion, and the related perception of the object as having the

[evaluative] property, tend to be idées fixes to which reason has to cohere. The phenomenon is a familiar one: when we are afraid, we tend unknowingly to seek out features of the object of our fear that will justify the fear." So we have an epistemic tendency to build an "epistemic landscape" that coheres with an evaluation and feeling. We lock ourselves into a specific emotional take. Self-empathy, as a contagious re-experience of emotion, may exacerbate a tendency that we already have and that itself requires intervention.

Similar worries emerge for the simulation view of empathy, for it would require that we take up, again, the very perspective from which we are trying to free ourselves. In the cases I detailed above, the emotional subject's focus is framed by guilt and shame that "capture and consume attention." Self-empathy requires dwelling again in that perspective, and so re-experiencing the same emotions. In the case of traumatic emotions, it may involve re-traumatization.

These objections may be limited, but they make clear that if a notion of self-empathy is to be part of a model of emotional and moral growth, something more than simulating and re-experiencing traumatic events and emotions (whether through narration or other representational forms—e.g., artwork or dance) is required. Here, not surprisingly, the notion of empathy in psychotherapy is helpful. Psychotherapy of various stripes, and especially psychodynamic models, depends on a patient revisiting and reliving painful emotions, characteristically in the context of an empathic listener who can both bear compassionate witness to the pain and through various interventions and gentle corrections of bias, interpretations, or reframings help break the repetition and defenses. The therapist's empathy involves "tracking" a patient's emotion—sometimes through her own congruent reenactments or counter-transferences, other times more cognitively. But it also typically involves a conveyed sympathy—compassion, trust, rapport, and a nonjudgmental stance that help build a "working alliance." Empathy, in this rich context, involves access but also benevolence and trust. The stance is both protective and transformative, helping the patient safely to remember, revisit, and feel painful reactions to traumatic events, as well as to reconstrue what happened in ways that may involve fairer self-judgment and less rigid notions of success and failure that ultimately help loosen self-destructive feelings.

All this is relatively familiar stuff. Less familiar is the notion of self-empathy and what role it can play in moral healing, not as a competitor or replacement for second-personal empathy and its role in formal or informal therapy, but as something in addition that has an important place in its own right.

One way to think about self-empathy is as a conceptually or causally derivative notion. We look at ourselves as if from outside, from a spectatorial point of view. Adam Smith develops the stance: "Whatever judgment we can form concerning [our own conduct], accordingly, must always bear some secret reference, either to what are, or to what, upon a certain condition, would be, or to what, we imagine, ought to be the judgment of others." So, individuals may come to self-empathy by internalizing a second-personal instance of it, say, when they learn a measure of self-empathy through the empathy of a therapist toward them. In this case, they may internalize another's stance. But they may also internalize the stance that they take toward others.

So, too, a rape victim in a support group may come to feel self-empathy only after first feeling empathy toward others in the group who were similarly victimized. "Oh, my God, that's what happened to me," the victim might come to say to herself. The recognition of experiences similar to her own and the ensuing empathy toward others may enable her now to look at herself through new eyes. Second-personal empathy, both the receiving and giving of it, may thus prepare one for first-personal empathy. One gains an outside perspective on oneself that is qualitatively different from the punishing and shaming stance that has held one hostage until now. Veteran support groups may similarly enable self-empathy through the validating experience of empathizing and being empathized with.

In thinking about self-empathy, it is useful to turn to Aristotle's remarks about self-love (or self-friendship). He is aware that the idea of self-love may be a bit strained, both because it requires that we stand as subject *and* object toward ourselves, and more importantly because it connotes a problematic sort of selfishness. However, there is room for a good kind of self-love, he insists, that is the capacity of a self to listen to practical reason with equanimity. He associates this kind of self-love with nobility and the sacrifice characteristic of virtue and practical wisdom, and contrasts it with the baser kind of self-love that involves taking material advantage for oneself.

However, in the soldiers' stories that are my focus, there is no short-age of nobility and sacrifice. If anything, that aspiration for virtue is too hard-driving, giving way to too much self-punishment when luck runs out. Even so, Aristotle's idea of finding the right way to befriend oneself is useful here. The best kind of friendship—that of character friendship, he tells us—is an arena for character critique and moral growth, which like all friendship requires positive feelings (*philēsis*) toward one's object and feelings of good-will (*eunoia*).

Self-empathy, as I am imagining it, involves a similar kind of self-friendship and requires a minimal measure of goodwill or compassion. I am also imag-ining it in the service of moral growth and in the cases I have limned of moral repair, of being called forth when one has held oneself accountable in a way that begins to seem unfair, or at least requires further reconsideration and reassessment of the nature of that accountability. And so the self-empathy I have in mind emerges as part of a moral process and is *earned* as a coun-terweight to overbearing self-judgment. This helps deflect various popular images of self-empathy as essentially self-kindness or self-compassion, a "going gentle on oneself," or, relatedly, the kind of self-esteem that is a con-trived boost to undo self-deprecation, or a narcissistic self-absorption where gaze turns too much to the self and not enough to others.

But equally, I am not thinking of self-empathy as a minimization of self, a putting of self in its place, as Cicero redacts the Epicurean teaching: these are "the restrictions under which all humans live," "you are not the only one to have this happen," "to endure these things is human." The Epicureans are saying, in effect: Get over it; what you suffer is just a part of the shared human condition. But this is not the kind of self-empathy I have in mind. I am envisioning self-empathy as an emotional attitude that predisposes one to a fairer self-assessment, especially, in the cases I have focused on, where luck and accident and power ceded to others squeeze out one's moral efficacy or cast doubt on one's goodness.

As a kind of felt reactive attitude, self-empathy operates by drawing us in, in the way that *emotions*—and not less charged mental states do—rein in our attention on what is morally salient and significant to our moral agency and well-being. One way of thinking about Tom Fiebrandt's experience is that he entreated himself to look back at the specific evaluations in his self-condemnation and the need for reopening the case. He went back to the very scenes that caused so much pain and assessed them from a new perspective that time and distance allow. In the dialogue of expressed reactive attitudes, overwrought guilt calls on the self to consider the reasonableness of showing oneself some compassion and empathy, in the same way that resentment asks those who have transgressed us to now give us reasons for reassurance or trust. The call in each case has the standing to expect a reply.

As suggested, the notion of self-esteem doesn't get at this reparative idea, but neither does that of self-respect. The underlying notion behind self-respect is that one is not servile or subordinate to others but, rather, an equal among equals. Yet someone may have no doubt about that, stand in no need of its reaffirmation, and yet still need a fairer hearing about whether "could have done's" entail "should have done's" in the case of guilt feelings, or about how fixed or severe the damage done to the self is in the case of shame feelings.

This reparative or therapeutic view of self-empathy presupposes the possibility of narrative distance and what one author has called a "narratable" conception of self: "We are able to deploy in thought and feeling a narratable conception of oneself: with a narratable past, which one now remembers, interprets, and evaluates in various ways; with a present; and with a narratable future, about which one can make plans, have hopes and aspirations, and so on. This conception of oneself is the narrative sense of self."

One is "in effect seeing oneself as another." And this creates an evaluative and epistemic gap essential to reappraisal and reevaluation: "One now knows what one did not know then; ... one can now take an evaluative stance which differs from the stance that one then took."

My notion of self-empathy adds to this narratable conception of self an ability to see from beyond or outside without radical dissociation or alienation from the old self and its ways of seeing *and* feeling. That is part of the force of the notions of affective and cognitive reengagement. In this sense, self-empathy allows for self-reintegration (a kind of connectedness), rather than serial reinvention or radical conversion. Though one may have psychologically and emotionally moved on, one can still remember how one saw and felt things. One can still be affected, even if slightly, in some such way.

As I am imagining it, in a case like Prior's, he can still feel a bit of the bite of the old guilt. It doesn't rattle him any longer, but in narrating the story, he is nonetheless affected by the remembering, in some way as he once was. That is not all he feels with respect to the events, though. He now sees circumstances far more completely and his emotions reflect those changed appraisals. But it is not just that he is now *tolerating* what he used to feel or think, or *accepting* and *owning* it for what it was, as therapists might put it. Rather, he also knows how it feels, as if in *muscle memory*. That is part of his self-empathy. Similarly, in Jeff Hall's case, we can imagine him experiencing a flush of shame as he retells the story and brings to mind the faces of the father and daughter or hears the commander's intonation as he gives him the order to deliver the envelope. The shame is no longer intrusive and paralyzing, as it is in posttraumatic stress. But it is still accessible. Self-empathy, as I am using the term—in addition to a compassionate, less judging regard—involves this kind of affective, empathic access.

Obviously the degree of access will depend on how changed a person's psychological make-up has become. Access exists along a continuum. When the narrative distance is great, an individual may be able to remember only coldly and cognitively, with little emotional valence. He isn't much alive to how circumstances felt then. At this extreme, a limit to self-empathy has been reached, at least for a while.

A STOIC LESSON: THE SAGE AND THE PROGRESSOR

To illustrate the idea of self-empathy as empathic access, the Stoic writers discussed two conceptions of emotional change. One characterizes the path to emotional enlightenment of the sage; the other, describes the emotional reforms of the "progressor"—that is, the student who makes moral progress but never reaches sagehood (namely, you and I, and all those I interview!). Self-empathy, both as empathic access and as compassionate, fair regard, can play a role in the progressor's life, though not easily at the point of sagehood. And it's the reasons that help underscore the notion of self-empathy I am after.

But first, some very brief background is helpful. The Stoics hold that emotions are ways of accepting certain impressions or construals about the world, And so, they are cognitivists. The impressions constitutive of ordinary emotions (and there are four basic ones) have to do with goods or bads in the present or future: *appetite* is directed at a future good and *fear* at avoiding a future bad, while *pleasure* is directed at a present good and *distress* at a present bad.

The Stoic prescriptive claim overlaid on top of this is that, in experiencing these ordinary emotions, we are assenting to *false* impressions about what is good and bad and what will make us happy. So, in experiencing ordinary desires and appetites, we mistakenly think the objects of those desires and appetites—food, drink, comfortable homes, and beloved children and spouses—are real goods and fail to grasp that the only real good in life is virtue, and that it alone constitutes well-being or happiness (*eudaimonia*). Everything else is an *indifferent*—it makes no substantive difference to our happiness. To be a sage is to be free of all those ordinary emotions and their clingy attachments, and prize virtue as the only real good. The sage who arrives at this enlightened state will not be emotion-free—truly *a-pathetic* (without emotion): he will have cultivated or "good" emotions (*eupatheiai*), hygienic versions of three of the four basic emotions (there is no good kind of distress for a sage) that will function as handmaidens of virtue and gatekeepers against vice.

The taxonomy is clunky. But the point of introducing it is that to be a sage who sees externals as truly indifferent requires *radical* transformation, a conversion of sorts, with a discrete break from a past self. You are either a sage or a fool, in one of the many hyperbolic Stoic formulations, and to become a sage is to leave behind what you used to experience as a fool. Stably recalibrating externals so that they are now seen as indifferents removes the sage from the emotional vulnerability to them that the fool still experiences. But crucially, for our purposes, this also means that the sage remembers his past in a way that is *affectively disengaged* from how he used to experience it. The remembered events simply don't touch him in the way that they were felt. They have lost their charge and emotional valence. They are not relived affectively, not even faintly. There is no "Proustian madeleine." Thus with equanimity comes a change in phenomenological access. And so the sage loses empathic access to who he was, but also, presumably, empathic access to those who are still emotionally like he used to be. In short, on this interpretation, the price of being a sage is that you lose connection to what it feels like to be a fool. This may be a blessing that makes achieving the most stable kind of happiness possible. But it definitely puts the sage at odds with most of humanity, including who he once was. This is a radical picture of conversion that requires dissociation from the past as part of an embrace of an enlightened future.

Admittedly, the picture is complicated by the Stoic concession that the sage still can shutter and shake. A sage's hair may stand on end at the sight of awful physical danger, "the knees of even the fiercest soldier [may] tremble a little as the signal is given for battle." Still these are not full-blown emotions, insist the Stoics. They are protoemotions (*propatheiai*), *physiological* disturbances that don't impugn the sage's pure virtue. They are caused by seductive impressions that only when assented to become proper emotions. "If anyone thinks that pallor, falling tears, sexual excitement or deep sighing or a sudden glint in the eyes or something similar are an indication of emotion … , he is wrong," insists Seneca. "He fails to see that these are just bodily agitations." Emotion "never occurs without the mind's assent." The sage knows not to give assent to these seductive presentations.

This idea of a "protoemotion" drives home the point that the sage still can *feel* what he used to feel and so preserves empathic access with his past. (And I have made this point myself in some reconstructions of the sage.) But the congruence of feelings, here, is thin and merely physiological. The battle cry is sounded, the sage's knees tremble, presumably as they used to, in the old preenlightenment days. But it is a physical sensation in his knees, like a startle reflex. Even if he can remember, cognitively, the thoughts that were part of an earlier set of reactions—that the enemy is fearsome and death unnerving—those are old appraisals no longer infused with affect. He doesn't relive the fear. Nor does he assent to impressions of present threats that would bring on similar feelings now. His body is just "acting out" involuntarily. He knows that to have the old emotions is both unfitting morally and unfitting epistemically, misrepresenting what is good and bad out there. And his character is in line with those new judgments. The upshot is that empathy with his past self is precluded as a condition of equanimity, but so too, it seems, is empathy with others who still feel and see through pre-enlightened sensibilities. This may be a new kind of numbness.

Contrast this picture of a sage with the less idealized model of emotional change that the Stoics also offer. The progressor aims for the sage's goal, to recalibrate values and emotions and thus achieve the self-sufficiency that comes with grasping inner virtue as the only true good. But the goal is always only asymptotic, and there is progress but also the possibility of regress. Even when the aspirant is most zealous, there is still empathic openness to what it feels like to be emotionally vulnerable and hurt. This is the best most of us mortals can expect.

Seneca, at times, takes up this stance when he writes to his moral tutees, his progressors, from the vantage point of a fellow progressor who is just a bit further along. He is the doctor as well as the patient: "Listen to me, therefore, as you would as if I were talking to myself, … lying ill in the same hospital." In a letter to Lucilius upon the death of his good friend Flaccus, Seneca urges Lucilius to move beyond his grief and "not … sorrow more than is fitting," though take comfort in the fact that the "the ideal soul"—the sage—can himself be "stung by an event like this." Still, if the sting (*morsus*) is a reference only to the physiological protoemotions to which the sage remains vulnerable, then Seneca is not offering much of a bone.

The real concession comes when Seneca confides that "he who writes these words to you is no other than I, who wept so excessively for my dear friend Annaeus Serenus that, in spite of my wishes, I must be included among the examples of men who have been overcome by grief." He suffers real grief, and not just protogrief—*lachrimae* that are an involuntary, physiological drip. Granted, the mature Seneca now "condemns" (*damno*) this behavior and believes he might have avoided it had he practiced then the Stoic consolations he now embraces. But what catches the reader's attention, and no doubt Lucilius's, is the empathic stance both toward himself and toward his student. Despite the psychological progress, Seneca remains alive to what he once felt. We can imagine him remembering the narrative details of the loss of Serenus and the actual feelings that he felt then—the helplessness and grief as he shed excessive tears, the shock and surprise, as he says, that someone so much younger than himself should predecease him. The feelings are repudiated but not disowned. Seneca, *qua* progressor, doesn't pity his former self for having been so vulnerable or fear for his current self that he will be derailed by the glance backward. In contrast, the sage both condemns his former behavior and feelings and has made them alien. The progressor maintains a kind of self-empathy with his past as he moves forward.

Self-empathy Is Not Self-forgiveness

Some readers may have the nagging thought that what I have been after all along is not self-empathy but self-forgiveness. Isn't it forgiveness that can really heal the guilt-wracked soul? Isn't it self-forgiveness that helps Tom Fiebrand move forward, or Jeff Hall leave behind the awful weight of guilt and shame?

Even if a notion of *self*-forgiveness is coherent in cases where one has transgressed against another, still it seems an ill-fitting notion when there is no real intentional wrongdoing for which to demand forgiveness, as in the case of these soldiers. True, as a more general idea of foreswearing anger and blame, it may have its place in the surmounting of self-reproach, irrespective of whether that reproach is deserved or not. But even so, self-forgiveness doesn't expose the more complex evaluative and affective mechanism I have been keen to explore—of surmounting certain emotions with compassion while preserving empathic access to them.

And why is that access important and worth preserving? I suspect it is because I don't believe that difficult conflicts and the emotions that express them are ever so completely resolved that all residue of such conflicts disappears. Self-empathy is a way of remaining attuned to those tugs and pulls as they morph into new shapes on new landscapes. It is a compassionate form of keeping self-vigil. That said, we may also need self-empathy in the cases where we have, in fact, transgressed or acted morally wrongly and forgiveness, toward ourselves or from others, doesn't seem quite right—perhaps because the wrongdoing was so heinous (and unforgiveable).

We've traveled a long and winding path in this sketch of the role of therapeutic self-empathy in a homecoming, uncovering along the way historical and philosophical resonances in the notion of self-empathy. As I have developed it, self-empathy is a composite notion that resists easy unification. A quick recap of some of its features will helpful. Self-empathy involves:

+ **Affective access** to past emotionally imbued experiences, such that one is able to "feel" and recapture something of the tone and valence of those experiences. This is the force of "being alive" to those experiences, not numb or dissociated. (This picks up on Hume's notion of empathy as a way of "catching" affect.)

+ **Cognitive and imaginative engagement** such that one can reinterpret, reframe, and so reconstrue emotionally powerful and, in some cases, traumatic experiences. This will often involve reassessment of the evaluative dimensions of that experience—one's sense of betraying or being betrayed, or letting oneself or others down, and so on. (This idea resonates with Smith's cognitive gloss on empathy as involving imagination or "fancy.")

+ **Compassionate and benevolent regard** toward oneself, especially in cases where it is needed to counter harsh self-rebuke. In the cases I am most interested in, this attitude can often amount to a fairer and more equitable assessment of responsibility that's crucial for moral repair. (Relevant here is Aristotle's notion that all friendships, including those toward self, involve feelings of affection and goodwill, and that the best friendships involve moral growth.)

+ **Reactive attitude structure,** in the sense that self-empathy is an emotionally charged way of calling out to oneself with the normative expectation of a reply. We can think of the narratives I have retold as involving moral calls to self about how to hold oneself accountable. Soldiers such as Tom Fiebrand and Jeff Hall are exposing their shame and guilt and demanding of themselves a shift from blame to *credit* for doing what was at the time reasonable or appropriate or simply the best that they could do.

+ **A narratable conception of the self,** in the sense that in understanding one's past actions, one narrates as if from outside, with a perspective not shared by the self that is inside the narrative: one knows now what one didn't know then. This notion of self invokes a historical perspective; one now has an epistemic and evaluative advantage that only time affords.

✦ **Self-forgiveness** may figure as a companion notion in this account of self-empathy. However, forgiveness typically connotes an objective wrongdoing that one forswears and seeks atonement for as a condition of reentry into a moral community. Insofar as the kinds of moral injuries I have been focusing on do not typically involve objective wrongdoing, self-forgiveness seems inapt. Granted, I have spoken of self-exoneration in places, but I am bending that term to capture the psychological sense of release from reproach and the move toward credit giving and self-trust, without commitment to the *fact* of a wrongdoing.

Perhaps the best way to capture that move from negative to positive self-reactive attitudes is by thinking about the shame or guilt that can come with nonperfect fulfillment of imperfect duties, and the ultimate acceptance of one's bounded but nonetheless honorable and creditworthy engagement. So, I couldn't save my buddy, but I was still a good soldier or Marine and I did nothing that intentionally or through negligence or incompetence or self-serving ends exposed them to undue risk or harm. To arrive at that point is no small achievement for many service members. And it may take the kind of self-empathy that is hard to come by for many a tough soldier.

To sum up, in thinking about self-empathy I have focused on moral injuries that may *seem* only apparent because the wrongs *are* only apparent. But the injuries are no less real. And the soldiers' suffering is no less real. Soldiers routinely impose moral responsibility on themselves in the face of factors that make light of their own agency, whether flukish accident, the tyranny of bureaucracy and public indifference, gappy intelligence, or all too lethal high-tech and low-tech weaponry. All this begs for healing, in part, through the consolations of self-empathy that allow one to touch the past in a way that doesn't devastate and to see a future filled with some sense of trust and hope in oneself and others.

How deep is trust within the ranks?

CHAPTER 5

———★———

REBUILDING
TRUST

"A Deer in Hunting Season"

In late 2005, "Sally," then twenty-two, deployed to Iraq from an Air Force base in the Midwest. The walk into the chow hall each day was a routine reminder of her perilous state as an attractive woman in a predominantly male and fairly sexist military. "I would walk in and everybody would stare at me," she said. "I felt like a deer in hunting season." She felt guilty relief when another woman would come on base, and eyes were redirected. What particularly upset her was that officers led in the staring: "The first ones that I noticed ogling me were the commanders, the higher officers, and after two seconds, they would look down or look away. So they are feeling kind of ashamed, and they know that they all have simultaneously reached that point in ogling and feel like, 'I shouldn't be doing this.'"

Sally wasn't the only woman I interviewed who told me of the chow hall ordeal. "When I would go into the dining room, I mean *everybody* is looking at you. There will be tables of guys elbowing each other: 'Hey, check it out,'" a mid-level Air Force officer told me on a recent visit I made to give a talk at the Air Force Academy. The leering wore on her, though she was no stranger to that kind of gender-drenched environment. In 2003, she was a freshman cadet at the Academy when it was roiled by sexual harassment and assault scandals. She now teaches there and sees an all too familiar pattern of sexism persisting in many of her classes and pervading life on the base, in subtle and not so subtle ways.

In Sally's case, downrange, her officers' predatory leers inspired little confidence in their leadership: "When all else fails, they're who I should be able to go with problems ... but they're having a hard time, just struggling with my presence." Still, she felt conflicted throughout her deployment, and afterwards, about whether she was empathetic enough toward many of the males and took seriously enough their sense of sexual deprivation. She worried that she was putting her own fears before their needs. "We're sexual creatures, I understand this," she told me. "So, I'm sure in an all-male shop the sexual urge was a little bit more rampant and the frustration dealing with that built up.... I think I always fought with whether I was compassionate enough for them.... I always struggled with how much I could put up with, and how much I couldn't."

Two harassment incidents forced her to turn to her superiors for intervention. In the first, a unit member began to stalk her, spreading rumors that they were sleeping together. Given the daily chow-hall ogling, she was "already hypervigilant; then, on top of that, I had to look out of the corners of my eye all the time to see if someone was following me. It was really stressful." In a second incident, she noticed that her underwear went missing while she was doing her laundry one day. She had stepped outside the laundry area to take a break for a few minutes; when she returned to fold the dry clothes, her panties and bras had vanished. She felt embarrassed and exposed, and ashamed even to have to write to her mother to ask, without explanation, for a care package, not of goodies but of a new supply of underwear.

After the theft, she decided it was time to report what was going on to her immediate supervisor, a male NCO (noncommissioned officer). Though she was reluctant to burden him with her problems in the midst of a war, and especially embarrassed to have to expose "the weird" underwear theft, she felt threatened and needed help. It got to a point, she said, where "I just couldn't take it anymore." We might say that she took a stab at trust.

Trust and trustworthiness are irreducible elements in the fabric of military life. They are the glue of any good military and are key to the willingness of battle buddies to fight and die for each other. Ordinary trust is the confidence that people won't betray you or waylay you in an alley or fail to bring you your soup, if they're your waiters. The bar is obviously higher for battle buddies than for waiters and diners. And yet trust is constantly tested in war among those who are supposed to be one's archdefenders. Betrayal by command or peer or institution is all too common a theme in military life and a significant cause of moral injury. The residue of those betrayals is part of the long afterwar in need of repair, in part through the renewals of trust at home.

The issue can be especially acute for women in the services, at home and abroad. Overall, women make up about 14 percent of the active-duty force, and on some bases abroad during the recent conflicts, they have been only 2 percent of the personnel, or 1 in 50. Betrayals in war zones can leave women with a profound sense of isolation, unprotected on American bases in a foreign enemy's land. On ships, where battle can quickly turn internecine in the absence of an outer enemy, women often feel especially alone and at risk. Trust's call, so critical to a band of warriors—that one can count on a buddy to cover one's back—falls on deaf, and sometimes hostile, ears. The reasonable expectation that battle buddies will be trustworthy, motivated by goodwill, or respect, or conscientious performance of duty—or more minimally, interest in reputation bound up with being regarded as trustworthy—is too often violated. Systemic biases underlying gender betrayal in the military, including sexual assault, harassment, unwanted contact, and inequities in prosecution, have been slow to be exposed, and only now, as I write, are making their way to the Senate floor, with proposals and responses of service chiefs. High-profile cases are exposing a broken judicial system and ill-thought-out responses to political pressures that can make worse the inequities.

It is not just *women* who are abused sexually inside the wire. In a recent report on sexual assault, the Pentagon estimated that 26,000 service members experienced unwanted sexual contact in 2012, up from 19,000 in 2010. Of those cases, 53 percent involved attacks on men, mostly by other men. This should not be surprising, given that men make up the bulk of the force and predatory sexual behavior has long been a form of bullying and entertainment in an all-male force. When I taught at the Naval Academy in the mid-1990s, the masculine entrenched environment made life for some of my women students desperately uncomfortable. A more recent high-profile sexual assault case at Annapolis, and campus-wide shunning of the female accuser, suggest that patterns of sexism have not changed much in twenty years and may even be more entrenched now than then. Given the difficulties for victims of sexual abuse, male and female, to come forward, the statistics likely underreport the incidences. Victims are left to suffer with shame and humiliation and trauma that are often overlooked in favor of more traditional combat exposure trauma.

But what the public debate presumes is that we all understand well enough what trust is and how to rebuild it. I don't share that presumption. Given how critical trust is within the military and to reentry at home, it warrants our careful scrutiny. In this chapter, we listen to several female service members and the serious challenges to trust that they face. And we listen to an ancient Greek male warrior whose willingness to trust the Greeks after a massive betrayal gives general insight into the conditions necessary for trusting again.

WHY TRUST OTHERS?

I conceive of trust as I have the other reactive attitudes, as implicitly involving a call to a person that you are holding him to account, with a normative expectation of an appropriate reply. Specifically, it is a summoning of another to recognize that you are in need or dependent in a specific way and require attention or assistance in that domain. In a most general sense, it is an exposure of vulnerability to another of one's finitude as a practical agent, with the expectation that the other will be responsive. Trust is as basic to the military as forming a cadre.

But why think you can trust another, especially when you lack strong beliefs that the other won't let you down? Why should a trustor trust a trustee to do something?

Consider Sally again. In coming forward, Sally might think, this man may be no more concerned about my well-being than my harassers. But in his role as supervisor, he is *constrained* to help me, and if he cares at all about compliance and conscientious fulfillment of his duties, then he should behave reasonably. In the philosophical literature, some have objected that this line of thought amounts more to *reliance* on another person than real trust (where reliance is a predictive notion that could be answered by the workings of a machine, stable patterns of nature, or a person's dependable psychological habits). Trust, in contrast, is a normative notion, an expectation based on a belief about how people *ought* to behave toward you, given your normative standing or status. Specifically, it is an expectation of another's genuine interest in your well-being or dignity. As one philosopher has argued in important early work on trust, trust is the expectation of another showing you goodwill. But while conscientiousness may be a thinner kind of moral (or normative) motive, it still seems to ground a kind of trustworthiness. Indeed, in Sally's case, knowing that her supervisor is motivated by conscientiousness in taking care of his troops might be enough for her to feel she can count on him. In this regard, conscientiousness as motivating trustworthiness works like goodwill. As a conscientious teacher, it is just part of my role to be responsive in various ways to my students—and so, too, a doctor toward her patients and, similarly, a first-line supervisor toward his soldiers. His job just is to take care of those under his command.

The rub, of course, is that in practice, in the context at hand, an entrenched male military, what constitutes the ideal of a conscientious commander is often laced with deep-seated bias and built-in institutional prejudice that can harm and disadvantage women and other minority and marginalized groups. (The issues can range from sexual harassment and assault [of women and men alike] to gender "naivete" with regard to hygiene requirements that can mean downrange port-a-potties that can't handle tampon disposal and stench.) The more general point is that social norms can compromise positive responsiveness to need, whether the responsiveness is in the form of goodwill (respect and benevolence) or a blander conscientious performance of duty. Each alike can be blind. On their own, they are abstract ideals that don't necessarily meet the needs and capabilities of real people in concrete cases.

Others have argued that the ground of trustworthiness has little to do with moral motives, thick or thin, and reduces simply to self-interest.

To be regarded as trustworthy by others satisfies a person's basic need for self-esteem: We desire and take pleasure in each other's good opinions. And being trusted is one such important opinion. The "cunning" of trust, as one philosopher puts it, is that it takes a motive that might be thought of as problematic and tames it for its social capital. In a parallel vein, another author argues that it is in a trustee's own self-interest to maintain a trust relationship and so in her interest to "encapsulate" the trustor's interests within her own. Trust banks on that confidence: "You can more confidently trust me if you know that my own interest will induce me to live up to your expectations. Your trust is your expectation that my interest encapsulates yours." But while it may be useful at times to ground trust in another's self-interest, relationships built on mutual self-interest (such as utility, as Aristotle argued long ago in cataloguing different kinds of friendships) tend not to be all that stable: "The useful is not permanent but is always changing," he reminds us. Self-interest is a wobbly ground for friendship, in part because what's in one's interest doesn't always coincide, or coincide for long, with the interests and needs of another. Similarly, self-interest is too transient a ground to motivate stable trust. Self-advantage can pull apart from what others are counting on one to do. And when it does, and prevails, trust and trustworthiness give way.

This is the backdrop for thinking about Sally's narrative. Imagine for the moment what she was probably hoping: that her interaction with her supervisor would be trusting in the sense that he would show her some goodwill. In coming forward, she is hoping he responds to her with genuine interest in her well-being and with an acknowledgment that she has been mistreated and threatened. Her trust overture may well be tentative. It's as if she is asking her supervisor, implicitly, if she can trust him before she trusts him. We do this kind of thing all the time when we make general inquiries: "Can I ask you a question?" is sometimes the preface to asking a question. What we are trying to do is establish our listener's standing, or maybe "instate" it through some prep work. We roll out the substantive exchange slowly so that we can build confidence in a partnership. In *deciding* to come forward, Sally is doing some of this. She's setting up a meeting, asking her supervisor to make time, asking him, in a way, to warm to the idea of being interested in her well-being and her personal safety on base.

Once they meet, his goodwill toward her would be communicated in just that kind of responsiveness, adapted, of course, in the way that attitude always is, to our personalities or temperament and professional codes of conduct. But the point is that goodwill is normatively expected. But so, too, is conscientious fulfillment of his office as a good supervisor, role modeling by example, and setting the right kind of nonsexist tone for the command climate within his unit. When she exposes her vulnerability, she in essence is saying, "I'm counting on you. I can't handle this one on my own." The interaction, ideally, puts in motion a reflective loop: he knows that she is counting on him, and she knows that he knows, and so on. As Aristotle might put it, building on a metaphor from the ancient Greek Stoic Chrysippus (280–207 BCE), and preserved by Seneca in his account of the mutual interaction in benefit and gratitude: Each "does not fail to notice" that the other "has properly thrown and caught [the ball] from one pair of hands to the other." That mutual acknowledgment ought to reinforce the supervisor's sense of being held accountable and of Sally's holding him accountable. But she might also think about his potential trustworthiness in more strategic terms, as we've said: that it's in his basic self-interest to care about her opinion of him, and that of other women on base who, if he responds well, may come to view him as a trustworthy advocate and good leader.

However, from my conversations with Sally, it's clear that she didn't ever develop that kind of trust toward her supervisor, or other senior officers, male or female, for that matter. (There were no female officers in her unit, and the one female officer outside her unit was well above her rank and outside what Sally viewed an appropriate reporting chain.) In short, Sally never got the sense that her supervisor was particularly responsive to her. In the case of the stalker incident, he did step in and mediate. But in the case of the underwear theft, he wasn't particularly empathetic or much interested in following up. He didn't seem to think it threatened her in any serious way or made her feel less safe in a war zone. In the end, she relied on her supervisor in only a perfunctory way; she never felt like she was being cared for in the way that noncommissioned officers are supposed to "take care" of their troops. The suspension of trust exposed an irony not lost on Sally: "I remember I did seek service with a chaplain … and he happened to be a captain. One of my complaints was that I didn't feel like I could trust any of the officers. It was an awkward moment, because I'm telling an officer I don't think I can trust officers!"

In the end, in the absence of trust, she became self-protective. She "androgenized" herself, she said—never wore make-up and cut down on her use of shampoo after receiving flirtatious comments on how nice her hair smelled. "You just don't want to look pretty. You want to be clean. But that's it." And she began carrying an unconcealed knife to meals, clipped to her wallet and slung around her body on a string.

TRUST AS REPARATIVE

Sally's bid at trust was not successful. Her resentment and fear on base went unabated. She never got the reassurance that what happened wouldn't be repeated. Her wariness toward many of the males around her triggered a backlash of defensive hostility and more reactive vigilance on her part. Her supervisor did little to improve the climate. A year or more after her deployment, she was still cautiously working out "trust issues" back home: The knife was "only an Iraq thing," she told me. "I now carry mace in my car. For the most part, civilians take care of their sexual needs. And I have good enough judgment to know how to keep myself away from the wrong people." By and large, she was amazed at how much more easily she could breathe on a large coed university campus that had near gender parity in its student population. Her sense of being routinely toyed with as a woman was beginning to lift.

Put all this into the language of expressed reactive attitudes, the manifest attitudes by which we hold each other accountable as members of a shared moral community: expressed resentment is moral address mediated through anger. We react with hurt and pain to something that has been done to us that violates due regard or a norm, and we sanction the transgressor through blame. Resentment demands recuperation of respect and goodwill in a negative way, through direct or second-personal reproach. Indignation is a third party's reproach toward those who have injured you. In one sense, it is moral protest *on your behalf* for an injury against *you;* in another sense, it is moral protest more globally for an affront against *one's shared humanity*. Either way, it involves the kind of intervention and empathy Sally hoped she would inspire in her supervisor, in even the faintest way, when she came forward.

But of course we hold each other to account in positive ways, too, as I have been arguing throughout, and we build partnerships and engagements through more reparative forms of moral (and normative) address. Resentment sometimes paves the way for it. In a formulation used earlier, the "preventive fantasy" in retributivist attitudes is the thought that the other *might have* acknowledged me. There was room and reason in another's deliberations for a different, more positive response and regard.

Trust makes good that fantasy. As another philosopher has put it well, "the sought-for 'answer' to being 'addressed' in the mode of resentment is 'be assured, trust again.' " This is to say that trust can be reparative. To loosely repurpose Nietzsche's idiom for *ressentiment* (which we considered in chapter 2), trust is a *positive* "reactive pathos." It is a positive attitude of holding another accountable that may work to undo resentment.

While resentment looks primarily backwards, *reacting* to what another has done, trust along with hope looks primarily forward, imagining and *projecting*. Trust is anticipatory, and broadly speaking, takes the form of a confidence (albeit often mild or weak), or an expectation about a person that falls short of sure belief and that involves some exposure to vulnerability and risk-taking. When expressed and explicit, as we have said before, it signals to the other that one is counting on her to recognize and respond to one's dependency or entrustment in a certain domain. We are counting on her to be responsive to our trust and to mirror that trust through trustworthiness. Granted, as we've noted, there are often backward-looking (reactive) reasons that support one's forward-looking projection of trustworthiness in another, such as past evidence of goodwill or solidarity or conscientiousness. Still, in trusting, one takes a gamble. That is especially so for Sally. She comes forward hesitantly in a way that so many victims of sexual harassment and abuse do. She fears she won't be taken seriously or believed, and that talk of bras and panties will seem like girly patter. She's not playing along in the "bro" game. Still, Sally takes a chance in summoning help. It is clear that she is not asking for a moral bludgeoning against the stalker or underwear thief; reparative trust can be built on empathy. Empathy goes a long way—in this case, by the supervisor showing that he "gets it," understands why she might feel unsafe, inside the wire and not just outside. If she trusts, in part, it is in order to bootstrap trust with a trustee who hasn't yet fully earned it. Even if she fails, she reasons that she needs to take the risk—treat the supervisor *as if* he's trustworthy and responsive to her call. She doesn't begin by wearing the knife. That comes after.

"HE GAVE ME HIS HAND, BUT TOOK MY BOW"

Let us now enter the realm of Greek mythology and take up another complex tale of testing trust. The trust trial comes in the aftermath of a massive betrayal by command, a festering resentment, and an entreaty to trust again by an emissary of the group who betrayed. The strange trust relationship I refer to is that between Philoctetes and Neoptolemus in Sophocles's tragedy *Philoctetes*. The case has little on its face to do with women in the military. But it is has everything to do with betrayal and abandonment, and the bootstrapping of trust afterwards. And in this regard, it speaks to women *and* men in the services who may suffer betrayals by command, or by political leaders, or by public and private institutions of all sorts, or by civilians too ready to say to a service member, "I just can't imagine what you've been through" and so perpetuate the myth that the military are made of different stuff from the rest of humankind, and that their experiences and traumas are somehow unfathomable and unspeakable. That remark is part of an implicit call and response, antiphonal to a service member's own defensive retreat, "You wouldn't understand, you weren't there." From both sides, the remarks conspire to create a romantic view of the warrior class that too easily lets civilians off the hook and invites isolation and betrayal by distance.

Our tragic tale has to do with profound isolation and betrayal. But before recounting the story, it is important to remember that Sophocles (496–405 BCE) was himself a Greek general whose plays, like *Ajax* and

Philoctetes, were public reentry rituals of sorts performed before returning veterans. They served as a public homecoming, or *nostos.* The audience would likely include top brass in the front rows, and hoplites, or foot soldiers, in the upper reaches, in an amphitheater that could hold some 15,000. The audience knew war all too well. Sophocles was writing in a century in which there were seven decades of war. The reenactment, or *mimēsis,* of betrayals by command, awful separations from family and home, abandonments due to war-incurred disfigurements, and psychological maladaptions were among the themes. But so, too, especially in *Philoctetes,* was the theme of repair through trust and hope. The audience learning from the suffering (and growth) on stage, through the cathartic and identificatory emotions of pity and fear, could, as Aristotle teaches in the *Poetics,* engage in their own healing from war.

The story will be familiar to some readers. Philoctetes is a Greek warrior marooned for ten years on the island of Lemnos, abandoned by his Greek commanders as they headed on to Troy. He was left behind because of a fetid foot wound he suffered as the result of a bite from a poisonous snake guarding the tomb of the goddess Chryse. Shunned by his command and by a fleet that couldn't tolerate the putrid smell of his mutilated foot or the constant shrieks of his anguished wailing, he was left to die with his "weeping disease." But ten years into his solitary confinement, Philoctetes, or more properly his bow, becomes critically necessary for the victory of the Greeks against the Trojans. And so Odysseus, trickster and cunning speechifier, enlists a boy warrior, Neoptolemus, with the right credentials and ancestral lineage (he is son of the deceased and glorious Achilles), to do Odysseus's and the Greek army's bidding. The two arrive at the island, Odysseus keeping out of sight as he coaches Neoptolemus to capture the bow through a snare of trust: "You know I could never speak to him as you can / He will trust you, and you will stay safe."

Like a good military interrogator, Neoptolemus is to build trust in order to exploit it. Of course, it is not intelligence that he will gather, but the "unassailable weapon" itself. He is to say that he too has a grudge against the Greek commanders for not holding him worthy of inheriting Achilles's arms. And from that sense of shared *ressentiment,* Philoctetes will begin to make himself vulnerable to Neoptolemus's overtures. He will begin to trust.

The trusting at first seems odd. Why should Philoctetes trust this young stranger who has pulled in from Troy and arrived so mysteriously on his island? Moreover, is it trust or just desperation that disarms him of caution? For he is miserable and lonely, and above all else craves safe passage home. He longs for human contact, and after a decade of solitary confinement thirsts for any news a messenger can bring of the battlefront and the fate of his fellow soldiers. In light of all this, is he just too ready to gain a friend, as a possible meaning of his name suggests ("he who gains a friend")? Trust is an attitude born of dependency. But when the need is abject and the power others have over one is near total, trust is manipulated, not given. Indeed, as I said, Neoptolemus's narrative of betrayal by the Greek commanders might be seen as an ancient version of a rapport-building technique that a good interrogator uses. The good interrogator develops an intimate and empathic relationship with his subject, and may even sow the seeds for an erotic or idealizing "transference" onto himself that can then be exploited for further domination and advantage: Neoptolemus rehearses plausible grounds for rapport: "Abused and insulted, I am sailing for home / Deprived of what is rightfully mine / By that bastard son of bastards, Odysseus. / I hold the commanders accountable. / Philoctetes is moved, as planned. / We share a 'cargo of common grievances,' he says. / 'You and I sing the same song.'"

The trust is coerced by faked trustworthiness, or at least trustworthiness fashioned with bits and pieces of truth, designed to ensnare. That is the hoax, a kind of Trojan horse rolled onto this island, once again engineered by the wily Odysseus, with the "young warrior" Neoptolemus (which is just what his name means) being initiated by his side in the sorts of treachery often morally permissible in warfare, though typically not directed against one's own. But is there any genuine trust and trustworthiness displayed in this play? Is there trust and trustworthiness that is not part of an intelligence scheme? There is. But it has to be developed. And its manifestation is critical for Philoctetes's moral repair from the double moral betrayal he suffers by his command (the first in the original abandonment by his commanders, the second in this trumped-up trust hoax). The power of trust in this parable, and the fact that it comes into being in the very moment of a potential massive betrayal, is an object lesson, albeit an idealized one, of trust's generative capacities.

The pivotal moment comes when Philoctetes, persuaded to leave the island with Neoptolemus and set sail for what he believes is home, gathers his few belongings, including his famous bow. Eager to get his hands on the bow, Neoptolemus asks to see it. Without the slightest reluctance, Philoctetes begins to entrust Neoptolemus with the very bow that has kept him alive on this island, protected from predators and provided with food. "I will grant your wish. There's nothing I wouldn't do for you," obliges Philoctetes. Neoptolemus gently demurs: "Is it allowed (*themis*)? If not, I will relent." Philoctetes assures him that it is permissible, and more importantly, that he trusts him because he has shown him goodwill and kindness. In that, he says, he mirrors Philoctetes himself, who received the bow from Heracles as a gift for his own demonstration of kindness.

There are two wrinkles in this passage, and they mislead about what is most fundamental in the trust exchange. The first is the apparent worry about background norms, implied by the question of whether it is right or permitted to hold the bow. Can he, Neoptolemus, really hold this sacred bow? Will it offend the gods? Is it okay to touch it? Is Neoptolemus really concerned about acting in conformity with a divine norm, or is he just exhibiting fake decency in order to mask his intention to steal? I suspect it is the latter. But whatever the answer, the basic trust isn't grounded in Philoctetes's expectation of Neoptolemus's compliance with some external norm. Rather, I want to argue that it is essentially grounded in the interaction itself—in Philoctetes's calling out to Neoptolemus saying, "Look. I'm counting on you as competent here." "I'm counting on the idea that you'll take seriously my dependency and be responsive to it in your own reasons for action." Moreover, that trust is projective. The trust is expressed here as a way of trying to elicit trustworthiness from Neoptolemus. It scaffolds trust, nurses it along, and helps it to grow through the expectation that he ought to be trustworthy. That is part of trust's cunning and perhaps why, at times, it can create not just trustees but also dependents, manipulated into collaboration.

The second wrinkle is that Philoctetes's own remarks bury this point. He suggests that his trust is based on his anticipation of Neoptolemus's continuing to show goodwill and compassion toward him in his suffering. Neoptolemus has become a "priceless friend," and friends act out of goodwill and benevolence. I can trust my bow with a friend, he thinks. He won't steal it. He won't "stab me in the back," as we would say. But even in this kind of case where trust imputes goodwill to the trustworthy, there is something more basic going on. Philoctetes is telling Neoptolemus that he is counting on him. And that expectation can itself, at times, motivate. So Philoctetes assures Neoptolemus, "Don't worry [*tharsei,* have confidence], the bow will be yours to hold / And then hand it back to the hand that gave it." He plies on additional reasons for his trust, namely friendship, goodwill, and compassion. And they too, no doubt, can incentivize and bring Neoptolemus around. But in a barer, more minimal way, Philoctetes is fostering trust simply by projection of his trust, implicitly saying I'm counting on you to keep safe the bow and then give it back. Being responsive to another's dependency is the bare bones of trustworthiness.

Moreover, in this staged case of trustworthiness, though Philoctetes presumes Neoptolemus's goodness, we as audience have an ironic distance that Philoctetes does not yet possess (and will have only in retrospect). We know that despite the fact that he seems genuinely moved by the islander's suffering, Neoptolemus is still in the employ of Odysseus, and his goodness, even if native and genuine, may just be instrumentally deployed here. So we are suspicious, rightly, from our position of knowledge, that his antecedent goodness or good name is doing any work here other than that of ensnaring his prey.

But, despite this, it would be hard to come away from this scene without seeing a genuine spark of trust and trust responsiveness being kindled. What we see, and probably what Philoctetes also picks up in Neoptolemus's response, is that he is answering an address to be trusted and trustworthy. He is responsive to the address, "I am counting on you." And recognizing that he is being so addressed, and acknowledging it, however thinly, back to Philoctetes, adds a new level of being counted on by him. Put differently, Neoptolemus's "catching the ball" is the first step in the reciprocation. And that acknowledgment, that one is being counted on, is then thrown back and caught by the trustor in a way that reinforces the trust.

There is much more to say about trust and trustworthiness in this play. Neoptolemus insists repeatedly on his trustworthiness with respect to the safekeeping of the bow, and his sincerity seems to grow the more he is exposed to Philoctetes's excruciating suffering. Philoctetes's utter dependency on him makes it hard for Neoptolemus to carry through with the plot. And he opts to return the bow to Philoctetes rather than continue as Odysseus's lackey, despite the consequences for the mission. It takes a *deus ex machina*, in the form of Heracles, to resolve the plot and assure Philoctetes that his (and the bow's) return to Troy will bring both victory to the Greeks and the cure for his noxious wound.

So goes the plot. The take-home lesson is that in this story Philoctetes, though traumatized by betrayal, still reaches out through trust, and thereby elicits trustworthiness in a potential enemy bent on subjecting him to yet more betrayal. Part of the work is done by the cunning of trust and not just by Philoctetes's generous and resilient spirit or by Neoptolemus's potential compassion, pity, and remorse. These other factors no doubt play an important role in a richer trust relation that can be read into this play, but I don't want to overmoralize the story or lose sight of a ubiquitous, more easily available form of trust that is also part of this story. I am keen to show what a basic display of trust itself can sometimes do, by calling out that one is counting on another to do something (or be competent in a certain domain), and how the fact of dependency may become a compelling reason in that other's deliberations. Whether it is an overriding reason is another matter. And what Neoptolemus must do is to figure out precisely what Philoctetes is counting on him for and whether he can comply in a way that minimizes conflict with his other important standing obligations, including trust relations. But the general point is that expressing trust can bootstrap trustworthiness. It projects onto another a normative expectation that can have causal efficacy.

Trust from the Bottom Up

But trustors, of course, need to be wise and make their addresses to those who are plausibly competent to aid and assist in the domains that are relevant. And those who are competent also need to signal their competencies, and in some cases contribute not just interpersonally but also institutionally, through networks of support. In the case of returning veterans, there can be a familiar shutting out of civilians, even family members, as potential recipients of trust: those who don't put on the uniform don't know what war is like. As we have seen, the resentment toward a civilian "Thank you for your service" can carry just that thought. And the retreat of veterans to their own circle gives permission to too many civilians to withdraw or believe that it is meddlesome or presumptive to think one has something to offer in helping a soldier process war's effects. But that's a myth that needs to be debunked by both sides.

I myself may have once, in a significant way, been complicit in perpetuating the myth. And the insight speaks to a more general point about elicitations of trust responsiveness. My dad was a World War II veteran (an Army medic) who died several years ago. I was left to clean up his effects in the hospital room. And in putting away his belongings, I found his key chain, with his dog tags (Army identifications) attached. They were well worn, and his name, "Seymour Sherman," was just visible. They had been touched and rubbed and fingered for some sixty-five years. My mother said he had carried them during their whole marriage. But I never noticed them before, and he never showed them to me. Perhaps it was a case of willful ignorance on my part, and willful concealment on his, a "don't ask, don't tell" policy of sorts. But his war experiences were by and large not something to be shared with his children. They were his private burdens, not ours. And we complied. Despite the remnants of World War II in our house—what I remember best was the pile of scratchy brown-green Army blankets that were spare bedding in our hall linen closet—we didn't talk about the war and how it could have affected my dad—or for that matter, all my uncles who also served. It was taboo.

I mention this because many returning veterans do feel, as my dad did, that the inner landscape of war is for soldiers and not for the civilians to whom they return. Why spill out the gore or the doubts or ambivalence to one's innocent family? War is a moral maze about killing and being killed, about liability to lethal and nonlethal harming, about the boundaries of wartime and peacetime, and adapting to the fuzzy boundary crossing. The most resolute Marine may still wonder if he did enough to prevent harm to innocent civilians or avoided undue risk to his troops. Guilt, shame, and a sense of betraying others can easily commingle with adrenalized pride, bravado, and the overwhelming sense of purpose and meaning that participation in war, even an unjust or imprudent war, can offer. The psychological and philosophical mess is hard to untangle and easy to wall up. And there is a certain comfort in thinking one is protecting others, innocent others, from one's toxins. But it comes with a price—of alienation and isolation. In this regard, Philoctetes becomes a bold metaphor for the anomie of a veteran, war-wounded, resentful, still "at sea," alone. Philoctetes's homecoming (*nostos,* in Homeric idiom) is all too uncertain—will he come home and in what condition? How will he be seen? How will he reenter? We are now bringing home the remaining service members from the longest and some might say endless war in American history. It should not surprise us if many return with "nostalgia," meaning literally, in this seventeenth-century, Greco-derived medical term—homecoming pain (*nostos algos*).

And yet Philoctetes heals, or at least begins to. And so he is also a remarkable symbol of the power of transformative trust and how it can bootstrap trustworthiness in the right set of conditions. Trust embeds hope, hope *in* others, that they may be responsive to one's need. Philoctetes pleads to Neoptolemus: "Have mercy, my son.... Don't let it be said in scorn that you tricked me.... You're not a bad lad, but I think you've been trained by bad men." He invests "parental" hope in the youth; Neoptolemus can overcome the bad influences. And even if his empathy is a bit out of sync at times, misattuned, and subjecting Philoctetes to fresh soul wounds and narcissistic injuries, even if there are many good reasons for him not to risk more vulnerability, the price of that protection is high and at the cost of connectivity with self and others.

Sometimes those who signal competence and interest may be representatives of important institutions responsible for key policy changes and the behavior of scores of others. Neoptolemus symbolizes that, too: he is an emissary of the Greeks. And his tender relationship with the needy Philoctetes will change the view of those in power toward this forsaken bowman.

This brings us to our own stage and to the Senate floor where there has been a recent massive campaign in support of victims of sexual harassment and assault in the armed forces. A few words are appropriate here, as the case illustrates well how, as in the case of Philoctetes and Neoptolemus, counting on another and being counted on can be a catalyst for change at high levels of power. In the background to the advocacy is the documentary *The Invisible War* (which premiered at the 2012 Sundance Film Festival and was later broadcast on PBS) that features interviews with veterans of the different branches of the armed forces who recount the incidents that led to their assaults. The documentary is harrowing. I have shown it to students—women and men, civilians, veterans, ROTC cadets and active-duty officers, including one high-level Army Ranger battalion commander, married to an Army colonel and West Point sweetheart. What he saw struck a deep nerve. He had just returned from ten years of back-to-back commands in Afghanistan and Iraq. During one of his commands, one of his troops got an emergency call in the midst of a tense engagement: his wife, serving in country in a different unit, had just been assaulted and raped by a fellow soldier. He needed his commander's permission to leave his post immediately and go to her aid. My class froze in hearing the account. The vulnerability that the Ranger commander felt, himself in a dual-career Army marriage, was raw and in the room. All of a sudden my students were looking at a brawny, brainy, invincible-seeming soldier who was not so invincible.

There was another moment that brought the reality of inside-the-wire sexual assault close to home. The film culminates with the exposure of a horrific rape, perpetrated not far from the Georgetown campus, at the prestigious Washington, D.C., Marine Barracks, "the oldest post of the Corps," and home of "The President's Own" Marine Band that plays "Hail to the Chief" at parades and ceremonial missions. Barracks Row in Capitol Hill S.E. has itself become a trendy scene of bars and restaurants, with military pageantry punctuating one corner as Marine sentinels stand guard at the gated courtyard of the historic Barracks. But after watching the film, it would be hard to look at those gates without deep suspicion about what takes place inside.

I leave to the side the harrowing testimonies of the victims and their loved ones. I urge readers to watch the *Invisible War*. The deep misogyny depicted in the film will not come as a surprise to some. The history of U.S. servicemen's treatment of women in regions where they have served, whether in Normandy during the invasion in World War II or in Subic Bay in the

Philippines during Vietnam, has not been pretty. Prostitution and objectification of women have gone hand in hand with U.S. military engagements. It may not be too cynical to say that what was turned against occupied women is now turned against those within. (I have my own stories here: My father, treating troops returning from Normandy on the *Queen Mary*, told me in one of the few conversations we did have about war that, in addition to amputations, what he was treating in his many trips was rampant syphilis and gonorrhea, amid the pleading of his soldiers to not tell the wives at home. And while I was teaching at the Naval Academy, a colleague and retired Marine colonel who commanded troops in Vietnam told ethics classes of how he ordered the bulldozing of prostitution sites his Marines were frequenting that put missions at risk and made light of the humanity of too many women.)

What is crucial to our narrative with regard to beginning to restore trust for today's women who serve is that several of the survivors featured in the film (in particular, Kori Cioca, beaten and raped by her supervisor in the U.S. Coast Guard; Ariana Klay, an Iraq War Marine who returned home to be raped by a senior officer and his friend, and then threatened with death; and Trina McDonald, who was drugged and raped by military policemen on a remote Naval station in Alaska) went on to tell their stories to senators on Capitol Hill, including two female senators, Senator Kirsten Gillibrand of New York and Senator Claire McCaskill of Missouri. Deeply disturbed by what they heard and by DOD statistics that confirm an epidemic of sexual assault in the ranks, each proposed legislation to give victims greater power in the legal process. This is not the place to track legislative reform. Nor is it the place to track whether these milder reforms have enough muscle to do real work in fair adjudication for victims of sexual assault within the ranks. The outcome of two high-profile court cases just in the news as I write suggests a system that is still broken.

What I do want to expose, though, is that these bills (and especially Gillibrand's) represent direct personal *and* institutional responses to the testimony heard and to the systemic fear victims describe of not coming forward because they won't be believed. It is an illustration of the call and response of vulnerability and the bid for trust ratcheted up to an institutional level through individual engagement—in this case, women listening to other women.

Building trust is a complicated matter for those who have been violated, whether the trust bond is with a producer making a documentary that might change a national conversation, or with a senator who tries to change adjudication procedures, or with a young warrior who shares your grievances, seems of noble cast, and promises you a way out of your desperation. There is risk, exposure, potential betrayal, and sometimes re-traumatization. But significantly, even in the case of restoring trust in an institution or organization, the trust is typically built bottom up, in one-on-one interactions, as in these examples, in conversations with an empathic producer, in private hearings with a public official who seems to "get it," in an enigmatic relationship with an emissary who reaches out and recognizes anguish. The interaction moves both ways: there is exposure and vulnerability, on the one hand, and recognition of the dependency, on the other—there's empathy often, and an acknowledgment of the need to respond, in part precisely because one is being counted on. Trust even in institutions as lumbering and bureaucratic as Congress often begins in one-on-one engagements, where there is some sense of uptake, mirroring, and recognition of value. The reach of even that uptake, though, is limited. A senator may not convince enough fellow senators. Military court cases may still embed entrenched sexism by keeping the case within the chain of command. Test cases may founder because of bungled prosecutions and weak or inconsistent testimony from the plaintiffs. Still, getting some senators to take seriously the sexism in the military and begin to fix a broken system is a start.

"I'll Be on the Big White TV Screen"

We have been talking about trust among adults. But coming home from war is often coming home to children, the children a mother or father has left behind. And we would be naive to think that these trust bonds are not among the most fragile. We know from famous developmental research conducted by British psychoanalyst John Bowlby in the wake of World War II, and evacuations of children during the London Blitz, that attachment and trust go hand in hand, and that separations early in life can affect a child's sense of "secure base" that's critical for social and emotional growth.

Concern about the effect of separation on her children must have been in the background of a remarkable set of practices that Air Force Colonel Stephanie Wilson put in place as she prepared to deploy to Ul Adeid Air Base in Qatar for a year-long senior deployment in the Air Force. I came to know Stephanie at the Woodrow Wilson Center in Washington, D.C., where we were both public policy scholars during the academic year 2011–12. Stephanie is an African American engineer with a master's degree in organizational management from George Washington University, who entered the Air Force through the ROTC program at Georgia Institute of Technology. By May of our year at the Wilson Center, Stephanie was preparing for her next mission, commanding some five to six thousand persons in logistical mission support for Iraq and Afghanistan. It would involve leaving behind her young children—her then five-year-old daughter Mikalya and her two-year-old son Liam. It was her second long deployment in three years; the last overseas deployment was in Ramstein Air Base in Germany.

This time round, Skype would be the family glue, with her husband Scott Wilson, a retired Air Force flyer working on a Ph.D., in charge of the home front and of rounding up the children daily for Skype time on the TV screen with Mom. The kids just had to be in the room, playing and chattering, with Mom in the background as part of their daily routine. True, she wouldn't be hugging them: "Skype hugs are not real hugs," as one Air Force colonel's wife once told me in describing the hug "good night" her son had each night from her husband. The touch, the smell, the feel, so crucial in early attachment, would not be there. But Stephanie would be there in voice and image on the screen, and in that sense, with them physically every day. The time difference was seven hours. The chat would take place in the morning for the kids: "I'll be on the big white TV screen while the kids are running around in the living room talking to me. So, they don't have to sit in one place. They can continue life, and Mom can just observe and be part of that life for half an hour every day. That's my goal; half an hour every day.... During the previous deployment, the attachment bond got built in a different way: My daughter was one at the time, and I sat down before I left and read about thirty-five books on videotape—by video recorder—and my husband would play one a night for her. And so that's how she got to see who Mom was: I was the girl reading books at night. My daughter was at the age where she didn't need to see the book. She was just fascinated drinking her bottle, listening to her mom."

In this new deployment, roles would be reversed: her daughter would be reading a book to her once a week over Skype as part of the routine.

Not all parents, military or otherwise, are as creative or as conscientious as these two. I suspect the fact that Stephanie is a logistics expert and engineer by education and training explains how she tackles a problem. But also, not all parents have had to face the same trials. At age three, Mikayla was diagnosed with kidney cancer, and within days, Stephanie and Scott were able to change their career plans so that they could be based in Washington, with access to Walter Reed Hospital, where they would have the best fighting chance of beating the cancer. And they did. Mikayla has had a remarkable recovery after aggressive rounds of chemo and radiation—"I'm leaving her healthy, she's completely healthy"—Stephanie tells me with enormous relief, when we spoke over lunch one day just days before her departure from Dulles. Anything is "a cakewalk," she laughed, compared to fighting your child's cancer.

Still, she knew the departure and separation for a year was its own trial. It would begin with two and a half long hours of waiting in the airport lounge. And then, in civilian clothes, she would step onto the plane and leave Scott and the children behind: "That's probably the hardest part—it *was* the last time I went— that first step on the plane. I've jumped off a plane before, out of a perfectly good airplane before. The first step is the hardest. Stepping into nothingness is the hardest. Stepping onto the plane is the hardest."

For Air Force Colonel Stephanie Wilson, stepping onto that plane was parachuting into the abyss. The metaphor absolutely paralyzed me. I imagined myself ejected into a black chute with no chance in hell of a soft landing. But for Stephanie, a wingman trained in parachuting, the metaphor had its comforts. And imaging it afforded her a "pre-rehearsal," as the Stoics would say, to anticipate perceived danger and detoxify some of the sting that comes with being unprepared. "That's how I think of it mentally. I'm mentally prepared to jump out of this perfectly fine airplane. So, mentally I have that. So how am I now going to take *this* first step? I am going to allow myself to cry. I'll have my box of tissues there. I'll have my pictures there. I've totally war-gamed this thing in my head. It's okay to cry."

Her Stoic pre-rehearsal had its own twist. She would "war-game" it so it was okay to cry. She could cry with advanced permission, and so with a kind of resolute control. The tears would flow—there would be no surprise there. The only issue, she joked, was whether she would have enough tissues.

A year is a highly abstract concept in the mind of a young child who can barely understand the passage of time. And so again, the logistics of counting a week was a problem to solve. There would be jar of goodies in the kitchen, and every Friday, each child would reach in and pick out a treat, "marking each week Mom is gone."

All this is a way of laying down the trust bond in advance, or at least its means. Colonel Stephanie Wilson is anticipating her responsiveness and the conduits that will have to be in place for mutual responsiveness to grow—the nursing story hour, the Skype half-hour, the weekly countdown that brings a young family closer to real time together. Thousands of other military families, some strained by a decade of separation, have been enacting some version of this. It is an enactment to keep the trust exchanges alive.

Trust, Betrayal, Emotion, and Ache

Trust is a future-leaning, reactive attitude, directed toward others and also, by extension, toward oneself, self-reactively. It is a mental attitude that is an emotion, felt and often explicitly expressed. But in what sense is it really an emotion? In what sense is the soldier who, acting through and living with emotion, trusts civilians to understand, or supervisors to not betray her, or senators to acknowledge her defilement, or an emissary to take her home? Aristotle tells us that emotions are accompanied with pleasure or pain. But trust doesn't have a strong valence, a lot of zing, or wing, or heat. Even if it isn't a belief, in the sense that the reason we turn to trust is precisely because we lack the evidence that would ground firmer belief, still trust doesn't have that excitable feeling we associate with many emotions. Of course, many emotions have their own quietness, and we know well by now that an emotion's "feel," as the critics of William James on emotion long ago pointed out, is not a reliable indicator of either emotion in general (we could just be feeling edgy) or of an emotion in particular (resentment, for example, rather than shame).

But perhaps the better way to get at trust as an emotion is by what it *does* rather than how it *feels*. To trust someone is to organize one's attention in a certain way, to notice what another is signaling or open to, to block out some doubts or suspend suspicion and build up an "epistemic landscape." But trust doesn't just see someone in a certain light. It makes an investment in that person to do something with the thing or confidence that is entrusted. Trust digs us into vulnerability. And we expose that vulnerability—show it to another, in our face, or voice, or expectant or beholden tone. And we disclose that dependency to ourselves, often by externalizing it to others or by trying it out in a performance. But trust in another may not so much see or find value as help build it, elicit worthiness, as we've said, that isn't yet obvious or proven. And all that can motivate us to share burdens, entrust intimacies, seek succor, come out of a shell, and be less alone.

The bottom line is that trust, *qua* emotion, makes us vulnerable to others: to their help and hurt, to their power over us, and to our desire that they be responsive to us. Trust, as emotion, is a basic form of attachment. It is dependence writ large. And as important as trust is to a military corps, the idea of dependence is not something many soldiers, Marines, wingmen, or sailors want to embrace full on. To be self-reliant, stoic, to suck it up, and soldier on are the mantras. Trust may be basic to a cadre, but willful determination and control are how one survives. Or so goes the myth.

But even if there is ideological resistance to the deep dependency and vulnerability that goes with trust, the violations of trust make the fact of dependence all too emotionally clear. And that is what we have been detailing—the ache and agony of betrayal and the cautious resowing of seeds of trust in its aftermath.

TWIN TALES

Ancient stories, like that of *Philoctetes*, are our own stories through which to understand betrayal and the possibilities for trust's renewal. Other war stories are also ours.

A Civil War Philoctetes is perhaps Summerfield Hayes, fictional as well, nineteen years old and a Union soldier from Brooklyn, whose three days of battle take place in the opening campaign of the North against the South in the Battle of the Wilderness. Like Philoctetes, Summerfield is abandoned by his command, in his case as punishment for failing to rise from sleep at the bugle's reveille. He lost his hearing from an intense mortar attack the day before and slept through the call. His commander strips him of his rifle and identity papers, and blasts him with the humiliation that would leave him stunned and mute, "I have no time to be playing nursemaid." With that, Summerfield Hayes is deserted, left to make his way between enemy lines in the smoke-shrouded forests of northern Virginia, with no weapon, no buddies, and no name. He finds his way somehow to a Washington hospital, unable to utter his name, or his circumstances, framed by his command as a malingerer. One missionary nurse, named "Walt," with a gray beard, soft wrinkles under his eyes, a tattered haversack, and a fondness for verse, recognizes that Summerfield's invisible and silent wounds must tell a story as grave as those that can speak through gushing blood and sawed-off limbs. Summerfield keeps looking for his wounds; he must have them if he is so sick. Nothing else could cause him to waste away as he does. He strips down over and over. He knows they must be somewhere.

They are there, wounds of betrayal, distrust, and abandonment. And they ache intensely. It is a fictionalized Walt Whitman, a nursemaid of the soul, who trusts the realness and hardness of this nameless Union soldier's wounds and who helps him to find them, and recover them, in voice and memory.

That overture of trust, an act of faithfulness, is the beginning of a long and arduous healing for Summerfield.

Summerfield has neither the agony nor the luxury of Philoctetes's fetid leg as tangible legitimation of a deeper moral hurt—indeed, he wants that validation desperately and contemplates often returning to the front to secure the badge that can prove his wound. It is only through the work of friendship and trust (of Walt) that he comes to accept that the hurt of being deserted by one's own troops is no less real than the hurt of losing an arm or a leg by enemy fire.

We shouldn't be glib here. Philoctetes's wounds are physical as well as psychological and moral. And presumably that festering, foul-smelling leg is the cause and putative justification of the moral betrayal: he must be cut off from the whole if the whole is to be saved; with a little utilitarian logic chop, the sacrifice of one soldier preserves the army of many. War always puts its human assets, and not just its matériel, at some risk. *Philoctetes* is just another case of balancing force protection against the exigencies of the mission.

But there is something insidious, haunting, cruel, and inhumane about Philoctetes's sacrifice, and it has to do with the trauma of isolation. Philoctetes has been a prisoner in solitary confinement for a full ten years. In his case, he has nature and the beasts as his companions. Not all are so lucky, especially those who have spent the past decade in the U.S. detention center at Guantanamo, set up as a part of the "global war on terror." Still, Philoctetes was put into solitary by his own side, by his own command, and that is perhaps the unkindest betrayal. And that's the reason his trust in Neoptolemus is so fascinating. Why should Philoctetes trust this emissary sent by his betrayers? And why should Neoptolemus be moved to renege on his plot? The moral address in this interaction, the signaling of dependency and the projection that it will be recognized and acknowledged as legitimate, are the components of this new trust bond. (And perhaps that was also so with Summerfield and his Walt.) Trust and trustworthiness are built here from the ground up, on the ashes of soul-shattered living. This is an ancient and abiding lesson for veterans coming home and for civilians to whom they return.

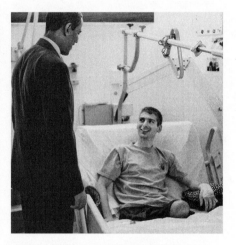

Dan Berschinski leading troops in Kandahar in July 2009

President Obama visits Dan in fall of 2009 at Walter Reed

Dan with new legs in summer of 2012

CHAPTER 6

——— ★ ———

HOPE AFTER WAR

DEFIANT HOPE

I begin with an example that is from war, but is not about its combatants. It draws from the documentary movie, *Defiant Requiem,* about the Nazi camp of Terezin (in Theresienstadt, outside Prague), which portrays the Jewish inmates singing for their life through performances of Verdi's *Requiem.* The movie follows conductor Murry Sidlin's recreation of that *Requiem* performance recently in the extant walls of Terezin.

As is well known, many of the inmates at Terezin were accomplished artists and musicians, performers, conductors, and composers. And one, Raphael Schächter, a talented pianist and opera-choral conductor, captured by the Nazis in 1941, brought with him just one piece of music, Giuseppe Verdi's demanding choral work, his 1874 *Requiem.* During the internment and with complicity of the guards (for Terezin was a "show" prison and central to the Nazi propaganda machine), the prisoners gathered nightly in the dank basement of the compound, around a piano, and learned the complicated Lain choral parts of the piece, with Schächter holding the only copy of the score. They sang, with hope against hope, to change minds, to have the Nazi leadership hear the humanity of their voices and rescind their death sentence. That hope became increasingly futile, as one death train after another rounded up Jews and took some of them on death marches or to Auschwitz. And when that happened, they would reconstitute their chorus, over and over, with winnowed and frail population, and repeat the defiant act of hope. The Nazi brass eventually did come to hear the chorus in a culminating performance on June 23, 1944; it was entertainment for them, but for the singers and Schächter, it was survival of the soul. And as Sidlin implied in remarks at a showing of the documentary in Washington, D.C., the sequence in the *Requiem*, "Dies irae," that the "day of wrath" would come, was ironic for these Jews, unpracticed in the rituals of Latin Masses, a moral protest that they could deliver face to face to their torturers, concealed through art. It was their retribution.

But singing the *Requiem* also expressed their hope. And it was hope with two interrelated facets. The prisoners sang to express hope *for* a future outcome or eventuality—to be saved, rescued, and redeemed, whether by God's hand or human hand. And that hoped-for outcome nourished some as food, despite desperate hunger, as one survivor of the chorus recalled. Singing to be saved brought back to life near-corpses.

But another aspect of their hope, far more galvanizing, I suspect, was the hope they had *in* each other and the aspirations they placed in their humanity. By singing together, after backbreaking days of labor and beaten servitude, they raised their voices and followed an extremely complex musical score. They worked on their parts, put them to memory, and saw mirrored in each other their high humanity. They kindled hope in each other and in themselves, in their potential to rise above the most subjugating circumstances, and to not just survive but also to thrive, in a sliver of a way, for a sliver of time, as artistic and spiritual souls. In the very act of choral singing, in answering a soloist's vocal call with responses and intricate recants, they reciprocally addressed and recognized each other, and in this context, *acknowledged* each other's hope in humanity. Moral address was woven into the interaction and was communicated as part of the choral activity. Perhaps, too, they had hope in the Nazi leadership that their art would awaken their own humanity. But I can't imagine that this energized as much as the reciprocal hope they placed in each other, a calling out to each (through music) of the potential of the other's humanity, and an echoing back, in acknowledgment, that each has been appropriately recognized. Singing Verdi's *Requiem* to each other, night after night, was an act of defiance, but also was an act of resilience, a way of being buoyed by a commonwealth of humanity, at work in recreating a piece that must have been appreciated by the performers as itself an exquisitely fine and noble expression of humanity.

This is a powerful example of the promise of *interpersonal* hope, even in futile conditions. Hope can be about eventualities—"nonnormative hope," following Adrienne Martin's usage—but it can also be about aspirations we hold on behalf of persons—"normative hope," as she calls it. And in some cases, though not all, part of the point of addressing others with hope is that the recipients might take up the values or principles deemed worthwhile and aspired for on their behalf. Hope can "scaffold" normative change.

Aristotle makes clear this last point in the *Ethics*. His remarks also go some way toward showing the intermingling of normative and nonnormative hope. He reminds us that we don't accurately attribute happiness or flourishing (*eudaimonia*) to a child; but in calling him "happy," we invest hope in him that he will become that: "It is natural, then, that we call neither ox nor horse nor any other of the animals happy; for none of them is capable of sharing in such activity [of reason and its excellences]. For this reason also a boy is not happy; for he is not yet capable of such acts, owing to his age; and boys who are called happy are being deemed happy by reason of the hopes we have for them."

Calling the child "happy" *misattributes* to him the developed rational capacities requisite for character excellence (or virtue) and that, when exercised properly, with the experience of years and adequate external goods, constitutes happiness. But the misattribution can be pedagogic: "deeming" or "congratulating" the child as happy sets a goal worth aspiring to and begins to "bootstrap" (or "scaffold") the requisite development and behavior for it. It gives the child "a job" and the parents a job, and encourages a two-way set of emotion-inflected behaviors that will communicate assessments in making progress on completing that job. Hope and disappointment, the parent's and the child's own—and, in turn, responses to each other's reactive uptakes and "updates" in the face of various interim goals—will populate the path. These are back-and-forth volleys—mirrorings and challengings—that are the familiar stuff of interpersonal engagement from childhood on up.

Given that hope for happiness in Aristotle's lexicon is not just hope for successful outcome (to conceive of happiness that way would be "a very defective arrangement," he insists, that would mistakenly "entrust to chance what is greatest and most noble"), the hope he points to here is *primarily* normative—that is, hope *in* the child that he will undertake the right "kind of study and care," as Aristotle puts it, requisite for realizing a flourishing and happy life. To be sure, the Stoics will press Aristotle on just this point, arguing that he has fudged on the issue and still left too much to externals and luck. Virtue is sufficient for happiness, they insist, following Socrates. There is something to this charge, and perhaps for our purposes what it shows is that *hope for* happiness, for an Aristotelian and probably for most of us, slides between *hope in* one's agency and reason (and in that of others) and *hope that* the world in which we exercise our individual and shared agency will be hospitable. Normative and nonnormative hope mix and mingle.

The point is a familiar one, especially in war. Good commanders place express hope *in* their troops that they will embrace the rules of engagement and have the skill bases necessary for good and just fighting. But they also hope *that* they will fare well in addition to do well. And the wisest among them will hope that in doing well, they will have the resources to accept and internalize judicious discriminations of responsibility.

This is background for a number of themes I explore in this chapter, among which are: how to conceive of hope in persons as something like a reactive attitude; what the relation of that kind of hope is to hope that a particular outcome will eventuate, as in the case of a soldier's initiative to relearn how to walk after losing both legs and a hip in a mine blast in Afghanistan; how nascent self-hope, as in the case of a young injured Marine, can be bootstrapped by others hoping in the Marine. The narratives are based on extensive interviews with individuals. They are not meant to yield easily generalizable lessons for all to follow. But they are intended to open a conversation and begin the call and response of moral engagement within relationships and communities.

POSITIVE REACTIVE ATTITUDES: SOME BRIEF BACKGROUND

As we have been saying, one way of thinking about expressed reactive emotions is as a means of calling out to another that you are holding him to account, and thinking you are owed an appropriate reply. In expressing reactive attitudes, we are not making detached appraisals, but we are engaging the other, calling out, with the presumption of some kind of connectedness and shared community. We're addressing him (and, in reflexive cases, us) with the demands, expectations, or aspirations implicit in those emotional expressions. And we are looking for an appropriate response to our call.

Until fairly recently, the focus on reactive attitudes has been on the negative ones—such as resentment, indignation, and guilt. But in the original articulation of reactive attitudes, positive emotions were always meant to be an important part of the continuum: "In general, we demand some degree of goodwill or regard on the part of those who stand in these relationships to us, though the forms we require it to take vary widely in different connections. The range and intensity of our reactive attitudes towards goodwill, its absence or its opposite vary no less widely. I have mentioned, specifically, resentment and gratitude; and they are usefully opposed. But, of course, there is a whole continuum of reactive attitude and feeling stretching on both sides of these and—the most comfortable area—in between them."

A number of philosophers have been exploring of late just what kind of demand or looser notion of expectation or aspiration is involved in various positive reactive attitudes. The details of that work are not our immediate concern here. What is important for our discussion, and what is implicit in the *Defiant Requiem* example, is the structure of reactive attitudes as a call-and-response, and that hope preserves that structure. Hope in another, like resentment toward another, is an address to another that we are holding him to account. But crucially, in the case of hope, we are doing it in a way that is aspirational rather than binding. As one philosopher has put it in original and important work on normative hope, hoping in someone is investing in a norm or principle on his behalf; it is a way of "treating a principle as worth aspiring to, without *insisting* on compliance." The fact that it is not a demand shows up in the sequel of appropriate reactive attitudes. In the case of someone hoping in you, you might be praised if you succeed, but not blamed if you fail. Disappointment is not the same as reproach, even if it sometimes has that flavor.

In lived life, hope in persons, in their agency and effort, is tangled up in hope for outcomes. Still, it's important to try to distinguish these two facets of hope. We shall come to hope in persons shortly. First we turn to hope for outcomes and its role in moral recovery after war.

WEARING LEGS, AND WALKING AGAINST THE ODDS

Returning service members sometimes tell me that they feel like they have lost meaning and purpose in their lives. Some desperately miss the sense of being part of something much larger than themselves in the way that a war effort is; others miss the fast operational tempo of missions that can intensify that sense of purpose and belonging. Some long for the respect and status earned in uniform, as Eduardo ("Lalo") Panyagua does. The twenty-some-thing Marine corporal we met in chapter 3 rose out of the L.A. barrio and its gangs to serve three deployment in Iraq and Afghanistan, his last as a platoon leader in charge of thirty-five Marine and Afghani National Security forces outside Marja, in extremely dangerous and demanding engagements in November 2009 to June 2010. For his "outstanding leadership and tremendous patience" in twenty-seven partnered combat patrols often under small-arms fire, he received a Navy and Marine Corps Achievement Medal. Though a corporal, he often filled the billet of a sergeant. Lalo is just not sure he can find that kind of standing in civilian life. In his case, the loss is profound, the despondency at times unbearable, and the hunger for replacement meaning palpable. Others come home missing limbs and some with severely disfiguring facial scars or brain injuries that severely challenge a notion of good functioning after war. For some, unhappiness as despair—the sense that reality falls short of longed-for ideals and that one can't close the gap—descends. Recent spikes in suicide rates within the military point to real and urgent concerns here.

This is where hope can get a foothold. Paradigmatically, hope—substantive hope—looks with desire (or perhaps with its own special kind of motivation) to the future, with its possibilities but also its uncertainties, and in normative cases, to self and others, and to positive differences each can make in a life. Hope presumes that possibilities—however bare—(and people) are *open* to one, and that prospect can galvanize energy. Hope presumes a kind of "possibilism," that can stabilize focus and fortify resolve.

One prominent philosopher develops the idea this way: "To form the hope that something is the case or that I or someone else will manage to make it the case, I have to invest that scenario with a level of confidence" that may exceed "the confidence of my actual belief in the prospect and with a degree of stability that will certainly exceed the stability of my actual belief." In this sense, hope is a *pragmatic* rationality. It redirects attention and desire and imaginative planning to possibilities that a more fact-processing, probability-assessing, evidence-seeking mentality might reject: "Forming the hope that a particular scenario will eventuate, or at least eventuate in the event of your taking a certain initiative, is a way of handling the hurly burly of belief. It frees you from the bleakness of beliefs that wax and wane unpredictably in level of confidence. It gives you firm and friendly coordinates in an uncertain and uncompanionable world. To have hope is to have something we might describe as cognitive resolve.... Without hope, there would often be no possibility for us of asserting our agency and of putting our own signature or stamp on our conduct. We would collapse in a heap of despair and uncertainty, beaten down by cascades of inimical fact."

Hope, on this picture, is deeply connected with practical agency, or as it sometimes put, is a form of "agential investment." In this regard, it is distinct from *mere* or *idle* wish, such as for the impossible or near impossible— "for immortality," as Aristotle says. And, too, it is distinct from wishful thinking—at least in the way Freud sometimes understands it, as a "turning away from reality" with wishful fantasies "regarded as a better reality." For similar reasons, the notion of wish fulfillment, in the sense of satisfaction fully hived off from the constraints of reality, does not capture the meaning of hope, either. To be sure, substantive hopes typically involve a kind of ego satisfaction, in the sense of a desire for one's own thriving, or *eudaimonia*. And these kinds of hopes may be expressed in the constructions of fantasy and its narratives, as vehicles for practice and for trying out future possibilities. I expand upon this shortly. But the point for now is that fantasy can be an important way of *engaging* reality and, not of retreating from it, in a fully separate, disconnected track.

It's hard not to think about hope when you meet Dan Berschinski, a young Army veteran from the war in Afghanistan. On August 18, 2009, Dan, then a twenty-five-year-old first lieutenant from West Point, in command of an infantry platoon in Kandahar, Afghanistan, stepped on a bomb while trying to retrieve the remains of his unit observer. A botched-up medevac left Dan bleeding profusely, and his family was pretty sure he was not going to make it out of Afghanistan alive. In the end, he was stabilized enough to be put on a plane to Landsthul Regional Medical Center, though too fragile to actually leave the plane. Within a week, he was flown to Walter Reed, where his parents awaited him. Bob and Susan Berschinski were warned that if Dan somehow pulled through, the hemorrhaging would likely result in severe brain damage. Dan miraculously did pull through, with no trace of traumatic brain injury. As Susan said to me, "once they brought him out of the coma, it was rapidly apparent *he* was still there."

But his body wasn't all there. He had lost nearly half of his skeleton and the joints that held it together, now so much dust in the Afghani desert: "My guys found a boot ... mostly intact actually, and they said to me later that they played rock-paper-scissors to see who would have to stick their hand inside the boot to see if there was any flesh inside. But there wasn't. It was empty.... I don't know what happened."

When Dan came to, he knew much of his body was gone, but under a protective white hospital sheet he couldn't really take in the damage, and his parents kept up a brave face. "He was a mess ... There was not a place on him that you could touch that didn't hurt," said Bob. After more than a dozen operations, and being pinned together by an exoskeletal frame to stabilize his remaining limbs, Dan officially became a double above-the-knee amputee, with a reconstructed left arm and hand, minus a pinky. But critically, he was missing a right hip joint. With that much skeletal damage, and profound socket challenges for a good-fitting prosthesis, it was fairly clear that Dan would never walk again. Without sit bones, he even had trouble sitting in a wheelchair without sliding off.

The evidence confirmed that prognosis. Others in the Army had suffered his kind of injury, but no one had walked again. Walking wasn't just about ambulating. As I learned from other amputees, walking was about standing, and being eye-to-eye with others.

In Dan's case, a shard of hope emerged. Dan soon learned of one "successful" (i.e., ambulatory) missing-hip, above-the-knee amputee. Andre Kajlich, a civilian living in Seattle, was hit head-on by a train while studying chemistry in Prague. Ten years later, Kajlich now walks with two prosthetic legs and a single cane. A YouTube video shows his jerky movements and his falls going downstairs without quadricep muscles. But it also shows that he clearly walks. And he not only walks, but he is a world-class paratriathlete.

Kajlich soon became an emulatory model for Dan, and was evidence that walking with his meager skeleton was humanly possible. And that possibilism set in a motion a *project* of hope not unlike a complex master plan with embedded initiatives, both collaborative and individual. Those initiatives included consultations that brought Kajlich to Walter Reed Hospital in Bethesda, Maryland, to discuss his case with Dan and other similarly injured vets. But gruelingly, for Dan, it involved two and a half years of intense physical and occupational therapy at the rehabilitation gym on Walter Reed's campus, and a deep immersion in the mechanics, fit, and usage of prosthetics. Dan became expert in the metrics of gait, stride, and balance and, more basically, in "wearing legs": how to keep stumps comfortable inside a silicon sleeve and carbon socket all day; how to get a good fit in the morning, when the stump is thin and not yet swollen from rub and wear; how to maneuver and feel comfortable wearing the heavy belt needed to hoist up the leg that is missing its hip bone and socket. All this was in aid of making possible an independent and ambulatory lifestyle.

Dan's case illustrates well how hope can be pragmatically rational. We can speculate that, in the course of his recovery, Dan puts the counterevidence and low probabilities—the examples of "unsuccessful" similarly injured military guys that would stand between him and ambulation—to the side. They become background information, though presumably still accessible at some level. True, in taking up this stance of hope he restricts exposure to evidence, but does that much in the way that we do many emotions—by narrowing our focus to certain patterns of salience that then dispose us to building ways of seeing, or "epistemic landscapes," that cohere with those patterns of salience. In this sense, hope is not systematically different from other emotionally laden ways of seeing. Dan, like many vets, carries a mental calculation of where his war injuries fit relative to those that others suffer. He has it easy, he thinks, compared to arm amputees or veterans who suffer severe brain damage. But he has it a lot harder than below-the-knee amputees: they're mere single or double "paper cuts," as he affectionately calls them! Also, he doesn't take for granted that he is a veteran with a college education *behind* him, and that he has had strong resources in a loving and upper-middle-class family and supportive friends. "All that helps," he says. "Others aren't as lucky." These considerations factor into Dan's hope. His hope is ardent, but it isn't blind.

It is also not entirely different from a more common, pragmatic stance of *confidence*. A philosophy colleague who works with surgeons on medical ethics issues reported a view of the ideal surgeon as one who has a ratio of confidence to ability that is slightly higher than 1. The idea is that the good surgeon gives himself "a little boost" before going into a difficult surgery; he "psyches" himself in the way an elite athlete does before a race. He has a kind of *confident anticipation*. Hope involves that kind of pragmatic boost, and perhaps even a stronger dose of it. But it also involves something we haven't yet explored and that's not typically an element of confidence. And that is imagination and fantasy.

I suspect, at some level or another, Dan fantasizes that he is like Kajlich, and that some day he will be able to do the things that Kajlich can do. He "trades places in fancy," as Adam Smith would say, with Kajlich. And in the space of imagination, Dan is able to practice and anticipate constructively, to "pre-rehearse," to use a Stoic term, what a possible future reality might look like, and so avoid the paralysis of idle fears and the futility of empty hopes. Kajlich's precedent means that Dan does not have to have *radical hope*—imagination from scratch. Here, I have in mind the concept of transcendent hope as one philosopher has developed it in his portrait of Plenty Coup, the Crow leader, who must and does imagine (through the interpretations of dreams and fantasies) a totally novel way of thriving for himself and his people in the face of the annihilation of Crow culture that comes with the death of the buffalo. Crow concepts of courage and virtue that depend on the warrior life of hunting buffalo no longer have application; radical hope and radical fantasy are required to create new, thick content for virtue if a people are to flourish again. Dan's conceptual and moral challenge is not as great. Still, in a related way, imagination, fantasy, and interpretations make concrete his hopes and help to shape and revise plans that are expressions of his hopes.

Dan trades places with Kajlich, but I suspect Kajlich also "trades places" with Dan. Through a biographic, retrospective narrative of what it was like to take his first, post-accident steps, he puts himself in Dan's "shoes" and comes closer to Dan's current frustrations and challenges. This also puts him in a position of investing *hope in* Dan (aspiring on his behalf), which presumably helps inspire Dan's hope in himself.

HOPE IN OTHERS

Dan's hope, in this reconstructed narrative, is for an eventuality when he can walk. But that hope is interlaced with normative hope. He invests hope *in* the medical and therapy staff at Walter Reed and in the institution that supports its remarkable, rehabilitative gym—the MATC, short for Military Advanced Training Center (and affectionately referred to by another double amputee, Army Lieutenant Colonel Greg Gadson, as the "Gold's gym of guys that are missing things"). Dan puts hope *in* the civilian contractors who make and fit prosthetics for veterans; he puts hope *in* his immediate circle of family and friends, including his new "family" of injured veterans at Walter Reed, like Tyson Quink, whom I met, a West Point football player who lost both legs three months into his deployment to Afghanistan; he puts hope *in* Congress in myriad ways: to authorize adequate allocations for veteran spending, to deliberate wisely about future military and humanitarian engagements, to support worldwide rights for persons with disabilities. And he puts hope *in* the American electorate to elect the right people to office who will make these decisions. Equally, he puts hope *in* American business and education leaders to create opportunities for veterans, like himself, to be re-integrated into the workforce and to return to school and training programs. And others invest hope *in* him—his therapists, coaches, mentors, fellow amputees at the rehab gym, his family, peers, and so on. And he invests hope *in* himself in ways that are mutually reinforced by his investments in others and their investments in him. Normative investments underlie his hopes for himself (and others) to be able to function well after military service in war.

As in the earlier *Requiem* example, to expressly communicate hope to a person is to morally address that recipient, to call her in a way that normatively anticipates a response. As with trust, the anticipation falls short of confident belief and involves exposure to vulnerability and risk-taking. The "caller" could be disappointed; the "target" might not take up the call. Or she may recognize that she is being hoped in, counted on, so to speak (to use the language of trust), and acknowledge that she has been appropriately recognized; but still she may not fulfill the aspirations invested in her or wholeheartedly take up the challenge. As Aristotle implies, our sons and daughters may not do what is required of them to meet the challenges implicit in our hopes for their happiness. We may hope in them on credit, but then be disappointed.

In *De Beneficiis (On Benefits)*, Seneca, the first-century Roman Stoic and tutor to the Emperor Nero, rehearses a colorful example of the call-and-response trope of recognition and acknowledgment in gift-giving and gratitude. His example is prescient as a sketch of the reiterative looping characteristic of reactive attitudes and the need for good attunement for successful uptake. Doing a kindness returned with gratitude is like a game of catch. You should know to whom you are throwing the ball. The passage bears a close look: "I would like to take up an analogy which our own Chrysippus drew with a game of ball. It falls to the ground through the fault either of the person throwing it or of the person receiving it, while it only remains in play by passing, properly thrown and caught, from one pair of hands to the other. A good player needs to send it off differently to a tall partner than to a short one. The same principle applies to a favour. Only if properly accommodated to both the persons involved, bestower and recipient, will it leave the one and reach the other as it should. Again, if the game with a trained and practised player, we shall be bolder in throwing the ball. No matter how it comes, his hand will be ready and quick to drive it back. Against an untrained novice, we shall not throw it so hard or so vigorously but be more relaxed, aiming the ball right into his hands and simply meeting it when it comes back. We should use the same procedure when doing favours....As it is, we very often make people ungrateful and welcome the idea that they should be so, as though our favours could only be great if we cannot be thanked for them....How much better and more considerate it would be to see to it that recipients too have a part to play, to welcome the idea that you could be thanked."

Obviously, doing someone a good turn is best geared to what that recipient needs and is capable of using. As Seneca goes on to tell us, giving books to a country bumpkin or a heavy coat to someone in summer is probably not a well-placed pass likely to be returned with much gratitude! Similarly, trust given to someone who has signaled no competence or interest in the domain in which one is asking her to be trustworthy is not a wise exposure of vulnerability, nor a likely way to scaffold deeper trust in that person.

But hope in others is somewhat different from trust. We may not fully trust persons and their readiness to receive us appropriately, but we still may hope in them; and in an even more robust way than trust, hope that our hope in them makes them responsive to our call. Thus, hope in others can presume a clearly developmental stance. We want to move a recipient along and hope she will rise to the challenge and catch the ball. Still, we are often willing to accommodate somewhat—throw the ball, with the recipient's limits in mind—all the while still trying to get her to catch. And where we simply can't engage the other properly (or are met with deep resistance), we may enlist others' help to throw the ball for us.

To make this concrete, consider the following narrative of a service woman I interviewed. "Roberta," with a distinguished record of academic laurels and military awards, is told to her face by her new commander that, despite her promotion to a highly coveted senior job on his base, he "fought against" her going there and would continue to do everything he could to undermine her appointment. As she put it, miming the lingo of her "brothers" on base, her very presence was "disrupting the status quo" and "tearing down heritage and tradition." In her case, she turned to a male mentor to help break into the "bro network," and plead her cause. There was no way that her new boss could recognize directly from her that her hope in him to accept her on an equal footing with her male peers was legitimate and something he had moral reason to commit to. He had to hear that through different channels. It is not even clear that he recognized the moral call in the end, and may only have felt pressured for political reasons to act in conformity with regulation and policy. To revert to Seneca's metaphor, this is a case where an individual (Roberta) is already in a game of ball, but can't get successful uptake from the recipient. And when she finally does, only through the intervention of another player, the "successful" catch may reflect changed behavior more than changed attitude.

In this case, Roberta's hope presumably devolves to disappointment. And her disappointment in the commander is compatible with any resentment she might feel toward him, or indignation her mentor feels toward him. The resentment or indignation has as its evaluative content that she has been demeaned and degraded by her commander, forced to work in a hostile environment where he encourages sexist values protective of the old military as a male-only club. Any resentment, were she to express it directly to him, would hold him strictly accountable for his wronging her. Her disappointment, in contrast, has as its evaluative content that she is let down by his impoverished leadership and by his failure to recognize her bid to him (or that made on her behalf) to take her military service seriously and on an equal footing with any male's. Her disappointment, in part, is that he doesn't invest hope in her.

One more caveat is important here. We might think of this normative disappointment as a tamped-down or suppressed version of resentment. We hold back, suppress the full force of our blame or resentment, and feel only a milder version of it. But I don't think this gets it right, even though on occasion we may *replace* our resentment with disappointment, in deference either to the youth and inexperience of the moral "progressor" or to the difficult challenges, external or internal, the target faces in meeting aspirations. But even in such cases we are taking up a different normative stance in disappointment than we are in resentment. In the first case, our aspirations on behalf of someone are frustrated and we feel let down; in the second, we feel violated, transgressed, toyed with, and we hold the target responsible for the transgression. We blame him in a way we don't in the first case. (That is, the counterpoint to praise, in the first case of meeting aspirations, is not blame when there is failure.) Moreover, disappointment, in others or in oneself, needn't be inherently a mild emotion. It can be felt as profoundly and intensely as the most bitter kind of resentment or guilt. It can cripple and paralyze and lead to the bleakest kind of despair. Again, Aristotle's remarks about parental investment in a child's happiness (however guided or misguided) makes this all too clear. The difference between disappointment and resentment is qualitative, not scalar.

HOPE IN ONESELF

We have been focusing on hope and disappointment in others. But many who return from war are dogged by profound disappointment in themselves and the sense that they have fallen short of ideals of what it is to be a good soldier. Sometimes the disappointment stems not from wrongdoing or evil, but from an over-idealized sense of good soldiering, or an intolerance for good and bad luck in war. In a related way, some may feel (subjective) guilt that doesn't track culpability or wrongdoing. In some of these cases, there may be causal but not moral responsibility at work, such as when an individual is the proximate cause of a nonculpable accident. In other cases, merely surviving when a buddy doesn't, without any sense of being the agent or cause of that buddy's death, unleashes deep guilt and despondency.

Hope in the face of evil is another matter, either when one is the victim of evil or when its perpetrator. There is no shortage of evil in going to war and killing and maiming for a cause that may not be just or at least is imprudent, as many in the public increasingly regard the wars in Afghanistan, and—especially—Iraq. This has not been my central focus, largely because the soldiers who are my focus have not made it theirs. This may speak to all sorts of issues, including an enlisted military and not a drafted one, a conservative-leaning military, a military that swelled in the wake of a patriotic surge after 9/11, or wars that have wound down only to be reignited. I suspect there will be far deeper disillusionment as the experiences of investing $2 trillion and too many lives in Iraq and Afghanistan leave little lasting impact in those regions.

The experience of some of the Marine veterans of the bloody Fallujah invasion of the Anbar region of Iraq in November 2004 may be indicative here. The battle that wrested the insurgent-held city was fierce and costly, and for the Corps a defining moment of the twelve years of war in Iraq and Afghanistan, with nearly 100 Marines killed and hundreds wounded. When the city fell back to insurgent Sunni forces with Al Qaeda links in January 2014, shock waves of disbelief ran viral through the close-knit Marine community who fought in that battle. With the fall came a lost sense of the mission and what they took themselves to accomplish. As Kael Weston, a State Department political adviser who worked closely with Marines in Fallujah and later Afghanistan put it, "This is just the beginning of the reckoning and accounting." The reckoning will come, and with it the shifting grounds of hope or despair. This is a future story to be told for these veterans and for many others who have served in these wars.

But for now I want to focus on a different reckoning: hope in the face of accident and the hope one should have. That is, hope that is appropriate and fitting, and that can update and correct earlier reactive uptakes. That hope can also be therapeutic—literally, life saving, lifting one from suicidal self-rebuke and despair. But coming to that self-hope is not easy. And it often requires the hope others invest in us.

Self-hope is self-address. But first, it might seem a stretch to think of *self*-reactive attitudes as moral addresses. After all, in the self-reflexive case, we don't have to *express* the attitudes to *disclose* them to ourselves. And so, if address is primarily *expressed* attitude, then the idea of moral address to one-self seems strained. Moreover, the background notion of call and response in speech acts, or in Gospel music of the Church and later absorbed in rock and roll patterns (stereotypically with a solo woman or "girl group" chorus answering the call of the male lead singer—think of Lou Reed's "A Walk on the Wild Side" and the controversial call line, "and the colored girls sing" with the reply, "Doot, doo doot, doo doot, doo doot doo doot"), makes vivid that idea of public and, paradigmatically, oral address and response. The vocal model isn't an easy fit for private, normative self-review.

But this is too literal and restrictive a read of moral address. Even in second-personal cases, we still may hold each other *responsible* without holding
accountable, where additionally the latter involves imposing sanctions that
only make sense when our blame or reproach is expressly communicated.
Moreover, insofar as evaluative attitudes are *emotions* that draw us in or rivet
attention, an important part of expressed address, which is to get someone
to pay attention to you, is already at work in the self-reactive case. All this
of course is to put aside the fact that we often do openly express emotions to
ourselves—in talking to ourselves, in singing to ourselves, in journaling, in
screwing up our face muscles, and in scores of other communications. Some
of these communications may need decoding and unmasking, but when
they are, they are the beginning of interpretive narratives, again, that we *tell*
ourselves.

But to return to the question I began with, in what sense can
self-hope act as a corrective update on harsher reactive attitudes we
hold toward ourselves, particularly when those attitudes—of guilt,
shame, or self-disappointment—are not entirely apt and are the cause
of deep anguish? Self-forgiveness, self-empathy, and self-compassion all
can play a role, as we have seen in earlier chapters. But so, too, can normative hope. Insofar as hope invests aspiration rather than normative
demands for strict compliance, we begin by giving ourselves some lati-
tude in the face of significant internal and external challenges we may
face. We take up the "progressor's" stance, not the perfectionist stance
of a "sage," to deploy Stoic idiom. For some, this will involve recognizing the limits of agency in the face of luck and embedded existence.
And this willingness to tolerate luck may combine with the resources
of hope to engage imagination in order to rethink and renarrate the
traumatic or nagging scenarios in a less "stuck" and less self-punishing
way. So, in time, a Marine may come to imagine those who have died
under his watch as *in fact* not condemning him. Or he may no longer
imagine himself exposed, under another's critical gaze, in a way that
compromises self-presentation and brings on shame. In short, new possibilities open up in how he holds himself responsible and how he views
others as holding him responsible.

With this in mind, let's revisit Marine Corporal Lalo Panyagua and his wife, Donna Hernandez. Recall that Lalo had sustained multiple injuries—traumatic brain injury, nerve damage in his arms, some vision, speech, and memory impairments, severe posttraumatic stress, and chronic insomnia. But what anguishes him the most is moral injury—in particular, the guilt of losing three Marines. One incident, which we've already detailed, keeps eating him up. It is the loss of Corporal Justin Wilson in Marja. It was bad luck. Wilson had to take a shit at the wrong moment and got blown to pieces. But Lalo didn't remind him to watch his step. That was Lalo's fault, and not a matter of luck, thinks Lalo. The citation on his achievement medal, "Corporal Panyagua adapted and overcame any challenge," offers little comfort in facing the self-rebuke and the suicidal fantasies that come with it.

Donna, his wife and my former student, is a powerful mix of sass, humor, dark beauty, street smarts, and academic sophistication. She is on an even keel, and while fiery about her interests and academic independence, she is a devoted partner, endlessly patient and empathic. Early on at Georgetown she decided on a career in the Foreign Service, and won a prestigious Pickering Foreign Affairs fellowship to do her master's at Yale in security studies, as part of her preparation for postings abroad.

All this is important background to Lalo's project of self-hope. Donna brings to bear her exceptional gifts and personal resources in her relationship with Lalo. And they have been critical for his recovery back home. Lalo is a "progressor" in her eyes, and his own project of hope in himself depends in critical ways on her hope in him. Still, the journey has not been easy.

To recap, with next to no transition time, Lalo returned from war to a stateside base where he became a combat guy at a desk job, surrounded mostly by those who had not gone to war and a commander who viewed him as a malingerer for taking off time for his medical appointments. It was Donna who got him to seek psychotherapy (to see "the wizard," as he puts it), two years after his return and after a pile-up of frightening incidents, where he flung her out of bed across a room as he relived a flashback, held her to knife point when she came up on him from behind during a thunderstorm, and nearly killed others on street corners in D.C. in attempts to protect her. She took away his knife. He took up archery in its place: "He can't really hurt me with a bow and arrow!" she laughs. The bow and arrow have now been confiscated, too. "No weapons," she told me. "It's too dangerous."

Donna is herself good at compartmentalizing, and since childhood, academic study has been her sanctuary and salvation. It's her safe retreat. Nourishment. But as separate as her bookish world is from the Marine Corps, Lalo has always been a part of it. In part, it's through her vision. She has a sustained vision of Lalo as someone who is absolutely winning and loveable—"everyone falls in love with Lalo," she has said to me on several occasions, meaning not just that he charms but also that he is *worthy* of her love and that of others.

Estimations of worth and goodness, of course, needn't have anything to do with estimates of a person's psychological capacities to overcome crippling and harsh guilt, or to accept the limits of agency and what is beyond one's control. But *admiring* another's goodness or capacity for hard work in the service of important and worthwhile ends *may* have such an influence. And Donna knows well and deeply, in a way that Lalo can forget, just how good a Marine he is and how he surpassed expectations in every mission he was assigned. When he wears his regalia, at her request, such as at their wedding when they eloped when she was a freshman, and at her graduation from Georgetown, she is reminding him of his honors and his capacities. She is trying to reconnect him with his capabilities and his confidence in them.

These are public addresses of sorts *to* him of her hope *in* him. They are nudges, offerings of content for introjections that will renourish his own self-images. They are attempts at tempering and updating his self-blame for being a leader who lost troops. Of course, uptake, especially in this kind of case, can be partial and primarily a performance, outer posturing of normative hope, perhaps in showing up for psychotherapy appointments, say, but also in resisting the hard work and trust alliance with a therapist required to really invest in the possibility of therapeutic change. But just as a therapist's finely expressed trust in a patient can elicit trustworthiness, so, too, can a partner's artful and finely attuned hope in one bootstrapping one's own. Donna is able to do this for Lalo.

Lalo's nascent self-hope, in this case, mirrors Donna's hope in him. Early on in the philosophical record, Aristotle invokes that image of a friend as "another self," a "mirror," not for narcissistic reflection, he insists, but for self-knowledge "when we wish to know our own characters ... and direct study of ourselves" is near impossible. The background assumption in Aristotle's claims is that we are not empty vessels for others' aspirations, but we are aspirants who can't do without others' support, trust, and compassionate critique in articulating how to live well and then trying to live that life.

It would be hard to spend any time with this couple and not pick up on this dynamic in their relationship. Donna's hope is neither sweet, nor supine, nor Pollyannaish: She has lived war and knows too much about the war that keeps going on. She is a survivor of war no less than he. But he is also now a student, at a community college in New Haven, where he takes classes four days a week, with one day free for himself and VA appointments. And he's enjoying being the student again. Each has invested in the other's future. Donna and Lalo partner one another by "trading places in fancy," and sometimes, in fact.

We human progressors engage in complicated moral and psychological interactions. We elicit change in response to each other's investments in us, as well as in our own. For a returning veteran, recognizing that another has invested hope in you can be profoundly transformative. It can nourish hope in oneself and sustain hope for projects that rekindle a sense of meaning and purpose after war. It is an important moment in healing.

A homecoming for a sailor and a new beginning for a family

CHAPTER 7

HOMECOMING

Lieutenant Alysha Haran is a thirty-seven-year-old naval officer, whom I first met in 2006 when she was a midshipman in the NROTC (Naval Reserve Officer Training Corps) program at the University of San Diego. I was giving a lecture honoring the late Vice Admiral James Bond Stockdale, the senior POW held by the North Vietnamese for seven and half years who attributed his survival through brutal isolation and torture to adherence to the teachings of Stoicism, and its call to let go of everything outside one's control as extraneous to inner virtue. Alysha had her own Stoic awakening around the time of the terrorist attacks of 9/11. She was a California actress and producer, whose L.A. career in film and commercials started to seem vapid, fat with material objects but lacking in "authenticity" and a sense of service. Shooting car ads, chasing the California summer daylight for seventeen hours a day to get the right angle and shot, struck her then as a worthless pursuit: "Making Mercedes commercials—what does it really matter?" The Navy, in contrast, offered a life of public service where her age and experience (she was ten years older than most of the other midshipmen on campus) and love of mentoring could have a solid place.

What clinched the Navy for her was a sense of a woman's place at sea. There was nostalgia, too. Her grandmother was in the WAVES (the Navy's Women Accepted for Volunteer Emergency Service) during World War II. When she died in February 2001, Alysha saw a picture of her in uniform for the first time. She was overcome with wistful longing: "She looked beautiful," she sighed. "It was a moment filled with nostalgia. The smell, the feel was right." In joining the Navy, Alysha had something of a conversion experience. A romance with a uniform became a romance with the sea and a romance with ships: "I love the ships. I love the efficiency with which you can get a city at sea to run," she told me recently. And she found her calling in a dedication to sailors, who for the most part grew up with neither her privilege nor her sense of expectation in life.

Alysha graduated USD and was commissioned into the Navy on May 27, 2007. Two months later she was an ensign, aboard a 300-person destroyer, at sea in the Middle East. Within five weeks of boarding the ship, she qualified in her watch station in aft steering, having had no prior training before deploying. Just around her commission time, the Navy shrunk its training program and jettisoned a six-month course for Surface Warfare Officers (SWOs; a program that they have since reinstated). Alysha was forced to learn on the job, by the book, with the help of the enlisted at her side. She had little doubt about the importance of her office. Aft steering was the "last line of defense," she explained to me, in ensuring the safety of your crew. And she had always been committed to performing to the highest standards of excellence. She always pushed herself. She had walked on the ship ready to be a professional, ready to lead, and ready to being given the standing of an officer. But she also knew she needed formalized training to do her job well. The Navy didn't treat surface warfare as it did aviator training and learning to fly, she said: "I had zero training before boarding that ship."

New on the job with her mint new credentials and little training, she was the officer in charge at the aft station when a supervising officer happened to walk in, did a routine inspection, and barked out "Unsat." He made a beeline to the commanding officer to share the unsatisfactory review, Alysha said, rather than seizing the occasion as a moment for her training. Within a day, three enlisted sailors and Alysha, their junior officer, were brought before a mast hearing with the commander at the helm. The proceedings commenced against the enlisted, with Alysha forced to watch from the rear, feeling helpless in her role of taking care of her enlisted.

The procedures for the watch were gone over at mast in far greater detail than she had ever heard before. She was here, at captain's mast, getting the kind of formal training she should have had before stepping onto the ship. The charges against the sailors were dropped. It was now Alysha's turn. In a moment of weight and gravitas, the commander moved the location of the mast to the more formal officer's podium. It became a spectacle. And she was certain she was about to lose her commission and be publicly disgraced. Her Navy career, her dreams of a woman's place were shot. But then the charges were dropped, just as they had been for the enlisted. But the spirit of indictment and the public shaming never lifted: "I became the Jonah of the ship," she said, using sailor's lingo for a person who brings bad luck on board. "Given who I am, I took it seriously to the point that I felt I had nowhere to go." She was trapped at sea. She later learned that the captain never had any intentions of putting her in the brig. "His motivation was to send a message to the wardroom." In an odd, perverted way, they used theater against me," she said, referring to how she felt stigmatized from the start for her unusual theater background. The captain had made a leadership decision: she was the object lesson to be put on stage. She was the plaything of the deterrent punishment, or at least the threat of it. And though she was never put in the brig, the public mast was humiliation enough.

This incident set the tone for her deployment. She became a Philoctetes of sorts (to recall the discussion in chapter 5), marooned on an island, struck down only after five weeks of becoming an officer, shunned by her fellow sailors. I was taking "my first step," she said to me, seven years later, with no time to become "toughened up and have allies." She did have one ally, a woman who was her department head, who knew that the charge would be dismissed. But as a matter of professional propriety she chose not to tell Alysha before the decision was formally delivered.

Alysha fully acknowledges that she and her enlisted companions made mistakes. And she was forthright and apologetic to the commander at the time. She had been given assurances by others who had aft duty that it was okay to bring a non-Navy book with her to read during the long lulls at watch. That was ill-advised and became a bone of contention with the supervisor. It also turned out that one of the enlisted men was not easily visible when the supervisor passed through—at that very moment he was behind a large piece of equipment mopping up an oil puddle. In addition, the whole team was lethargic in the 117-degree heat. That, too, didn't help. Still, the disgracing left a "black spot" on her psyche: "To this day, I still feel it. They picked the worst possible officer to do this to. Others could shrug it off. But it had a lasting impact on me, with four months left of deployment on the ship. That was the only time I came close to contemplating suicide. I would go to the transom on the ship and look at the wake and just want to jump.... Still, I got up for every watch, and did it all. But I internalized it all—down, down, down—a complete severing of my previous life. All that happiness I found in San Diego, all that happiness dried up. I stopped writing to friends and family. I had no way to tell them I was a complete failure. And I was failing on the ship without anyone to help me. I think I was 112 pounds. I stopped eating in the wardroom because I had no friends. So I slowly started to disappear."

Alysha was vulnerable. As often in the case of trauma, there is a history. The third sister of four girls, she was often blamed for mishaps. And she was the working daughter who brought home the paycheck as a child actress. She felt exploited: "I was only valued for *what* I was as a kid, and not for *who* I was. I was an actress. And as an actress, you never let down your mask." She internalized the blame and became expert in shaming herself. The perfectionist military, demanding blemish-free performance, suited her own harsh superego. And that she was different, an actress, a writer, a dancer who loves yoga—all that made her an easy target, on a ship on edge, combat ready with no enemy in sight except the one within. "The war is *in* the ship," Alysha says. "The *Lord of the Flies* syndrome sets in." And on a small destroyer of 300 persons, unlike an aircraft carrier that is a virtual city of 5,000, there is nowhere to hide: "You are confronted by that hostility every day." Even the most efficient ship can devolve into a moral snake pit: "When you take in all lines from a ship, you lose your perspective."

It is easy to see Alysha as cut from a different cloth than many in the tradition-bound male Navy. An actress and dancer with a background in the arts, she didn't fit into a familiar pattern. She is extremely wary of pinning her uphill battles on sexism, though. When I ask her if there was discrimination involved in the commander's picking her out for an object lesson, she is adamant: "No, no, no. He wasn't sexist at all; the three enlisted sailors were all male. He made a leadership decision." She says emphatically, "The gender issue was irrelevant." Still, when I mention the term "implicit bias," the idea behind it resonates: "When you regard a male and female junior officer, somewhere on an unconscious level, you automatically assume the guy is going to be more successful than the girl." And she suggests that disparities in the elevation rates up the ranks in surface warfare "definitely confirm the bias."

Alysha returned from that deployment badly traumatized and feeling desperately alone during the next postings at sea. Despite her anguish, she surprised herself at how she managed to do well at the job, got "pegged high," and went on to serve as an aide to the commander of the Navy's Central Command and 5th Fleet, based in Bahrain. Her second boss in that posting, Vice Admiral John Miller, quickly gained her trust in a way few commanders ever had. "I was really, really on the brink. I was fine at work because I have mastered control, keeping it all in, not letting my face crack. And then I was talking to my grandfather one day. He's passed away, but he was in the Navy and I was calling on him, so to speak: I was lost. And then arrives this admiral who looks like my grandfather, talks like him, and completely accepts me. He accepted the artistic side of me. It wasn't a big deal for him."

In psychoanalytic terms, what Alysha experienced is a kind of double transference, an attachment to a beloved grandfather mirrored anew in a professional relationship with an admiral who admires and respects her, in a way that allows her to incorporate that positive image into her own self-regard and self-esteem. In the terms we have been developing in the previous two chapters, she experienced a reciprocal positive moral address of trust and hope: Alysha can now reliably *count on* a senior naval officer who has a stable vision of her as a talented, young naval lieutenant in whom he is willing to invest publically. This positive call becomes critical for her sense of self-trust and self-hope, and self-empathy. His mentorship was sustaining and Alysha went on to apply for a highly competitive Olmstead fellowship (a kind of

Fulbright scholarship for mid-level officers), which she won and is now working on for two years in Tokyo."The healing came through championing not
what I was but *who* I was, raising me up, acknowledging me ... accepting
me, allowing me to come to work as an entire human being. He trusted me
enough to allow me to trust the *whole* of myself."

The lesson should not be trivialized. The military is very much a stage of
masks and managed hearts, roles and demeanor—outer performances that
often keep at bay inner conflict and turmoil. The temperate Stoic, as I call
it and have written extensively about in *Stoic Warriors*, is the valorized role.
But even *well*-tempered Stoicism comes at a cost. And the ability to access
what one is really feeling, and not wall it off into lasting numbness or disdain
or fear of exposure, needs to be part of doing well and thriving, even in the
military.

I recently gave a seminar at the Naval Postgraduate School in Monterey,
California, to Special Forces officers just back from ten years of war and
selected by that prestigious institution to pursue mid-career master's degrees.
One officer spoke candidly before the others of the trauma he suffered as a
child, and the pain of multiple adoptions and foster parents who were emotionally abusive and obtuse. He now has his own child, and he doesn't want
to transmit those absorbed habits into an abusive tough, "truck it on" parenting style. These were issues he could think about now, in leisure and in an
academic setting, while he was home with his wife and child, not downrange,
leading troops, surviving on little sleep, primed to be hyperreactive, ready to
pounce as the intelligence demanded, a man of action, who has to ward off
the appearance of softness and vulnerability.

* * *

My aim in this book has been to tell the story of many different kinds of
homecomings, from lonely ships, from dubious missions, from assaults inside
the wire, from accidents that make human perfection laughable, from Greek
islands where the wounded are abandoned, from off-duty poolside R and
R where life-saving intel sits idle, from rooftops in Marja where crouching
versus standing means life rather than death, from picking up your buddy's
remains from a bomb blast and then losing the whole bottom of your body
from another blast, from not giving your troops the warning "to take care"

normative cases, to self and others, and to positive differences each can make in a life. Hope presumes that possibilities—however bare—(and people) are *open* to one, and that prospect can galvanize energy. Hope presumes a kind of "possibilism," that can stabilize focus and fortify resolve.

One prominent philosopher develops the idea this way: "To form the hope that something is the case or that I or someone else will manage to make it the case, I have to invest that scenario with a level of confidence" that may exceed "the confidence of my actual belief in the prospect and with a degree of stability that will certainly exceed the stability of my actual belief." In this sense, hope is a *pragmatic* rationality. It redirects attention and desire and imaginative planning to possibilities that a more fact-processing, probability-assessing, evidence-seeking mentality might reject: "Forming the hope that a particular scenario will eventuate, or at least eventuate in the event of your taking a certain initiative, is a way of handling the hurly burly of belief. It frees you from the bleakness of beliefs that wax and wane unpredictably in level of confidence. It gives you firm and friendly coordinates in an uncertain and uncompanionable world. To have hope is to have something we might describe as cognitive resolve.... Without hope, there would often be no possibility for us of asserting our agency and of putting our own signature or stamp on our conduct. We would collapse in a heap of despair and uncertainty, beaten down by cascades of inimical fact."

Hope, on this picture, is deeply connected with practical agency, or as it sometimes put, is a form of "agential investment." In this regard, it is distinct from *mere* or *idle* wish, such as for the impossible or near impossible—"for immortality," as Aristotle says. And, too, it is distinct from wishful thinking—at least in the way Freud sometimes understands it, as a "turning away from reality" with wishful fantasies "regarded as a better reality." For similar reasons, the notion of wish fulfillment, in the sense of satisfaction fully hived off from the constraints of reality, does not capture the meaning of hope, either. To be sure, substantive hopes typically involve a kind of ego satisfaction, in the sense of a desire for one's own thriving, or *eudaimonia*. And these kinds of hopes may be expressed in the constructions of fantasy and its narratives, as vehicles for practice and for trying out future possibilities. I expand upon this shortly. But the point for now is that fantasy can be an important way of *engaging* reality and, not of retreating from it, in a fully separate, disconnected track.

It's hard not to think about hope when you meet Dan Berschinski, a young Army veteran from the war in Afghanistan. On August 18, 2009, Dan, then a twenty-five-year-old first lieutenant from West Point, in command of an infantry platoon in Kandahar, Afghanistan, stepped on a bomb while trying to retrieve the remains of his unit observer. A botched-up medevac left Dan bleeding profusely, and his family was pretty sure he was not going to make it out of Afghanistan alive. In the end, he was stabilized enough to be put on a plane to Landsthul Regional Medical Center, though too fragile to actually leave the plane. Within a week, he was flown to Walter Reed, where his parents awaited him. Bob and Susan Berschinski were warned that if Dan somehow pulled through, the hemorrhaging would likely result in severe brain damage. Dan miraculously did pull through, with no trace of traumatic brain injury. As Susan said to me, "once they brought him out of the coma, it was rapidly apparent *he* was still there."

But his body wasn't all there. He had lost nearly half of his skeleton and the joints that held it together, now so much dust in the Afghani desert: "My guys found a boot ... mostly intact actually, and they said to me later that they played rock-paper-scissors to see who would have to stick their hand inside the boot to see if there was any flesh inside. But there wasn't. It was empty.... I don't know what happened."

When Dan came to, he knew much of his body was gone, but under a protective white hospital sheet he couldn't really take in the damage, and his parents kept up a brave face. "He was a mess   ... There was not a place on him that you could touch that didn't hurt," said Bob. After more than a dozen operations, and being pinned together by an exoskeletal frame to stabilize his remaining limbs, Dan officially became a double above-the-knee amputee, with a reconstructed left arm and hand, minus a pinky. But critically, he was missing a right hip joint. With that much skeletal damage, and profound socket challenges for a good-fitting prosthesis, it was fairly clear that Dan would never walk again. Without sit bones, he even had trouble sitting in a wheelchair without sliding off.

and having that omission haunt for the rest of your life. And in some cases, too many cases, there are no homecomings. Or homecomings that later take lives—one's own or one's spouses or fellow soldiers on home bases. And then there are homecomings *to us*, in classrooms, in hospitals, in work corridors, in airports, where the lived worlds can seem alien until we morally engage each other and do what we humans do best: recognize and acknowledge each other, and invoke and convoke community through our emotions and understanding.

That is the work of emotions such as trust and hope and empathy. They are calls to each other, invocations to take responsibility. In the case of expressing trust, you let another know that you are counting on him or her, as Sally, the wingman did, often to her commander, though sadly, without adequate uptake. She had to resort to her own self-protection when she entered the chow hall. Hope is an investment in another, a setting of a challenge, in the best cases, with the kind of care and concern that helps the recipient bootstrap him or herself up to reach those new heights. This is what Donna does so well for Lalo, and what he now feels empowered to do through his own aspirations for himself. Empathy is a soulful connection with another—and in many cases, with oneself—that allows one to touch past hurts without their being toxic and paralyzing. After months and years of beating up on himself for not being in Tal Afar for Lt. Edens, Tom Fiebrandt came to the epiphany that he couldn't be the one-stop intel officer for all of the Army in Iraq. To think that one ever could, of course, sounds grandiose. But guilt can wrack in just that way that demands a full and merciless self-flagellation. Shame can even be more global in its self-rebuke, robbing a self of any sense of worth in any domain. Ajax fell on his sword because he felt fully emptied of honor. Jeff Hall felt stripped of all his goodness when hamstrung by bureaucracy in his repeated attempts to help a civilian girl bury her dead mother, father, and brother killed in the crossfire

Guilt and shame can tear a self into pieces, to the point that one loses sound judgment about who one is and who one can be. The task is to recover lost goodness, to renew a desire to live well, and to find meaning at home.

That is a kind of invocation of community, within one self and in one's own company. Service members long for that, too—to recognize themselves when shorn of the uniform and the side arms, when their old civilian self seems unfamiliar, alien, and maybe even hostile. Those of us who have not worn the uniform, and have sent others to war in them, have a sacred role in this peace process.

Afterwords

Where They Are Now

The healing continues for many of the service members I have interviewed. Here are some brief updates:

Jeff Hall is transitioning out of the Army with the devoted help of his life-long soul mate and spouse, Sheri, and their two grown daughters. He is "starting a new life," he reports, in two business ventures—custom wood milling and an art shop. Both are interests he took up during his convalescence from war, initially as therapy, carving intricately detailed war helmets and painting masks that glimpsed at the war within. Sheri is opening a coffee shop and following her culinary passion. They both remain committed to soldier and veteran advocacy. Jeff has had numerous surgeries and ongoing treatment in the wake of complicated war injuries that have taken a toll on his body and mind.

Josh Mantz recovered from his near fatal femoral wound of 2007 and redeployed to Iraq five months later to lead troops. After that tour, he worked stateside, as Company Commander in the Fort Riley Warrior Transition

Battalion, helping soldiers face up to the emotional wounds of war. Interested in Arabic since he was at West Point, he was selected as an Army Foreign Area Officer, and completed an advanced intensive Arabic language program at the Defense Language Institute in Monterey, California. He remains a close observer of the areas he served in, following Arabic newsfeeds and YouTube videos coming out of Iraq and the neighboring regions. I saw him in mid-June 2014 in Monterey. He was sickened by the sectarian bloodletting he was seeing on line, and was deeply disillusioned by the collapse of Iraq and the infrastructure that he and his troops fought so hard to build, at such high cost of life of life and limb. He still remains an advocate of counterinsurgency operations, but he is convinced that they can work only if troops have decades to implement the changes and far more resources and personnel. He is growing weary of Army bureaucracy and inflexibility in its care of troops, and is contemplating what might be next for him in his career. Promoted to a major, he is peparing to leave the Army, for medical reasons and more, and is pretty sure his next job will be in the private sector, away from the military and government. He has had a divorce, struggles with his own psychological and physical injuries, and has finally reached out to his father for candid conversation and support. He has a little sister at home in Pennsylvania whom he adores to pieces. During his deployment in Iraq, she and her classmates made tee-shirts for him to distribute to Iraqi children their age. Josh is just thirty years old.

Dan Berschinski is at Stanford's Graduate School of Business. He gets around the large campus on a Segway, donated to him by the charity Segs4Vets. A few years back, he started his own manufacturing company in plastic-injection molding, setting up a division of the company that serves military bases. He is hoping to do more partnerships with businesses that work with veterans and is in an incubation program this summer to explore that route. An ongoing interest is the development of prosthetics and joint replacements, including making safe and flexible, well-designed but inexpensive "legs" for nonprofits and Third World distribution. Though he is enjoying Stanford and the ease of being outdoors in sunny Palo Alto, he wishes that more of his classmates, outside the small veteran community, would ask him how he got injured. It's not that he wants to be known as the guy who lost his legs in war. He wants people to feel comfortable asking how it happened so that both sides can move beyond it, and he can be just Dan. During the past three summers, Dan has served as a counselor at a special wilderness camp for kids who have lost limbs.

T.M. Gibbons-Neff is finishing up at Georgetown University, having served as the president of the campus Students Veterans Association. He enlisted in the Marines, thinking that the second time round he would serve as an officer. He'd lead knowing what life was like in the ranks. But the writing bug has bitten him, and he is now firmly intent on a career in journalism. He was an editor at Georgetown's newspaper, *The Hoya*; a columnist for the blog, *War on the Rocks*; and is a contributor at the *Washington Post*. A number of his pieces have been published in the *New York Times, Time,* the *Washington Post,* the *Atlantic,* and the *Daily Beast.* He follows war correspondents closely, especially those who were themselves once Marines, like C. J. Chivers at the *New York Times.*

Tom Fiebrandt, a graduate of Georgetown's School of Foreign Service, does intelligence work for a defense contractor in the D.C. area, and hopes soon to become a Foreign Service officer. We reconnected in early 2014, just as Al Qaeda forces were claiming control of U.S. hard-won sites in Ramadi and Fallujah. He was disillusioned by the re-ignition of fighting and deeply concerned for locals, like those he worked closely with, trapped permanently in the crosshairs of war. I asked if he thought about going back to Tal Afar and Mosul, the cities in northern Iraq where he was posted. He hesitated before answering: "It's a possibility, but I'm not sure how I'd handle it, being back in the lion's den." The "lion's den" was not just the sectarian violence, but also the return of his own demons. Tom's fascination with the region dates back to childhood: "It's one of those places whose culture and history always gripped me since I was a young kid reading the Bible." The tale of the prophet Jonah begins and ends in the plains of Nineveh, in the northern region of Iraq near the Syrian border. It is the site, as I write now, of the violent Sunni takeover by ISIS (Islamic State of Iraq and Syria), in their assault to form an Islamic state in the region. And there are confirmed reports of footage that show jihadists taking sledgehammers to the tomb of Jonah as part of their attempt to eradicate Judeo-Christianity in the region.

After his tours in Iraq, Tom took classes at the community college in his home neighborhood, where he met Brittany, his wife of several years now: "We were both the oldest students in class." That was the initial draw. An accomplished equestrian, Brittany competes and teaches young children riding and care for horses. The couple has bought a foreclosed, 110-year-old house in rural Maryland that they are renovating.

Lalo Panyagua was medically discharged from the Marines in a formal ceremony at the VA elder residence in Virginia, where he and his care dog, Max, lived for several months while Lalo was in treatment at the Marine Wounded Warrior Regiment at Walter Reed in Bethesda, Maryland. In the audience were many elder veterans and widows of veterans who had become Lalo's informal support system during those months of psychological convalescence. He and Max have since relocated to New Haven to be with Donna. Lalo is thriving in his new life as a student at Gateway Community College. During the summer of 2014, he took classes at Yale as part of a warrior/ scholar program. One day during the summer, he told me with an exasperated voice that he was having "a love/hate relationship" with de Tocqueville! He had to read *Democracy in America* that week and was struggling with the nineteenth-century French-translated prose. I was caught by surprise a few weeks later when he announced that de Tocqueville had become a personal favorite. The change of heart came after Lalo visited Yale's Beinecke Rare Book and Manuscript Library and the librarian pulled out de Tocqueville's handwritten manuscripts. In an instant, an abstract work became concrete and even likeable! Donna Hernandez continues as a U.S. Department of State Pickering fellow at Yale's Jackson Institute for Global Affairs. Among her seminar teachers has been retired General Stanley McChrystal, now a senior fellow at Yale. On Lalo's twenty-sixth birthday, newly discharged from the Marines, Lalo joined Donna and her classmates for a beer with McChrystal after his seminar. McChrystal toasted Lalo. Lalo had a chance to talk directly to the commander who had been in charge of all American forces in Afghanistan, including the Marine presence in Marja where Lalo, in flashbacks, still returns to pick up the fragments of his buddies.

During the summer of 2014, while Donna was out of the country on assignment in Cambodia, Lalo took long, meandering walks with Max up the wooded hills in East Rock in New Haven. Protected by Max in the city park, Lalo could take in nature. After he finished his program at Yale, he was honored when the school invited him to return next summer to be on hand to help new vets who may be struggling with posttraumatic stress. Once the course was over, Lalo returned to his search for a psychotherapist in New Haven, someone, he tells me, "who can listen and is compassionate, and who he can trust." He's become a sophisticated patient and consumer of mental health treatment, open about his moral and psychological injuries and eager to get better. Still, there is a little-appreciated hurdle in the system for veterans like Lalo: though his Tricare health insurance allows him to go outside the VA system, the insurance pays only at Medicaid rates. And not many providers will accept those fees. Lalo and Donna, who eloped in her freshman year, will be wed again in a religious ceremony before parents and friends, in June, 2015 in California. As Donna put it, "Lalo and I finally bowed to our parents' pleas for a Catholic ceremony."

Most of the service women I have written about do not want their names disclosed. In those cases I have used pseudonyms. But "Alysha Haran" is the actual name of **Alysha Haran**. While at sea, and as a part of a master's program, she wrote a creative nonfiction book under her own name that draws from her experiences in the Navy. Under her Navy-sponsored Olmsted fellowship, which seeks to immerse military members in the cultures in which they serve, she is doing a second master's in Japanese Studies at Sophia University in Tokyo. As part of the immersion, she is directing a play with the 118-year-old theater company, Tokyo International Players. Her background in film and theater has also led to an unusual collaboration with Japanese public sponsors on a possible TV series that sets Louise May Alcott's *Little Women* in modern Japanese society. The collaboration is part of a push in Japan to gain some ground for women, long subordinated and kept out of the workplace and public life. Alysha is an unusual and unlikely sailor. As she jokes, "I'm glad the military repealed "don't ask don't tell," because once everyone is finally comfortable with the word *lesbian*, we can move onto the word *thespian*. To support others who have the same dream of finding room in a military life for a literary or artistic soul, she has founded with her sister Laurel Haran, "Artists in Uniform," a nonprofit organization that will bring accomplished writers, actors, dancers, and artists onto bases to talk about their art forms.

Alysha has recently married a retired Navy master chief who "is my family for the first time in a long time." Eager to go back to sea after her Japanese studies, she plans to serve for twenty years, all in, and then retire. At last she is making peace with the Navy and with her dream of serving honorably as a naval officer in whites.

"Stephanie Wilson" is also not a pseudonym. **Stephanie Wilson** returned from her command in Qatar, heading up security logistics for mission support, to take a post at the Pentagon under a three-star female Air Force general. She's a "supportive colleague," Stephanie told me, who understands the demands on working mothers and spouses. An engineer by training, Stephanie's current work focuses on environmental oversight issues affecting the Air Force, stateside. Stephanie's children, Liam and Mikayla, are healthy and flourishing and did well during Stephanie's year-long absence. Her husband, Scott Wilson, a retired Air Force lieutenant colonel, was at home at the helm. A few years back, when Stephanie was selected early for command, Scott supported her decision to accept the promotion, giving up his own opportunity to command. Had they both stayed on their career tracks they would have probably been commanding concurrently on two different continents. Scott was willing to make the sacrifice and retire early.

Stephanie is well aware that in her command position she is a role model for the military but also for the military family. Before she deployed to Qatar she and her family met the families of the squadron commanders who would be deploying under her. The challenges of juggling family and career were on her mind as she reached out to these families. Later, when we chatted, she put her rising career in perspective, in a way one wishes more men would: "Family relationships are so important probably in every job, every occupation, in every step of life, but especially in the military. It's what grounds you. It's what helps you. And sometimes, as military members, we have to remind ourselves about that as we get into the quagmire of our day and our duties, and the stress and strain. We have to remind ourselves that at the end of the day, when you retire, the Air Force is going to say goodbye to you.... You'll be forgotten by the system, by the organization the minute you are out the door and you are no longer working for them. But that family, if you've done your job right, being a mom and a wife, (or a dad and a husband) and balancing that with being an airman and a soldier, will be with you for life."

ACKNOWLEDGMENTS

I AM indebted, in writing this book, to the men and women who have served (and their families) who have been so willing to talk openly to me about the moral challenges of going to war and coming home. The book has incubated for over three years, some of its ideas taking shape while I was giving talks on *The Untold War*. The list of debts is long. Among those I owe gratitude to are: Michael Abbatello, Matthew Alexander, Ashley Anderson, John Anderson, Bill Andrews, Paul Baffico, Dan Berschinski, Bob and Susan Berschinski, Dave Blair, Phil Carter, Rhonda Cornum, Caitlin Davies, Max Despans, Joe Felter, Tom Fiebrandt, Greg Gadson, George Glaze, Erik Goepner, TM Gibbons-Neff, Jeff Hall, Alysha Haran, Dave Hodne, Colby Howard, Rob Kislow, Tim Karcher, Miriam Krieger, Fernando Lujan, Josh Mantz, Mauro Mujica, Steve Robinson, Jacob Sotak, Tom Vail, Peter Weinert, Corneila Weiss, Stephanie Wilson, and Jonathan Wong.

I am also indebted to conversations and symposia over the years with those in the behavioral health clinical and research communities who treat service members and veterans, or run and support advocacy programs and outreach. I owe thanks here to: Christina Biedermann, Joe Bobrow, Victoria Bruner, Robin Carnes, Abbey-Robin Durkin, Chuck Engel, Jerry Fromm, Sam Goodman, Chuck Hoge, Leslie Hunter, Helene Moriary, William Nash, Kathleen Quinkert, Elspeth "Cam" Ritchie, and Steve Xenakis.

I could not do my work without the circle of philosopher-warriors who are a part of my larger, academic community. Here I owe special gratitude to Tony Pfaff and Jim Dubik. I also owe hearty thanks to Ian Fischbach, Lon Olson, and Kevin Schieman.

And I am grateful, too, to the war journalists who have shared their insights with me as they have covered these thirteen and more years of war, especially Jim Dao, David Finkel, Greg Jaffe, and Mark Mazzetti. I owe thanks, too, to Celia Strauss for bringing together the "We Serve Hour" to work on media programing to help bridge the mil/civ divide.

My home base remains in academia and here the debt is large. Many have read or heard versions of parts of this book, given me comments on related chapters, or steered me in the right direction at the right time. My largest debt is to Francisco Gallegos and Trip Glazer, both philosophy graduate students at Georgetown, who have been at my side in the writing and rewriting, transcribing of interviews, compiling of references, and much more. I also wish to give special thanks to Christina Biedermann, Susan Brison, Alisa Carse, Victor Caston, David Konstan, Adrienne Martin, Peter Meineck, Sabine Roeser, Cain Todd, B.J. Strawser, Sam Rickless, Saba Bazargan, and Jessica Stern. Each read some bits of the book, in manuscript form or tailored for self-standing articles. I owe special thanks to Shira Nayman who brainstormed with me early on about resilience and just what aspects of it concerned me. I also owe deep thanks to Julia Annas, Jonathan Lear, David Luban, and Martha Nussbaum for their support early on of the project. I fear that I may have forgotten some who have helped me along the way, and I hope I will be forgiven for any oversights.

I have given many seminars and lectures, here and abroad, based on the ideas in this manuscript, and have benefited greatly from the lively discussions that followed. I thank all those who have extended invitations to me to visit and to the audiences who have been so willing to engage with my work. Among those lectures and institutions are: the Sidney Drell Lecture, Stanford; the Changing Character of War Conference, Oxford, England; the Kim T. Adamson Lecture in International Studies, Westminster College; Affective Dynamics Conference, Geneva, Switzerland; Moral Emotions and Intuitions Conference and Public Lecture, The Hague; the American Psychoanalytic Association Meetings; the Hans Bethe House Scholar in Residence, Cornell University; Empathy and

Ethics Conference Keynote, Indiana University; Virtue and the Life of Soldiers public lecture,Villanova University; They Also Serve Conference, the Woodrow Wilson Center; Educating Veterans' on America's Campuses Keynote, the Department of Education; Our Ancient Wars Conference, the University of Michigan; Sapientia lecture, Dartmouth; the Ethics Center, Kings College, Wilkes Barre; Keynote to faculty, US Air Force Academy; Soldiers within Society Conference, Reading, England; Untold Stories, Hidden Wounds War Trauma and its Treatment Conference, Austen Riggs Center; War Ethics Conference, University of California, San Diego; US Military Academy at West Point; Keynote, The Last Chapter Conference, Lehigh University; Loyola University, Baltimore; the Jubilee Center for Character and Virtue Conference, Oriel College, Oxford, England; Practical Philosophy Workshop, University of Chicago; University of Pennsylvania; Ethics of War Conference, Villanova University; the Onassis Center; the Tavistock Institute, London; Georgetown University Psychiatry Grand Rounds; Union College; plenary address at the International Applied Ethics Conference, Hokkaido University, Japan.

The writing of this book would not have been possible without the generous support and encouragement of the Guggenheim Foundation, whose fellowship sustained me during 2013–14. I remain deeply indebted to my academic home, Georgetown University, and especially my chair, Wayne Davis, for his unflagging support over the years. I also wish to thank Provost Bob Groves and Dean Chet Gillis for freeing me from academic responsibilities during the Guggenheim year. The book began life in 2011–12 while I was a Public Policy Scholar at the Wilson Center in Washington, D.C. The Wilson Center has been an exciting second home to me, both during my time as a policy scholar and my earlier fellowship year in 2006–07. I am grateful to Sonya Michel for bringing me on board as a Scholar, and to Rob Litvak, Lindsay Collins, and Mike Van Dusen for their continuing support over the years. Two scholar interns were at my side at the Wilson Center, 2011–12, to whom I owe special thanks. They are Kris Bradley and Dilbar "Tina" Rasulova. Kris was instrumental in helping me sort through the extensive psychological research on resilience. Tina was an invaluable transcriber of interviews. Her insights and striking maturity, and nuanced mastery of English, though a recent emigré from Baku, Azerbejian, continue to inspire me.

Some of the themes of a few chapters have close relatives in independent scholarly essays. Versions of chapter 4 appear in the following articles: "Recovering Lost Goodness: Shame, Guilt, and Self-Empathy" in *Psychoanalytic Psychology* 31, no 2 (2014): 217–33; "Self-empathy and Moral Repair" in *Emotion and Value*, edited by Sabine Roeser and Todd Cain (Oxford University Press, 2014); and "Moral Injury, Damage, and Repair," to appear in *Our Ancient Wars*, edited by Victor Caston and Silke-Maria Weineck (University of Michigan). A cousin of chapter 5 appears as "He Gave Me His Hand, but Took my Bow": Trust and Trustworthiness in the *Philoctetes* and Our Wars," in *Combat Trauma and the Ancient Greeks,* edited by Peter Meineck and David Konstan (Palgrave Macmillan, 2014). The themes of chapter 6 are explored in "Moral Recovery after War: The Role of Hope," in *War Ethics,* edited by Sam Rickless and Saba Bazargan (Oxford University Press, forthcoming).

Afterwar owes a great debt to my agent Jim Levine, and to my editor at Oxford, Peter Ohlin. Peter's enthusiasm and encouragement, from acquisition to publication, and his discerning editorial eye have made working with him a pleasure. I also wish to thank his editorial assistant, Emily Sacharin, for overseeing many of the production details.

As always, no words can express my abiding love and gratitude to my family. We are a close-knit team, and though Kala and Jonathan now reside in far away San Francisco, they are with us daily, as intellectual, witty, creative, and inspiring soul partners in life. To Marshall, whose good nature, humor, love, and sharp intellect have sustained me for well over half of my life, I thank you profoundly. And to my mother, Beatrice Sherman, who still comes in first in bridge and reads several novels a week, I thank you for the example you set of how to age with dignity, competence, and grace.

Nancy Sherman
Kensington, Maryland
July 15, 2014

Notes

Prologue

Page 4 **the Vietnam Wall or the beaches of Normandy:** Or, too, virtual memorials, such as the online Garden of Remembrance for the Falklands-Malvinas War. Royal Navy Surgeon-Captain Dr. Rick Jolly (OBE), who took troops to that war and served in the long conflict, established the site: http://www.sama82.org/garden/index.php. I interviewed Rick Jolly at his home in Cornwall, England, in July 2002, and I write about him in *Stoic Warriors* (Sherman 2005a, 110–12). At the time of the interview, he told me that the memorial was crucial: many troops were lost at sea or buried in a country far from home. Those who lived needed tangible graveyards to pay their respects to their comrades.

Page 4 **as General Stanley McChrystal called his counterinsurgency directive:** http://www.nytimes.com/2010/03/27/world/asia/27afghan.html?_r=0

Chapter 1: REBORN BUT DEAD

Page 7 **Captain Josh Mantz died in Baghdad:** I interviewed Josh Mantz several times, and at length, on March 14, 2012, March 29, 2014. We have also corresponded by email.

Page 8 **as I call it in *The Untold War*:** Sherman (2010).

Page 8 **the moral injuries:** The term "moral injury" is increasingly used in military behavioral health units. In the definition I offer here, I have been helped by Brett Litz's formulation below. In my own work, I have stressed the fact that transgressions can be real or apparent, and in either case, can cause deep and real moral suffering: survivor guilt may not arise from a real transgression, though it can represent a real sense of falling short and failing in one's care of another. See Litz et al. (2009); Maguen and Litz (2012); and Nash et al. (2011). Litz et al. (2009) defines moral injury as "perpetrating, failing to prevent, bearing witness to, or learning about acts that transgress deeply held moral beliefs and expectations." For a summary discussion of scientific research, see the National Center for PTSD website, and Maguen and Litz's (2012) review: "Moral Injury at War," (p. 700): http://www.ptsd.va.gov/professional/newsletters/research-quarterly/v23n1.pdf.

According to Maguen and Litz (2012), PTSD and moral injury should be distinguished in clinical settings: "PTSD is a mental disorder that requires a diagnosis. Moral injury is a dimensional problem—there is no threshold for the presence of moral injury, rather, at a given point in time, a Veteran may have none, or mild to extreme manifestations." Litz et al. (2009, p. 2) argue that the phenomenon of "moral conflict-colored psychological trauma among war veterans" has been understudied in the clinical science community, and propose models for diagnosis and treatment specific to moral injuries. They argue that trauma treatment, often based on fear extinction models, ill-fits the nature of moral injuries. While I have been an early reader of Jonathan Shay's work (1994, 2002), I came upon this newer clinical research after the initial drafting of many chapters in this book. I thank William Nash, M.D., and Navy Captain (Ret.) for conversations on these topics. I am in debt for his sharing his presentation to the Armed Forces Public Health Conference, March 23, 2011 (Nash and Westphal 2011). I also thank Jessica Stern for correspondence on this issue.

Page 8 **the preaching of Bishop Joseph Butler:** See, for example, Bishop Butler's Sermon VIII. "Upon Resentment and Forgiveness of Injuries," in *Fifteen Sermons Preached at the Rolls Chapel*, Butler (1964).

Page 10 **"universal soldier":** The term is folksinger Donovan's. And the song makes clear that the "universal soldier" is, in fact, no easily profiled stereotype. For lyrics, see: www.azlyrics.com/lyrics/donovan/universalsoldier.html

Page 10 **business executive Paul Baffico:** I interviewed Paul Baffico on March 4, 2012. He has written a memoir of his war experience as a way of coming to peace with his war. See Baffico and McNamara (2014). I return to Baffico's homecoming in the next chapter.

Page 11 **a psychiatrist presented at a war trauma conference:** Trauma psychiatrist Frank Ochberg presented this case at the Erikson Institute Conference on PTSD and Moral Injury, Austen Riggs, Stockbridge, MA, October 2012. For an interview with Ochberg on his interventions pursuant to this conference, see Fromm (2014).

Page 12 *believing* **one's activities are worthwhile:** On this, see Susan Wolf's insightful essay, Wolf (2010).

Page 12 **cognitive resolve:** On cognitive resolve and hope, see Pettit (2004).

Page 12 **Alarming peaks in suicide:** In July 2010, under Vice General Chiarelli's directive, the Army released what became known as the "Red Book"— "Army Health Promotion, Risk Reduction, Suicide Prevention," widely distributed to leaders to set in place an Army-wide discussion of suicide prevention and destigmatization of behavioral health treatment (Chiarelli 2010). In 2012 the number of military suicides outpaced the number of soldiers dying in combat. See Timothy Williams, "Suicides Outpacing War Deaths for Troops," *New York Times,* June 8, 2012, at: http://www.nytimes.com/2012/06/09/us/ suicides-eclipse-war-deaths-for-us-troops.html?_r=0. See also the Center for New American Security policy brief of October 2011, "Losing the Battle, The Challenge of Military Suicide," at: http://www.cnas.org/files/documents/ publications/CNAS_LosingTheBattle_HarrellBerglass.pdf. (Harrell and Berglass 2011) Finally, see Patricia Murphy, "Military Suicide Prevention Should Include Personal Weapon Disclosure, Retired General Suggests," *KUOW,* December 17, 2012, at: http://kuow.org/post/military-suicide-prevention-should-include-personal-weapon-disclosure-retired-general-suggests.

Page 12 **Positive psychology:** See Martin Seligman in the introduction to Snyder et al. (2011, p. 4).

Page 13 **$145 million Army-wide… Fitness program:** The price tag varies according to different accounts. In an announcement in the *New York Times*, the figure is $117 million. See Benedict Carey, "Mental Stress Training Is Planned for U.S. Soldiers," *New York Times,* August 17, 2009, at: http:// www.nytimes.com/2009/08/18/health/18psych.html?_r=0. In a *Harvard Business Review* article in which Seligman describes the program, the price tag is given as $145 million, a figure I often hear mentioned. See Martin Seligman, "Building Resilience," *Harvard Business Review,* April 2011, at: http://hbr. org/2011/04/building-resilience/ar/1. The program has had its critics. Early on, the absence of proper pilot testing riled the psychological community. See Seligman and Fowler (2011) and Tom Barret, "Soldiers of Optimism,"

Chronicle of Higher Education, October 30, 2011, at: https://chronicle.com/
article/Psychologists-Battle-Over/129580/. Most recently, a DoD requested
review from the National Academy of Sciences' Institute of Medicine delivered a stinging rebuke, claiming that most of the DoD's prevention interventions were not "theory or evidence based." The Army's Comprehensive Soldier
Fitness was singled out as problematic. See Denning et al. (2014).

Page 13 **as Cornum and her deputy described it to me:** I interviewed General
Cornum and her deputy Col. Tom Vail on December 14, 2011. Both were retiring from the Army that week. For more on Cornum's captivity, see Cornum and
Copeland (1992). I am also grateful to conversations with Air Force Capt. Bill
Andrews, March 12, 2012. In February–March 1991, he ejected out of his F-16 aircraft into Iraqi enemy territory, badly breaking his leg. It was he that Cornum was
headed out to medevac, when her helicopter was shot down and she was captured.

Page 13 **"catastrophizing":** See Reivich and Shatte (2002).

Page 14 **mixed messaging within the Army:** I am deeply grateful to conversations with William Nash, retired Navy Captain and military psychiatrist.
Nash has worked extensively with the Marines on issues of resilience and moral
injury. See, for example, Nash et al. (2009). I am also grateful for conversations
on this issue and more general issues regarding empirical research standards for
intervention programs with psychiatrist Ellen Liebenluft, Chief of Section on
Bipolar Spectrum Disorders at the National Institute of Mental Health.

Page 15 **few unifying factors:** For a discussion of suicide prevention in the
Army at the time, see Chiarelli (2010), or what became known as the "Red
Book." For a sensitive reporting of those meetings, see David Finkel's account
in Finkel (2013, p. 1398).

Page 15 **perturbations of the past:** I have written about this at length in
Sherman (2005a).

Page 15 **Figures from the recent wars:** Figures vary and can obviously depend
on tools and who is doing the surveying. See "PTSD: A Growing Epidemic,"
NIH Medline Plus 4:1 (Winter 2009), 10–14, at: http://www.nlm.nih.
gov/medlineplus/magazine/issues/winter09/articles/winter09pg10-14.
html. For the far wider claim that more than "half of the 2.6 million
Americans dispatched to fight the wars in Iraq and Afghanistan struggle
with physical or mental health problems, feel disconnected from civilian
life and believe the government is failing to meet the needs of his generation's veterans," see Rajiv Chandrasekaran, "A Legacy of Pain and Pride,"
Washington Post, March 29, 2014, at: http://www.washingtonpost.com/sf/
national/2014/03/29/a-legacy-of-pride-and-pain/.

Page 15 **traumatic brain injury (TBI):** See Hannah Fischer, "A Guide to U.S. Military Casualty Statistics: Operation New Dan, Operation Iraqi Freedom, and Operation Enduring Freedom," *Congressional Research Service,* February 19, 2014, at: http://www.fas.org/sgp/crs/natsec/RS22452.pdf.

Page 15 **TBI as high as 23 percent:** See Terrio et al. (2009).

Page 15 **"signature injuries":** See Bryant (2011).

Page 16 **the mounting evidence:** See, for example, ESPN's coverage, "NFL at Crossroads: Investigating a Health Crisis," at https://www.ire.org/resource-center/stories/26223/.

Page 16 **symptoms of TBI overlap with those of PTS:** See Bryant (2011).

Page 18 **"reactive attitudes":** The notion was first developed by Strawson (1962/1993) and the subject of much rich, current philosophical research. Strawson's seminal idea is that reactive attitudes, of the sort we have been talking about, are constitutive of moral responsibility, and not a side effect of some independent, underlying belief in responsibility. See, for example, Strawson (1962/1993), Watson (2004), Wallace (1996), Darwall (2006), Walker (2006), Macnamara (2011), Hurley and Macnamara (2010), Martin (2008, 2010, 2011), and Smith (2005). As I will go on to say, the expressed emotion targets an individual and calls attention to the fact we have taken normative review and are now calling on the addressed person to respond appropriately. The expressed emotions are thus reactive and vocative—they respond to persons but also address them (in*voke* and con*voke)* with a demand or aspiration. See McGeer (2012), Macnamara (2012), and Kukla and Lance (2009).

Page 18 **the important role of positive, reactive attitudes:** For an argument for a kind of hope, "normative hope," as a close sibling to a reactive attitude, see Martin (2010). For gratitude as a reactive attitude, see Macnamara (2012). For the suggestion of trust as a kind of reactive attitude, see Jones (2012).

Page 20 **they feel resentment toward us:** For a historical perspective on this, see Wright (2012).

CHAPTER 2: DON'T JUST TELL ME "THANK YOU"

Page 23 **The remark broke the ice:** The event was sponsored by Intersections and their Veteran-Civilian Dialogue program.

Page 23 **T. M. (TM) Gibbons-Neff:** I first interviewed T. M. Gibbons-Neff in the summer of 2012. I have been in ongoing conversation with him ever since.

Page 26 **Jonathan Wong:** I interviewed Jonathan Wong on March 9, 2012.

Page 26 **"The ocean really doesn't care...:** As the Jewish twentieth-century theologian Martin Buber might put it, it was outside an "I-Thou" encounter of mutual vulnerability and accountability. It was not part of the to-and-fro of moral address and normative review (Buber 1970, p. 60): "The human being to whom I say You I do not experience. But I stand in relation to him.... Only when I step out of this do I experience him again. Experience is remoteness from You."

Page 27 **Air Force Colonel Erik Goepner:** I interviewed Erik Goepner in November 2011. At the time he was a fellow at the Center for International and Strategic Studies in Washington, D.C.

Page 27 **Taliban fighters poured into Zabul:** See Joshua Partlow, "Zabul Province Seeks U.S. troops, but Is Caught in Afghan Numbers Game," *Washington Post,* March 9, 2010, at: http://www.washingtonpost.com/wp-dyn/content/article/2010/03/08/AR2010030804916.html.

Page 27 **exacerbates vulnerability to insurgency:** See, for example, Erik Goepner, "An Enduring Argument against Counterinsurgency," *Small Wars Journal,* September 27, 2012, at: http://smallwarsjournal.com/print/13293.

Page 28 **a "personation":** For the notion of "personation," see Pettit (2009).

Page 28 **complicity and group identification:** Among the philosophical topics are: collective agency, shared intentions, shared benefits, consent to group membership and exit rights, group commitments, normative expectations that come with group membership, identification with group values, and so on. For selective discussions of shared and collective responsibility and attitudes, see Gilbert (2002), Cooper (1972), Kutz (2000), Huebner (2011), Searle (2009), Sepinwall (2010), and Tollefsen (2003). For a robust and critical review of the literature, I am indebted to Amy Sepinwall.

Page 28 **second-personal address:** Indeed, the reactive attitude can sometimes not have a present target, as when one voices one's resentment *toward* a group in their absence, *before* one's own group members, as a way of modeling and rallying further participation for that emotion. I take up cases like this later.

Page 29 **mental health care due a veteran:** For discussions of this issue, see Phillip Carter, "The Vets We Reject and Ignore," *New York Times,* November 10, 2013, at: http://www.nytimes.com/2013/11/11/opinion/the-vets-we-reject-and-ignore.html?_r=0; and also the NPR *Morning Edition* multi-part special series on vets with "bad paper" (or other than honorable discharges): Marisa Peñaloza and Quil Lawrence, "Other-Than-Honorable Discharge Burdens Like a Scarlet Letter," *NPR Morning Edition,* December 9, 2013, at: http://www.npr.org/2013/12/09/249342610/

other-than-honorable-discharge-burdens-like-a-scarlet-letter; Marisa Peñaloza and Quil Lawrence, "Path the Reclaiming Identity Steeps for Vets with 'Bad Paper,'" *NPR Morning Edition,* December 11, 2013, at: http://www.npr.org/2013/12/11/249962933/path-to-reclaiming-identity-steep-for-vets-with-bad-paper; and Marisa Peñaloza, "Filling the Gaps for Veterans with Bad Discharges," *WNPR News,* December 16, 2013, at: http://wnpr.org/post/filling-gaps-veterans-bad-discharges.

Page 29 **universal national service:** For some of the debate, see Phillip Carter and Paul Glastris, "The Case for the Draft," *Washington Monthly,* March 2005, at: http://www.washingtonmonthly.com/features/2005/0503.carter.html; Moskos (1988); Conor Friedersdorf, "The Case Against Universal National Service," *The Atlantic,* June 26, 2013, at: http://www.theatlantic.com/politics/archive/2013/06/the-case-against-universal-national-service/277230/; the latter, in response to General Stanley McChrystal's call for a national service program at the 2012 Aspen Ideas Festival, at: http://www.youtube.com/watch?v=rYdNcsE4998.

Page 29 **moral tribalism:** See Greene (2013) and Luban (2014).

Page 29 **"inside the wire":** I thank Phil Carter for this apt phrase.

Page 29 **20 percent of Congress's members:** See David Greene and Cokie Roberts, "Since Post-Vietnam Era, Fewer Veterans in Congress," *NPR Morning Edition,* November 11, 2013, at: http://www.npr.org/2013/11/11/244452613/politics-in-the-news.

Page 30 **Paul Baffico:** From an interview with Paul Baffico on March 4, 2012. Paul describes his homecoming in further detail in Baffico and McNamara (2014). In addition to his monthly trips to the Vietnam Wall where he volunteers as a docent, Paul is deeply involved in his home in Illinois in the ongoing work of the Lake-McHenry Veterans and Family Services. He is currently helping to set up a nonprofit foundation to sustain their work. For more on this veteran outreach program, and its wide-ranging services for veterans and their families, see http://www.lmvfs.org.

Page 31 **The homecoming left abiding scars:** My remarks throughout leave to the side the weighty national issue of civilian military contractors, who in the past decade have served in historically large numbers alongside citizen soldiers and yet are ineligible for most of the benefits to which citizen soldiers are entitled. For discussion of this important issue, see Dunigan et al. (2013); Josh Hicks, "PTSD Rates Similar among Defense Contractors and Veterans, Report Says," *Washington Post,* December 10, 2013, at: http://www.washingtonpost.com/blogs/federal-eye/wp/2013/12/10/ptsd-rates-similar-among-defense-contractors-and-veterans-report-says/; and T. Christian Miller and Doug Smith, "Injured War Zone Contractors Fight to Get Care," *LA Times*, April 17, 2009, at: http://articles.latimes.com/2009/apr/17/nation/na-contractors17.

Page 31 **Rolls Chapel in London:** A chapel that once sat on Chancery Lane, near the Strand, and the site now of a library at King's College, London. Interestingly, the church was initially established by Henry III as a residence for converted Jews. See http://www.londonancestor.com/stow/stow-church-138.htm

Page 31 **importance of voicing moral outrage:** See the helpful article on Butler by Aaron Garrett in the *Stanford Encyclopedia of Philosophy*, and especially the discussion in section 6 on compassion, resentment, and forgiveness: http://plato.stanford.edu/entries/butler-moral/#ComResFor.

Page 32 **different from a mental state like anxiety:** See Searle (2009, pp. 25–26). I am indebted to Searle for his clear elaboration on this issue.

Page 32 **Expressed gratitude:** See Macnamara (2012).

Page 32 **sacrifice at its vocational core:** See Luban (2014, p. 286).

Page 33 **a ritual that each tacitly recognizes:** For an interesting related discussion on collective acceptance or recognition vs. cooperation, see Searle (2009, p. 58).

Page 33 **an expression of respect toward another person:** Kant (1964, pp. 454–55); see also Buss (1999).

Page 33 **"to accept the occasion for gratitude":** Kant (1964, p. 455).

Page 33 **gratitude "is not a mere *prudential* maxim . . .:** Kant (1964, p. 355), second italics mine.

Page 33 **feel "used," sacrificial, exploited:** See Kahn (2008) on the notion of sacred violence and exploited sacrifice. Service members can feel played with by public displays of gratitude—say, ovations at sporting events—when the opportunities for gathering vets together with civilians could be better used for job networking or the like.

Page 33–34 **the words of Fitzroy Newsum:** From an interview by Nina Talbot on July 26, 2010, and part of a series of narratives (written up by her daughter, Sophie Rand) that accompany Talbot's remarkable portraits she has painted of veterans from her neighborhood in Brooklyn.

Page 34 **"Hey, there, you owe me an RSVP":** See Darwall (2006) and Walker (2006).

Page 34 **to show resentment is to call out to another:** Moral outrage is what we feel against moral monsters who subject us to the most unspeakable atrocities. Even here, I suspect in expressing the outrage, there is a sense that those monstrous individuals belong to that same community of humanity, but they violate, in the most awful way, the moral laws of its membership. I turn to this issue later in the discussion of Jean Améry.

Page 35 **liable for intentional harm in war:** Some of the debates hang on the distinction between combatant and noncombatant and the moral space between them, occupied by collaborators, supporters, and sympathizers. The implications of these important normative roles for battlefield ethics is a thrust in Pfaff (2012). For a discussion of related issues, see Pfaff (2011). For an important repudiation of the moral significance in the traditional distinction between combatant and noncombatant (and for a prioritizing of one's own citizen combatants), see Kasher and Yadlin (2006). For an influential reply in the just war debate, see Avashai Margalit and Michael Walzer, "Israel: Civilians & Combatants," *New York Review of Books*, May 14, 2009. For a reformulation and defense of the priority of the combatant, see McMahan (2010).

Page 35 **just and unjust combatants:** See McMahan (2010, p. 345) for a brief review of distinctions he draws. For his full view, see McMahan (2009).

Page 35 **"an equal right to kill":** Walzer (1977, p. 21).

Page 36 **degrees of moral responsibility:** This is Seth Lazar's (2010) approach in his review of McMahan's book *Killing in War*, McMahan (2009). I am indebted to him in the following discussion.

Page 36 **she deserves praise or blame:** Lazar (2010, p. 184).

Page 36 **reluctance to kill:** See Lt. Col. Dave Grossman's work on psychological inhibitions to killing, Grossman (1995). Much discussed in this vein is S. L. A. Marshall's controversial combat fire ratios about World War II—specifically, that less than 25 percent of American combat infantrymen in battle discharged their weapons. The point remains, that there are retreaters and nonfirers on a battlefield, as well as many others who have supporting and enabling roles not necessary for liability. See Marshall (2000).

Page 37 **Many noncombatants . . . make small:** Lazar (2010, pp. 193–94).

Page 37 **reasons others have argued for well:** Lazar (2010, pp. 193–97).

Page 38 **even if we could predict fairly accurately:** See Lazar (2010, p. 195) on the "radical unpredictability" of facts relevant for the proportionality criterion.

Page 38 **Civilians are proxies for service members:** For an important related discussion of alienated and insulated warfare, see Ryan (2009).

Page 38 **Those expanded responsibilities:** Or at least more exhaustive arguments would have to be made to demonstrate that specific contributions and roles constitute battlefield liability. For example, accepted liability lines may be currently drawn in ways that vastly outdate the massive blurring and commingling of civilian and defense communities that characterize the contemporary military/industrial/technological complex. Just which kinds of contributions or what kinds of roles would pull civilians into the liability net is not a topic I can take up here.

Page 39 **that sense of shared responsibility:** See Amy Sepinwall (2010). Like parents who are part of a collective project in sharing goals and expectations in raising their children, so, too, as fellow citizens do we share certain goals and expectations and do some common work to bring them about. That notion of group identity may be sufficient for some sense of shared credit and blame even when individual contributions within the group are vastly different, uneven, and not all goals are equally supported.

Page 40 **"emotional labor":** See Hochschild (1983). Hochschild distinguishes "emotional labor" from "emotional work" and claims that the former takes place only in the workplace while the latter can take place anywhere. I am using the term "emotional labor" to refer to all kinds of emotional work.

Page 41 **in … the *Washington Post*, Carter spoke candidly:** See Phillip Carter, "For Veterans, Is 'Thank You for Your Service' Enough?" *Washington Post*, November 4, 2011, at: http://www.washingtonpost.com/opinions/for-veterans-is-thank-you-for-your-service-enough/2011/11/03/gIQA67hZmM_story.html.

Page 41 **everyone's mutual advantage:** See Pettit (1995, pp. 208–12) on the mechanisms of loyalty, virtue, and prudence as bases of trustworthiness. Friendship is, of course, a privileged sphere of trust and, as Aristotle notes, is motivated by similar reasons: virtue, pleasure, and utility. See Aristotle (1984, *Nicomachean Ethics,* VIII. 2–3).

Page 42 **"thin crust of display":** Hochschild (1983, p. 21).

Page 42 **a more satisfying form of moral address:** Interestingly, I know British service members who would love some of those "Thank you's" thrown their way as a part of their homecoming. From conversation with David Ian Walker, a retired career soldier in the British Army who has worked extensively with soldiers exiting military service and their resettlement. See Walker (2010). I am grateful to conversations at King's College, London, Department of War Studies, during a seminar I gave in fall of 2010. I am especially grateful to conversation with Dr. Simon Wessely for helping me to understand some cultural differences in the American and British reintegration experience.

Page 42 **resentment became perceptible:** For an excellent discussion of emotional self-expression, see Green (2007).

Page 42 **untethered from their matching inner states:** For an exploration of these themes, I am indebted to conversation with Trip Glazer and his Georgetown Ph.D. in progress on emotional expression and communication.

Page 42 **on Seneca's Stoic view:** Seneca (1995, *On Anger,* II.14, I.6.1, II.11). See Sherman (2005a, p. 76 and notes).

Page 43 **sociologist Erving Goffman famously taught:** See Goffman (1959).

Page 43 **are the same across cultures:** See Ekman (1994) and Ekman and Rosenberg (2005). The question of whether the expressive behavior is the same across cultures can be detached from the question of whether the recognition of expressive behavior is the same across cultures. There's empirical research to suggest that individuals from different cultures will interpret the *same* behavior slightly differently, depending on, among other things, culturally relative display rules. I thank Trip Glazer for conversation here. See, for example, Jack et al. (2012), Ebner and Riediger (2010), and Plant et al. (2000).

Page 43 **interpretive challenges:** So, some languages and ethnicities seem to involve more emotional *expressiveness* on the part of their native speakers than others; contrast New York Jewish conversational style with, say, a Midwesterner style. See Tannen (2005). (I am indebted to Tannen's talk at Georgetown Program in Jewish Civilization, Fall 2013, on this topic, as well as private conversation.) Equally, American Sign Language uses facial expression as itself an element of expressing meaning, as a non-manual, or non-"signed" marker to intensify meaning; expressiveness, we might say, is built into the formal code of meaning. Women may stereotypically "perform" emotions more than men, or may be interpreted that way, as part of a gender stereotype. (On how gender norms and stereotypes affect recognition of men's and women's emotional expression, see Plant et al. [2000].) The military as a group may "underperform" emotions, especially in the context of formal bearing, and so on. The point is emotional expressiveness varies across persons and groups.

Page 43 **He's signaling a norm:** The same might go for the resentment that a service member addresses *at* civilians and *before* other battle buddies to rally and model participatory support.

Page 43 *social referencing*: On the social referencing literature, see Emde et al. (1976) and Sorce et al. (1985).

Page 44 **public enactment and recommendation of a norm:** Social media obviously take this point to new levels, but that is another subject. For debate on who has authority to have and express certain reactive attitudes, see Smith (2007) and Searle (2009).

Page 44 **shows others how to respond:** To put it in philosophical language, on the "call" side we are modeling implicitly as a "we." And on the target side the "you" addressed is implicitly in the plural, as a person who represents a group. So we are engaged in a second-personal address that is implicitly in the plural on both sides: It's less "I-You" address (with "You" in the singular) than a "We-You" address (with "You" in the plural). So it's a dialogic address in the plural.

Page 44 **Men are, one and all, actors...:** Kant (1974, p. 151). See Sherman (1997b) for further discussion of the affective dimensions of virtue training, especially pp. 121–86 for a discussion of Kant on emotional training.

Page 44 **Kant's Pietism:** Kant (1964, p. 473); see also Sherman (1997a).

Page 45 **efferent bio-feedback loops:** See Strack et al. (1988).

Page 45 **too deeply behind the façade:** Goffman (1967, pp. 60, 58). On faking it, see Miller (2003).

Page 45 **I am showing what I now feel:** For insight on the notion of self-ascription of current mental states, see Bar-On (2004).

Page 45 **opening a door for future interaction:** Cicero and Seneca are important sources again. Just how to play "*the role* of the good person" is of crucial importance, Cicero insists, in our effective communication to others. Creating the right appearances matters in fulfilling many of our offices and duties (*officia*). The *conveyance* is key. Seneca is rich in detail here: "No one can feel gratitude for a favour haughtily tossed down or angrily thrust on him" or given with groaning or flaunting, with an "insolent expression" or "language swollen with pride," or in a way that is "simply irritating." It is like giving bread with stones in it, he says! Of course, it is easy to run afoul and become mere poseurs, on the one hand, or disclosers, on the other, in the face of involuntary emotional emissions. The Stoics are well aware of pre-emotional phenomena that can escape the dictates of "assent," such as blushing, erections, or hair standing on end. Still, they hold that in matters of showing kindness and gratitude (and even in many cases of spontaneous responses to danger or loss), we are subject to far more emotional agency than we often give ourselves credit for. See Seneca (1995, *On Anger*). See also my discussion in Sherman (2005a, ch. 3).

Page 45 **we lock eyes, show interest, listen:** It seems obvious that third parties who are onlookers may not be privy to the full emotional communication. What I signal in indirect modeling to third parties might be thinner and not something they can fully pick up without being present as part of the direct address.

Page 46 **the basic worry really is:** I thank Trip Glazer for help with the thoughts in this paragraph.

Page 46 **that you undo that step:** For a colorful discussion of this, see Macnamara (2012).

Page 47 **sons and daughters... come home, or not come home:** For a moving narrative of Vietnam veterans watching their own sons and daughters volunteer to go to war, see the documentary movie *My Vietnam, Your Iraq*, by Ron Osgood. This is also the subject of the brilliant war novel by Israeli author David Grossman, *To the End of the Land* (2010). The novel depicts the trauma and recovery of war, relived in a family, first in one generation of soldiers and then in another, and the awful anticipation of losing one's child, announced by that awful knock on the door. The doorbell rang at the Grossman's own house on August 13, 2006, to announce the death of their son Uri, killed by Hezbollah in the Lebanese village of Hirbet K'seif. Grossman had nearly finished the novel a month earlier. Art foretold the awful reality.

Page 49 **"brandishing of emotional arms":** Walker (2006, p. 115).

Page 49 **"a weapon against injury, injustice, and cruelty":** Butler (1964, pp. 120, 127).

Page 49 **"one who has been in a moral sense injurious":** Butler (1964, p. 126). Indignation is the analogous attitude on behalf of others, though Butler uses the term "resentment" to cover both personal and impersonal reactions. Still, resentment can be normative without being narrowly moral, as when a fellow crook becomes resentful toward his buddy because he botched the burglary. Bernard Williams (1995, p. 40) discusses this general kind of blame in terms of "focused blame": "People can be blamed for missing their opportunities or making mistakes, and they can be blamed by non-moralizing people." R. Jay Wallace (1996) recognizes the same point in his notion of reactive emotions, such as resentment, sometimes being "quasi-evaluative," by which he means not strictly appealing to a moral conception or moral transgression. John Rawls is narrower in linking his conception of resentment with background *moral* conceptions. See Rawls (1971, pp. 416, 423, 467, 468, 472–74).

Page 49 **"reactive *pathos*":** Nietzsche (1994, pp. 21, 24, 26, 28, 32 n.41, 36, 52, 53, 99).

Page 49 **the depravity of revenge feelings:** For discussion of Seneca on anger, see Sherman (2005a, pp. 64–99).

Page 49 **holding another to account:** See Strawson (1962/1993).

Page 49 **These circumstances can give rise…:** Bernard Williams (1995, p. 73).

Page 50 **…who had a reason to do the right thing but did not do it":** Williams (1995, p. 42). On resentment being different from advice and the putting out of a piece of information, see Darwall (2006, p. 49): "Second-personal address makes a claim on the addressee's will (and not, like advice, only on her beliefs about what there is reason for her to do)."

Page 50 **neither moralistic disdain nor manipulation:** Williams (1995, p. 44).

Page 50 **to be guided by it in future interactions:** See Darwall (2006, pp. 70–81) and Kukla and Lance (2009, p. 142).

Page 50 **"is the little account which he seems to make of us…:** See Smith (1759/2000, II.III.1, pp. 138–39). I am indebted to Steve Darwall for pointing this out in his discussion of second-personal morality.

Page 51 **Georgetown Veterans Day celebration:** The speech was given by Gen. Dr. Richard Scales (Ret.).

Page 51 **"a bidding to recognize… a kind of relationship…:** See Margaret Urban Walker (2006, p. 134) and Bennett (2008a, p. 14).

Page 51 **They are fellow citizens:** I thank Tony Pfaff for pointing this out in Pfaff (2011). In making this point, Pfaff refers to James Dubik, who rejects Walzer's claim that soldiers give up their right to life to gain the right to kill. See Dubik (1982) and Walzer (1977).

Page 51 **the case of sexual assault within the military:** More pointedly, the fact that New York Senator Kirsten Gillibrand's bill recently rejected by the Senate—stripping military commanders within the chain of command of any involvement in the review of allegations of assault and rape—was so virulently protested by the top brass itself sheds interesting light on the dynamics of civilian–military power relations at the highest levels. See, for example, CBS News, "Military's Top Brass Prep Measures to Combat Sexual Assault," August 9, 2013, at: http://www.cbsnews.com/news/militarys-top-brass-prep-measures-to-combat-sexual-assault/. It exposes the challenges even the most well-placed civilian can face in trying to break down military insularity and respond, as a caring civilian and public civilian servant, to military injury and abuse. See Ed O'Keefe, "Gillibrand Wants Vote on Military Sex Assault Bill 'Right Away,'" *Washington Post,* December 10, 2013, at: http://www.washingtonpost.com/blogs/post-politics/wp/2013/12/10/gillibrand-wants-vote-on-military-sex-assault-bill-right-away/?tid=hpModule_f8335; also, Kathleen Hunter and Tony Capaccio, "Gillibrand Vows to Pursue Military Sexual-Assault Bill," *Bloomberg News,* December 10, 2013, at: http://www.bloomberg.com/news/2013-12-10/gillibrand-vows-to-pursue-military-sexual-assault-bill.html.

Page 51 **The needs here are profound:** See the Center for New American Security report on this by Phil Carter (Carter 2013a, 2013b). In 2012 the Department of Veterans Affairs "cared for nearly 6 million of the nation's 22 million veterans," with much of the care focusing on mental health issues, including posttraumatic stress and traumatic brain injuries. In 2013, there were approximately 2.6 million veterans of Iraq, Afghanistan, and other theaters of the war on terrorism. Among those, about 900,000 have sought VA care, and about half of those have been diagnosed with a mental health disorder of some type. And this data does not include veteran private defense contractors who have served in unprecedented numbers in the war zones in the past decade and have been exposed, like regular soldiers, to war's stressors. For discussion of this pressing issue, see Dunigan et al. (2013). On the financial legacy of Iraq and Afghanistan conflicts, see Bilmes (2013).

Page 51 **recent spikes in suicide rates:** For a discussion of the spike in suicides, which by some estimates has exceeded those in the civilian population, see Harrell and Berglass (2011). During his tenure as Army Vice Chief, General Peter Chiarelli tackled this issue head-on in monthly suicide advisory board meetings in which commanders around the world reported in detail on suicides under their commands during that period, and potential "lessons learned." I attended several of those Pentagon meetings.

Page 51 **profoundly altered in face and limb:** Consider face injuries, such as close-up wounds and burning due to explosives. According to one recent survey, facial wounds accounted for almost 40 percent% of injuries sustained by U.S. soldiers. Facial reconstruction in these cases is not primarily cosmetic and the results often not optimally aesthetic. The reconstructions are for basic human functioning so that a patient can breathe through her nose, open her mouth to take in liquid and food, hear, and see. Fresh scarring can ravage the best surgical results. See Claudia Dreifus, "Healing Soldiers' Most Exposed Wounds: A Conversation with Col. Robert. G. Hales," *New York Times*, December 2, 2013, at: http://www.nytimes.com/2013/12/03/science/healing-soldiers-most-exposed-wounds.html.

Page 52 **social and informal institutional reality:** See Searle (2009, p. 91) on different levels of institutional reality.

Page 52 **Jean Améry, an Austrian:** My discussion is indebted to Thomas Brudholm's excellent discussion of Améry and the refusal to forgive. See Brudholm (2008).

Page 53 **"My personal task is to justify...:** Améry (1980, p. 64). The title of the above essay *"Ressentiments"* is translated in this edition as "Resentments."

Page 53 **"It desires two impossible things...:** Améry (1980, p. 68).

Page 53 **inserted into his agency "an acknowledgement of me...:** Williams (1995, p. 73).

Page 53 **"The Flemish SS-man Wajs...:** Améry (1980, p. 70).

CHAPTER 3: THEY'RE MY BABY BIRDS

Page 58 **Donna was immersed in her studies:** From extended conversations and an opinion piece in Georgetown's student newspaper that Donna wrote in Georgetown's undergraduate newspaper, *The Hoya*. She wrote the piece at the request of a classmate in a class I taught who happened to be the editor of *The Hoya* and realized few on campus had any idea of what it might be like to be an undergraduate at Georgetown and a military spouse.

Page 59 **"I had no idea . . .:** Interview from October 17, 2012.

Page 60 **. . . the stress 'thermostat' is reset":** Hoge (2010, p. xiv).

Page 63 **inflated sense of control:** I have been helped in thinking about this by Jonathan Lear's discussion of therapeutic action, in Lear (2003), especially chs. 2 and 3.

Page 63 **"thin crust of display":** Hochschild (1983, p. 21).

Page 64 **the one who is missing:** See Shay (1994).

Page 65 **even when photojournalists are onsite:** See the early work of photojournalism in the Magnum Photos, founded 1947, that included such giants as Henri Cartier Bresson, Robert Capa, and Chim (David Seymour). For a recent trove of film negatives of the Spanish Civil War, known as the "Mexican Suitcase," and shown in a recent New York exhibit at the International Center of Photography, see http://www.icp.org/museum/exhibitions/mexican-suitcase. For recent work on photojournalism, and an attempt to show the public more of what the agents, victims, and witnesses of war, see the exhibit War/Photography, Images of Armed Conflict and its Aftermath, at http://photowings.org/ann-wilkes-tucker-war-photography/, and especially the graphic and now iconic picture of the bombing of an Israeli bus in 1974.

Page 65 **hard to cognitively mediate and process:** For an accessible discussion of how brain biochemistry is altered during episodes of intense stress, see McEwen and Lasley (2002).

Page 69 **a preventive fantasy:** This is Bernard Williams's helpful term. See Williams (1995).

Page 69 **a version of strict liability:** There may be a more appropriate role for the imposition of strict liability in war conduct, and that is in combatant accountability for enemy noncombatant deaths, caused collaterally or discriminately. And it may be that accepting that liability should be better reinforced in soldier training, so that soldiers come to feel not just that they ought to take care of each other but that they ought to minimize harm done to enemy noncombatant innocents. Strict liability may make sense here insofar as armed soldiers, like hazardous materials (often discussed in the liability literature), can cause great harm, unintentionally and collaterally. Moreover, soldiers have protective advantages through troop defense and medical evacuation teams that noncombatants lack and that make them more vulnerable to harm. For discussion of related issues, see Luban (2014).

Page 69 **"When I endeavor to examine my own conduct...:** Smith (1759/2000, III.1.6, p. 164).

Page 70 **"judicious spectator":** Hume (1739/1968, III.1, p. 581).

Page 70 **invokes a spectator:** See Charlotte Brown, "Review: *The Impartial Spectator: Adam Smith's Moral Philosophy,*" *Notre Dame Philosophical Reviews,* November 18, 2007, at: http://ndpr.nd.edu/news/23254-the-impartial-spectator-adam-smith-s-moral-philosophy/.

Page 70 **a technique being developed by some VA clinicians:** Brett Litz, a Boston VA psychologist, discussed a technique of this sort developed as part of Marine treatment protocol. An empty chair is part of the therapy. The buddy returns to the room in a face-to-face conversation. He knows you survived him. The goal is to make plausible a fantasized conversation in which he doesn't hold you liable or accuse in the way the patient does toward himself. He discussed this "empty chair technique" at a conference on war trauma and soldiers' moral injuries at Austen Riggs, October 2012. For abstracts and the proceedings of the conference, see the special issue of *Psychoanalytic Psychology: Untold Stories, Hidden Wounds, War Trauma and its Treatment* at: http://psycnet.apa.org/index.cfm?fa=browsePA.volumes&jcode=pap. See also Litz (2014).

Page 70 **On a cognitivist view of emotions:** See John Deigh's excellent review essay on cognitivist and neocognitivist views in Deigh (1994).

Page 71 **Even if resentment and guilt don't necessarily co-travel:** Amy Sepinwall elaborates upon this idea of non co-traveling in Sepinwall (2010).

Page 71 **But first he has to detoxify the image:** It might be argued that if there is a proper place for strict liability on the battlefield, it is not so much in a soldier's accountability to fellow combatants as it is in his accountability to noncombatants. David Luban suggests a notion of strict liability for combatant caused civilian injuries in Luban (2014).

Page 72 **He was threatened with a disciplinary separation:** At the Austen Riggs conference on war trauma, Brigadier General (Ret.) Stephen Xenakis, an Army psychiatrist, lambasted this "smoking out" of service members due to weight gain from psychiatric meds. He implied that the screening was an unconscionable cost-saving measure.

CHAPTER 4: RECOVERING LOST GOODNESS

Page 77 **Army Major Jeffrey Hall:** I first interviewed Jeff Hall in September 2010 and several times later that year and many times thereafter. I am also grateful to his wife, Sheri, for conversations about moral injury.

Page 78 **the Coalition Provisional Agency (CPA):** For an excellent account, see Chandrasekaran (2006).

Page 79 **The incompetence of Hall's superiors:** There may be comedic elements in the incredible incompetence that characterized much work off the Coalition Provisional Agency: "You couldn't invent more comedic war narratives," Rajiv Chandrasekaran (2006) said in a seminar at the Wilson Center, September 2011, reflecting on his own research and writing about that period of the war in Iraq.

Page 80 **It can be a way of calling out to oneself:** Here, I am influenced by the work of Kukla and Lance (2009) and Macnamara (2012) on Strawsonian models of reactive attitudes. See Strawson (1962/1993).

Page 80 **our very act of trusting may elicit:** See Jones (2012).

Page 81 **Theater of War:** For more on the Theater of War, and the larger umbrella theater group under the direction of Bryan Doerries, see: http://www.philoctetesproject.org/l; see also Patrick Healy, "The Anguish of War for Today's Soldiers, Explored by Sophocles," *New York Times,* November 22, 2009, at: http://www.nytimes.com/2009/11/12/theater/12greeks.html?pagewanted=all. For the performance of Greek plays by military veterans (some who also are trained dancers and singers, as well as actors) before civilian/military audiences, see classicist Peter Meineck's important outreach work as director of the Aquila Theatre based at NYU at: http://aquilatheatre.com/about/staff/peter-meineck/.

Page 82 **Ajax was "the bulwark of the Achaeans":** Homer (1990, III, lines 270–90; VII, lines 242–332). For a wonderful account of lessons to be learned from a retelling of the Ajax story, see Woodruff (2011).

Page 82 **"I will return from Troy...:** Sophocles (2007a, lines 464–65).

Page 82 **Look at the valiant man!:** Sophocles (2007a, lines 364–67).

Page 82 **There is ironic distance:** On narrative and ironic distance, see Goldie (2011, p. 87; 2007).

Page 83 **the role of shame as a precipitant:** See Lansky (1995, p. 1086).

Page 83 **"Never in your right mind...:** See Sophocles (2007a, lines 182–185).

Page 83 **"I can darken the sharpest eyes...:** Sophocles (2007a, line 85).

Page 83 **"He thought he was bathing his hands...:** Sophocles (2007a, line 43).

Page 83 **"You see the great deeds...:** Sophocles (2007a, line 366).

Page 83 **"He has been laid low by this evil...:** Sophocles (2007a, lines 320–25).

Page 83 **"Lift him up to me here...:** Sophocles (2007a, lines 545–50).

Page 84 **"The experience of shame:** For a penetrating study of the ancients on shame, see Williams (1993).

Page 84 **to be caught without your fig leaf:** Susan Brison has raised the question with me as to whether shame must have this sense of being exposed, in addition to the sense, I discuss later, of falling short of an ideal. She suggests that these may be two very different features of shame, and the latter is a more central part of the concept.

Page 84 **"eyes are upon you":** Aristotle (1984, *Nicomachean Ethics*, II.6, 1384a35–1384b1).

Page 84 **promise of redemption through moral repair:** See Lansky (1995, 2003b, 2007).

Page 84 **"accident guilt":** See Sherman (2010, ch. 4).

Page 85 **facts of moral responsibility:** For important work on disambiguating moral notions of appropriateness from those that have to do with epistemic warrant, see D'Arms and Jacobson (2000).

Page 85 **"room for play," as Immanuel Kant calls it:** See Kant's discussion of imperfect duties of care or, as it is sometimes put, imperfect duties of end, to self and others, in the *Doctrine of Virtue* (1964). I discuss the notion at length in Sherman (1997b, chs. 4 and 8).

Page 85 **falling short of an ideal:** On ego-ideals, see Freud (1974, pp. 14, 93–7).

Page 85 **more self-regarding than other-regarding:** On a related noted, Peter Goldie and Kate Abramson have recently argued that shame may not always have "insidious," "globalizing" tendencies that deny "all moral worth." In some cases of shame, one sees oneself from a perspective that allows for self-forgiveness and redemption. See Goldie (2011, p. 89) and Abramson (2010).

Page 86 **Epistemically fitting shame:** This seems to follow from the idea of construing it as a failure of imperfect rather than perfect duty, again to use Kantian terms. Kant famously leaves "playroom" (*Spielraum*) as to what degree and extent we are to fulfill imperfect duties of end, such as beneficence to others, though he does not himself develop the category of the supererogatory. For further thoughts on this, see Sherman (1997b, ch. 8). Also, see Sherman (1988), Hill (1971), and Baron (1995).

Page 84 **...by the subject's own lights, *already been answered"*:** Michael Brady (2009, p. 427, my italics); see also Brady (2006, 2007, 2008).

Page 87 **attention is taken away from factors that *are* relevant:** Brady is eager to put forth a neojudgmentalist (variant of cognitivist) view of emotions that steers a middle course between imputing too much irrationality to the subject of recalcitrant emotions and too little. On his view, the subject of irrational emotion does not hold two conflicting beliefs, as strict judgmentalists argue. Rather, the subject holds a construal and a belief, but the construal, while falling short of a belief is not simply arational; it has deep cognitive teeth, in that it *inclines* the subject to expend limited cognitive resources wastefully and hence take epistemic missteps. Thus, Brady is a neojudgmentalist who still can impute a fair degree of irrationality to the subject of recalcitrant emotions. See Brady (2009, p. 429). In a related piece, Brady argues that recalcitrant emotions are somewhat analogous to cognitively impenetrable visual illusions, but not strictly so. The "arational perception—say, that the stick appears bent when we know it is straight—unlike the "recalcitrant" construal (say of phobic fear), lacks cognitive teeth: the visual illusions do not "capture and consume" our attention; the illusions don't persist and waste our cognitive resources. See Brady (2007).

Page 87 **"incoherent evaluative profile":** See Brady (2009, p. 414). On irrational emotions, see Greenspan (1983).

Page 87 **whether one could have or should have known the consequences:** See Aristotle's case of forced, mixed actions, Aristotle (1984, *Nicomachean Ethics,* III.1). I should note that my view of so-called irrational/recalicitrant emotions is different from Rawls's notion of "not proper" guilt feelings, or what he also calls "residue guilt feelings" (Rawls 1971, pp. 481–82). He gives as an example a person who is raised to believe going to movies is sinful. He no longer believes that, but yet when he goes to the movies he feels guilty. This kind of case doesn't leave room for those where one is ambivalent or unsure about an evaluation that one has done nothing wrong. For a discussion of Rawls, see Wallace (1996, pp. 40–50).

Page 87 **what Freud called *Durcharbeitung*:** For use of the term by Freud, see "Remembering, Repeating, and Working Through," (1914) and "Inhibitions, Symptoms and Anxiety" (1959), in Freud (1974).

Page 88 **Tom Fiebrandt:** I interviewed Tom Fiebrandt in fall of 2010. I came to know him through a class I taught at Georgetown that fall on the ethics of war.

Page 91 **"despite believing that there are no genuine reasons ...:** Brady (2009, p. 429).

Page 91 **There are elements of this:** Similarly, a therapist who works with soldiers recently told me of a patient who repeatedly went over the site of where he lost a buddy, homing in over and over on the spot on Google maps, working out how he could have prevented the death if he only took this route rather than that.

Page 91 **prelude to self-empathy:** For my own overview of the subject with lengthy references and discussion of the literature, see especially Sherman (1998a, 1998b, 1998c).

Page 92 **developed by Theodor Lipps:** For discussion, see Eisenberg and Strayer (1987), Lipps (1903), and Titchner (1909). For Freud and his interest in empathy, see Pigman (1995) and Freud (1986, p. 325).

Page 92 **Hume's metaphor is intuitive:** Hume (1739/1968, pp. 316–24).

Page 92 **The second camp, led by Adam Smith:** Smith (1759/2000).

Page 92 **"coming to beat time with their hearts":** Smith (1759/2000, I.I.1, p. 4).

Page 92 **not only situational but also dispositional:** For reflections on becoming another, see Bernard Williams's "Imagination and the Self," in Williams (1973).

Page 92 **"enter, as it were, into his body...:** Smith (1759/2000, I.I.1, p. 3). On the notion of "becoming" the other person and the therapeutic work of empathic resonance, the writing of psychoanalytic theorist, Heinz Kohut is extremely helpful. See Kohut (1971, 1977, 1984). Note, for Smith, there is an ultimate interest in moral judgment and the fittingness of the emotion, and this requires a bringing back of that empathic connection to one's own bosom (Smith 1759/2000, I.I.1, p. 5) in a way that can both facilitate moral insight but also distort empathy with a projection from our own home base.

Page 92 **a secondary effect of the repetition:** See Freud on repetition compulsion in Freud (1974, p. 293). Also, included in the symptoms of posttraumatic stress are intrusive recollections. For a very helpful discussion of posttraumatic stress and its treatment, see Wilson, Friedman, and Lindy (2001). Note, there has been a move afoot, with some momentum from the Army, to drop the "D" in PTSD (posttraumatic stress disorder) because of the stigmatizing effect of the term. The argument is often made that service members returning from war with limb losses do not have "limb disorders." Why should those returning from war with psychological stress have disorders? There are other terminological shifts aimed to "normalize" the response to stress. For a history of PTSD and its inclusion in the *Diagnostic and Statistics Manual III* in 1980, see Herman (1992).

Page 92 **inbuilt biases of emotional construals:** "Construal" is Robert Roberts's term for the cognitive content of an emotion. For how Roberts distinguishes that notion from a stricter judgment, see, for example, Roberts (2013).

Page 93 **features of the object of our fear:** Goldie (2004, p. 99). This is similar to Brady's view with respect to recalcitrant emotion, that because emotions tend toward a "capture and consume" mode, through emotional engagement, we sometimes waste attentional resources for problems already solved. See Brady (2007).

Page 93 **"capture and consume attention":** Brady (2009, pp. 423, 425–26, 428–29).

Page 93 **congruent reenactments or countertransferences:** See Chused (1991) and McLaughlin (1991).

Page 93 **"working alliance":** Greenson (1967).

Page 93 **benevolence and trust:** And so the therapist is not just a blank screen or withholding (or "abstinent"), on the traditional Freudian view. For a discussion, see Sherman (1998b, 1995).

Page 94 **"Whatever judgment we can form...:** Smith (1759/2000, III.I.1, p. 161).

Page 94 **she might come to say to herself:** I thank Susan Brison for this point.

Page 94 **Aristotle's remarks about self-love:** After all, there is only one chapter in the *Nicomachean Ethics* on this odd kind of friendship (namely, IX.8) in a discussion that that goes on for 26 chapters (at least in the *Nicomachean).*

Page 94 **the baser kind of self-love:** Aristotle (1984, *Nicomachean Ethics,* IX.8).

Page 95 **The best kind of friendship:** Aristotle (1984, *Nicomachean Ethics,* IX.12 1172a). See also Sherman (1997b, ch. 5).

Page 95 **friendship requires positive feelings:** See Aristotle (1984, *Nicomachean Ethics,* VIII.2) for the criteria of friendship.

Page 95 **a narcissistic self-absorption:** See Neff (2003).

Page 95 **"the restrictions under which all humans live":** Cicero (2002, *Tusculan Disputations,* 3.77).

Page 95 **"you are not the only one...:** Cicero (2002, *Tusculan Disputations,* 3.78).

Page 95 **"to endure these things is human":** Cicero (2002, *Tusculan Disputations,* 3.34).

Page 95 **The Epicureans are saying, in effect:** The Epicurean teaching, more fully, is that distress occurs when we direct our attention toward something we regard as a relatively *great* evil compared to goods measured against it. The Epicureans hold that we are masters of our own attention, and so we can prevent this kind of stress by redirecting our attention to pleasures of various kinds. We also minimize our woes by realizing that others suffer similarly. See Graver's useful discussion of the Epicurean position in Cicero (2002, p. 99).

Page 95 **rein in our attention on what is morally salient:** See Sherman (1997b, p. 68) on the idea that emotions are ways of tracking, in defeasible ways, the morally relevant news. See also Hurley and Macnamara (2010).

Page 96 **reasons for reassurance or trust:** See Walker (2006), Williams (1995, pp. 42, 73). Just as blame "asks" a transgressor for "acknowledgment" of one's standing, so too does self-blame ask one's condemner for acknowledgment of the hurt and reconsideration of the charges. On the call and response nature of reactive attitudes, see Macnamara (2012).

Page 96 **We are able to deploy in thought...:** Peter Goldie (2011, p. 86). For a sharp and lively criticism of the idea of a narrative self, see Strawson (2004).

Page 96 **"in effect seeing oneself as another":** Goldie (2011, p. 86).

Page 96 **"One now knows what one did not know then...:** Goldie (2011, p. 87).

Page 97 **this kind of affective, empathic access:** See Schechtman (2001), whose work I came upon in revising this paper. She invokes Richard Wollheim's notion of "event memory," as discussed in *The Thread of Life* (1984), which, as she explains, "is not a cold cognitive relation to the past, but one which is thoroughly infused with affect" (Schechtman 2001, p. 248). Wollheim, when describing his World War II soldier years, recalls driving by mistake into the German lines in August 1944: Having described the event and the memory of it, he says, "and as I remember feeling those feelings, the sense of loss, the sense of terror, the sense of being on my own, the upsurge of rebellion against my fate, come over me, so that I am affected by them in some such way as I was when I felt them on that remote summer night" (Wollheim 1984, p. 106).

Page 98 **they are cognivitists:** For qualifications on cognitivism and neocognitivism (also judgmentalism and neojudgmentalism) of the emotions, see Deigh (1994) and Brady (2009).

Page 98 **(and there are four basic ones):** For further adumbration of Stoic views on emotions, see Sherman (2005). For a neo-Stoic view of emotion, see Nussbaum (2001). For an overall account of Stoicism, see Brennan (2005). For another in-depth account of Stoic emotion, see Graver (2007).

Page 99 **the sage at odds with most of humanity:** Again, the texts underdetermine a portrait of the sage. For my own alternative pictures, see Sherman (2005a). For John Cooper's compelling and more sanguine picture of a sage, see Cooper (2005). I am grateful to conversation on this issue with Margaret Graver, though I interpret the texts less sympathetically than she does.

Page 99 **"If anyone thinks that pallor...:** Seneca (1995, *On Anger,* II.3). The view is propounded in other Stoic texts. See Graver (1999).

Page 99 **the congruence of feelings:** One could get more mileage out of protoemotions by suggesting that they are a kind of re-enactment, of the sort a psychoanalyst might feel in listening to a patient and experiencing a fleeting congruent feeling—say of anger, or sexual arousal, or sadness. The analyst doesn't indulge the emotion in a full-fledged way, yet still the taste of that emotion is a moment of connection and attunement that allows access and understanding. See Chused (1991), McLaughlin (1991), and my (1999).

Page 99 **misrepresenting what is good and bad out there:** The texts can pull in other directions on just how to reconstruct the sage's equanimity. One of the "good" emotions (*eupatheiai*) the sage feels is *eulabeia*, wary or rational control that replaces ordinary fear (*phobos*). It may be watchfulness with respect to virtue, but also wary control to help keep a tight lid on potential entanglements with vice. If so, then the sage is still "alive" to what unnerved him in the past; he still "traffics" in the world of emotions and its vulnerabilities. See John Cooper's (2005) interpretation of the sage's equanimity, cited above, as pulling in this direction. Also, see my discussion of the role of Stoic good emotions, including this kind of rational wariness, in Sherman (2005a, pp. 81, 106, 109, 193, 205).

Page 100 **...as if I were talking to myself...:** Seneca (1989, *Epistle,* 27.1–2).

Page 100 **"he who writes these words...:** Seneca (1989, *Epistle,* 63.16).

Page 101 **the sage both condemns his former behavior and feelings:** In the case of anger, Seneca himself gives us a taste of that process of walling off: "conceal" it, keep it "hidden and secret"; give the mind an advance directive that should anger erupt, the mind must "bury it deeply and not proclaim its distress" (Seneca 1995, *On Anger,* 3.13). Perhaps anger is more toxic than grief and a greater threat to equanimity.

Page 101 **not self-empathy but self-forgiveness:** For the coherence of that notion, see Goldie (2011).

Page 101 **a more general idea of foreswearing anger and blame:** See Griswold (2007), Goldie (2011), Roberts (2003), and Calhoun (1992).

Page 102 **Reactive attitude structure:** In the background to all this is the rich discussion of reactive attitudes begun by P. F. Strawson. See Macnamara (2012) on the general view of reactive attitudes as having *a call and response* structure.

Page 102 **A narratable conception of the self:** This notion builds on Peter Goldie's views. Goldie (2003, p. 584; 2007, p. 303) refers to this as ironic. Though this kind of stance may be necessary for irony, it doesn't seem sufficient. I thank Sabine Roeser for comments on this.

Chapter 5: REBUILDING TRUST

Page 105 **"Sally," then twenty-two:** "Sally" is a pseudonym. The interviewee asked that her name not be disclosed. I interviewed this Air Force service member in June 2012.

Page 105 **"I felt like a deer in hunting season":** Others I have interviewed had similar experiences. I interviewed five faculty women officers, in spring 2012, during a visit to the Air Force Academy. Ashley Anderson was one of them. An Air Force officer in intelligence, she spoke of often being only one of twenty women on Army bases of about 1,000 in southern Iraq.

Page 107 **women make up about 14 percent:** See CNN Staff, "By the Numbers: Women in the U.S. Military," *CNN*, January 24, 2013, at: http://www.cnn.com/2013/01/24/us/military-women-glance/. West Point, for example, has a matriculation rate for women of about 16 to 17 percent. See Larry Abramson, "West Point Women: A Natural Pattern or a Camouflage Ceiling?" *NPR Morning Edition*, October 22, 2013, at: http://www.npr.org/2013/10/22/239260015/west-point-women-a-natural-pattern-or-a-camouflage-ceiling.

Page 107 **In a recent report on sexual assault:** See James Dao, "In Debate Over Military Sexual Assault, Men Are Overlooked Victims," *New York Times,* June 23, 2013, at: http://www.nytimes.com/2013/06/24/us/in-debate-over-military-sexual-assault-men-are-overlooked-victims.html?pagewanted=all&_r=0.

Page 107 **attacks on men, mostly by other men:** According to one report by military sociologists, "The risk of developing PTSD from sexual trauma is at least as high if not higher than, the risk of PTSD from exposure to combat." See Kelty et al. (2010).

Page 108 **A more recent high-profile sexual assault case at Annapolis:** See the coverage on the story, e.g., Helene Cooper, "Former Naval Academy Football Player Is Acquitted of Sexual Assault," *New York Times,* March 20, 2014, at: http://www.nytimes.com/2014/03/21/us/former-naval-academy-football-player-is-acquitted-of-sexual-assault-charges.html.

Page 108 **I conceive of trust:** See McGeer (2012, p. 303); see discussion of this in Macnamara (2012).

Page 108 **it is an exposure of vulnerability to another:** In broad brushstroke, here, I am following Karen Jones's recent excellent work on trust. See Jones (2012). Implicit in her account is an acceptance of a three-place relation analysis of trust and trustworthiness: "A trusts B in a certain domain of interaction where B has competence" (Jones 2012, p. 70). Or, A trusts B to do Z: "A trusts

B in domain of interaction D" (Jones 2004, p. 16, n. 1). She draws on Annette Baier's influential work on trust, specifically, "Trust and Anti-Trust," and the three-place analysis of, "A trusts B with valued item Z" (Baier 1986).

Page 109 **As one philosopher has argued:** See Annette Baier (1986).

Page 109 **conscientiousness as motivating trustworthiness:** As Karen Jones has put it, "though otherwise quite different, goodwill and conscientiousness are alike in one respect: it is constitutive of having goodwill or conscientiousness that, in certain contexts, the fact that someone is counting on you can, all by itself and without further incentive, activate responsiveness." "The mistake is in thinking that this goodwill is something distinct from the responsiveness itself." See Jones (2012, p. 69).

Page 109 **His job just is to take care of:** As an Army guide puts it, "A non-commissioned officer's duties are numerous and must be taken seriously. An NCO's duty includes taking care of soldiers, which is your priority. Corporals and sergeants do this by developing a genuine concern for their soldiers' well-being." See: http://www.armystudyguide.com/content/army_board_study_guide_topics/nco_duties/duties-responsibilities-authority-of-nco.shtml.

Page 109 **hygiene requirements:** From conversations with Army Col. (Ret.) Elspeth Cameron "Cam" Ritchie, MD, former Psychiatry Consultant to the Army Surgeon General and Senior Editor of the Army's updated combat behavioral health manual (Ritchie 2011).

Page 110 **"The cunning of trust":** See Philip Pettit (1995).

Page 110 **tames it for its social capital:** See Jones (2012) for this way of making the point.

Page 110 **in her interest to "encapsulate":** Russell Hardin (2004, p. 5).

Page 110 **"The useful is not permanent…:** Aristotle (1984, *Nicomachean Ethics,* VIII.2, 1156a22, translation slightly altered).

Page 110 **trust and trustworthiness give way:** Again, see Jones (2012) on this point.

Page 110 **the preface to asking a question:** I thank Trip Glazer for discussion of this in relation to recent work of my colleagues Rebecca Kukla and Mark Lance on the performative force of various locutions. See Lance and Kukla (2013).

Page 111 **thrown and caught [the ball]:** See Aristotle (1984, *Nicomachean Ethics,* VIII.2, 1155b30–1156a5) and Seneca (1995, *On Favours,* II.17.3).

Page 113 **The "preventive fantasy" in retributivist attitudes:** Bernard Williams (1995).

Page 113 **"be assured, trust again":** Margaret Urban Walker (2006, p. 135).

Page 113 *positive* "**reactive pathos**": Nietzsche (1994, p. 53). On strict vs. more inclusive reactive attitudes, see Wallace (1996, p. 27).

Page 113 **a positive attitude of holding another accountable:** In R. Jay Wallace's terms, "the defining mark of reactive attitudes is their connection to the expectations we hold people to." And holding someone to an expectation "involves a susceptibility to a certain range of emotions" (Wallace 1996, p. 26).

Page 114 **the military are made out of different stuff:** For a provocative opinion piece on just this topic, see Phil Klay, "After the War, a Failure of the Imagination," *NYT Sunday Review,* February 9, 2014, at: http://www.nytimes.com/2014/02/09/opinion/sunday/after-war-a-failure-of-the-imagination.html?_r=0.

Page 115 **their own healing from war:** I am indebted to Bryan Doerries for his many performances of the Theater of War in which he conveys so well to public audiences the relevance of ancient theater to our current wars. I am also indebted to performances by Peter Meineck and his Aquila Theater, which takes up similar themes. I participated in a talk-back after an incredibly riveting Aquila Theater performance of *A Female Philoctetes* on Veterans Day, 2014, at NYU, performed, in part, by veterans. For recent anthologies on ancient and modern war and trauma, see Meineck and Konstan (2014) and Caston and Weineck (2015). For a discussion of learning through a tragic hero's actions and suffering, see Sherman (1992).

Page 115 **The story will be familiar:** I use throughout Peter Meineck and Paul Woodruff's translation and notes in Sophocles (2007b).

Page 115 **constant shrieks of his anguished wailing:** For a plea not to minimize as a mere inconvenience the physical wound and the effect of Philoctetes's animal screams of pain on the Achaen troops, see Stephens (1995).

Page 115 **his "weeping disease":** Sophocles (2007b, p. 6).

Page 115 **"You know I could never speak to him…:** Sophocles (2007b, pp. 70–71).

Page 115 **the "unassailable weapon":** Sophocles (2007b, p. 77).

Page 116 **"he who gains a friend":** Sophocles (2007b, p. 673). See Meineck and Woodruff's note (Sophocles 2007a, p. 217) on this possible translation. See also Daly (1982) for the name's related connotation: "a friend better than any possession." The traditional meaning is "fond of gain."

Page 116 **The good interrogator:** For a discussion of interrogation techniques based on building rapport, see Sherman (2010, ch. 5–6, with notes). For the Army field manual on interrogation techniques in human intelligence collection, see https://www.fas.org/irp/doddir/army/fm2-22-3.pdf.

Page 116 **Abused and insulted:** Sophocles (2007b, pp. 381–85).

Page 116 **"You and I sing the same song":** Sophocles (2007b, pp. 404–405). For the theme of false and persuasive *logoi* used to lure Philoctetes, see Hoppin (1990).

Page 117 **"I will grant your wish...:** Sophocles (2007b, pp. 658–59).

Page 117 **...I will relent":** Sophocles (2007b, p. 660).

Page 117 **who received the bow from Heracles:** When Philoctetes, as a young boy, lit Heracles's funeral pyre. See p. 671n. in Sophocles (2007a), which fills out the background here. Also, see *Women of Trachis,* in Sophocles (2007a, p. 1214n.

Page 117 **manipulated into collaboration:** Pettit (1995). For a brief discussion of just when in the play Philoctetes addresses Neoptolemus as a friend (*philos*), see Konstan (2001).

Page 117 **"priceless friend":** Sophocles (2007b, p. 673).

Page 118 **"the bow will be yours to hold":** Sophocles (2007b, p. 667).

Page 118 **an ironic distance:** See Peter Goldie (2003) on ironic narrative distance.

Page 118 **So we are suspicious:** For a discussion of Neoptolemus's ultimate change of heart and his rejection of Odyssesus's "stratagems in favour of his natural honesty," see Gill (1980).

Page 118 **a new level of being counted on:** For this back-and-forth iteration of second-personal address, see suggestive remarks by Jones (2012), Macnamara (2012), and Kukla and Lance (2009). For suggestive and complementary remarks here about the "restoration of communication between man and man," see Segal (1995).

Page 118 **the first step in the reciprocation:** See Seneca (1995, *On Favours,* II.29.3–7) for an important "game of catch" metaphor showing the to-and-fro of gift giving, acceptance with gratitude, and acknowledgment of that gratitude. I discuss this in chapter 6 of this volume. Also, see the related metaphor of the three Graces' dance that "goes back on itself" (Seneca 1995, *On Favours,* I.3.2–4). For a related perspective on this reciprocation of gift giving with "thank you" and in return, "you're welcome," see Macnamara (2012).

Page 118 **his sincerity seems to grow:** For a complaint that Neoptolemus is motivated by an unexplained pity, see Sandridge (2008). For a more sympathetic view of the growth and motivational power of Neoptolemus's (and the Chorus's) pity, see Konstan (2006).

Page 119 **the cunning of trust:** See previous note.

Page 119 **the fact of dependency:** Again, I am indebted to Jones (2012, p. 71).

Page 119 **another a normative expectation:** There is an overlap here with the psychoanalytic notion of projective identification. The rough idea, first developed by Melanie Klein, is that an individual splits off negative represented parts of self (or ego) onto another in order to distance and defend herself from the anxiety those represented parts arouse. Projective identification is a defense mechanism. The projection I have in mind is not defensive, but more proactive and normative. It is a transference and then mirroring of one's own trust of another onto that other, with the aim of that target receiving, recognizing, and reciprocating (through trustworthiness) that trust investment. For a discussion of the history and meaning of projective identification, see Grotstein (1995).

Page 121 **the anomie of a veteran:** For a wonderful psychoanalytic piece on Philoctetes and the sense of abandonment of Vietnam veterans, see Lansky (2003a).

Page 121 **many return with "nostalgia":** For a powerful tale of nostalgia, see the novel by that name about the psychological trauma of a young Union soldier from Brooklyn, Summerfield Hayes, who finds himself aphasic with invisible wounds in a Washington, D.C. hospital, lovingly attended to by a gray-bearded civilian named "Walt." He is Walt Whitman. See McFarland (2013).

Page 121 **"Have mercy, my son...:** Sophocles (2007b, pp. 967–72).

Page 121 **narcissistic injuries:** On the concept of narcissistic injuries, see Kohut (1971, 1977, 1984).

Page 122 **a documentary *The Invisible War*:** For discussion by the director, Kirby Dick, of the film, see "Invisible War Director Kirby Dick on the Healing Power of Film," *PBS Independent Lens,* May 9, 2013, at: http://www.pbs.org/independentlens/blog/invisible-war-filmmaker-kirby-dick. See also the press kit for the movie, at: http://invisiblewarmovie.com/images/TheInvisibleWarPressKit.pdf.

Page 122 **"the oldest post of the Corps":** For information on this post, see: http://www.barracks.marines.mil/Parades/EveningParade.aspx.

Page 123 **It may not be too cynical to say:** See the insightful essay of Linda Gordon (2013) in her review of Roberts (2013). My colleague, Alisa Carse, has spoken to me often about the abuse of her mother in Germany at the hands of the occupying U.S. forces. For further discussion of crimes against women beyond the U.S. Armed Forces, see Barstow (2000) and MacKinnon (2006). For a remarkable account of the Russian occupation of Berlin, see Anonymous (2000). For a reading of the book (through the lens of a radical critique of the "governance feminist" argument for criminalization of rape in international criminal courts), see Halley (2008). For testimony of the private war of

American service women sexually abused while serving in Iraq, see Benedict (2009).

Page 123 **senators on Capitol Hill:** See Rebecca Huval, "Sen. Gillibrand Credits the Invisible War with Shaping New Bill," *PBS Independent Lens,* May 10, 2013, at: http://www.pbs.org/independentlens/blog/sen-gillibrand-cred-its-the-invisible-war-in-shaping-new-bill; and Eleanor Clift, " 'The Invisible War' Spurs Action Against Military Rape," *Daily Beast,* February 23, 2013, at: http://www.thedailybeast.com/articles/2013/02/23/the-invisible-war-spurs-action-against-military-rape.html. Former Secretary of Defense Leon Panetta previewed the film early on and apparently, two days after watching it, transferred power to prosecute sexual assault crimes from the level of unit commander to colonel.

Page 123 **an epidemic of sexual assault in the ranks:** According to a report released by the Defense Department Sexual Assault Prevention and Response Office (SAPRO), FY 2012 SAPRO, there were an estimated 26,000 cases of unwanted sexual contact and sexual assaults in 2012, representing a 37 percent increase from 2011. The report found that 50 percent of female victims stated that they did not report the crime because they thought that nothing would come of it. For an overview of the findings, see: http://www.gillibrand.senate.gov/mjia. For the complete SAPRO report, see: http://www.sapr.mil/public/docs/research/2012_Workplace_and_Gender_Relations_Survey_of_Active_Duty_Members-Survey_Note_and_Briefing.pdf.

Page 123 **each proposed legislation:** Gillibrand's bill took the prosecution out of the chain of command, and McCaskill's eliminates the "good soldier" legal defense from evidence rules unless a defendant's military character is directly relevant to the allegations. On March 10, 2014, though Gillibrand's bill fell five votes short of a filibuster-proof majority that would have cut off debate and allowed the bill to come to the floor in a final vote, McCaskill's bill, with its own more limited sexual assault prosecution reforms, passed on a 97–0 vote. See Darren Samuelsohn, "Claire McCaskill's Sexual Assault Bill Passes," *Politico,* March 10, 2014, at: http://www.politico.com/story/2014/03/claire-mccaskill-military-sexual-assault-bill-104499.html.

Page 123 **two high-profile court cases:** On the case of disgraced Army general, Brig. Gen. Jeffrey Sinclair, see Craig Whitlock, "Disgraced Army General, Jeffrey A. Sinclair, Receives Fine, No Jail Time," *Washington Post,* March 20, 2014, at: http://www.washingtonpost.com/world/national-security/disgraced-army-general-jeffrey-a-sinclair-receives-fine-no-jail-time/2014/03/20/c555b650-b039-11e3-95e8-39bef8e9a48b_story.html.

On the Naval Academy case, see Helene Cooper, "Former Naval Academy Football Player Is Acquitted of Sexual Assault," *New York Times,* March 20, 2014, at: http://www.nytimes.com/2014/03/21/us/former-naval-academy-football-player-is-acquitted-of-sexual-assault-charges.html.

Page 123 **systemic fear:** The Commandant of the Marine Corps General James F. Amos acknowledged the point when he said of victims, "they don't trust the chain of command." Transcript of Testimony, Senate Armed Services Committee, Oversight Hearing to Receive Testimony on Pending Legislation Regarding Sexual Assaults in the Military at 92 (June 4, 2013) as reported in: http://responsesystemspanel.whs.mil/public/docs/meetings/Sub_Committee/20131023_ROC/04_RoC_Gillibrand_Proposal.pdf. See also: http://www.gillibrand.senate.gov/mjia, and Lanny Davis, "Obama Should Back Gillibrand," *The Hill,* July 24, 2013, at: http://thehill.com/opinion/columnists/lanny-davis/313369-obama-should-back-gillibrand.

Page 124 **trust bond... with a producer:** See Eleanor Clift, "'The Invisible War' Spurs Action Against Military Rape," *Daily Beast,* February 23, 2013, at: http://www.thedailybeast.com/articles/2013/02/23/the-invisible-war-spurs-action-against-military-rape.html.

Page 124 **British psychoanalyst John Bowlby:** See Bowlby (1969/1973/1980).

Page 125 **Air Force Colonel Stephanie Wilson:** Col. Stephanie Wilson and I were both fellows at the Woodrow Wilson Center in Washington, D.C., during 2011–12. We talked several times that year about her coming home from war and getting ready to redeploy. The above conversation draws from an interview on May 2, 2012.

Page 127 **a "pre-rehearsal":** For discussion of Seneca's use of the notion, see Sherman (2005a, pp. 117, 145).

Page 128 **emotions are accompanied with pleasure or pain:** Aristotle (1984, *Rhetoric,* II.1, 1378a20ff).

Page 128 **not a reliable indicator:** See James (2003).

Page 128 *does* **rather than how it** *feels***:** I have argued in earlier writings that emotions play various critical and overlapping roles in our lives as practical and moral agents See, for example, Sherman (1997b) where I argue emotions function as:

(1) Modes that *discern* or *recognize salience*; that is, they direct, and often, rivet our attention to certain objects of value that we care about and take to be important for good living. They help us to *attend to* values.

(2) Modes that *convey and express values*; that is, when expressed, they communicate those values to ourselves and others; they *show* what we care about. In some cases, we may have not have corresponding inner attitudes we are externalizing. Rather, we are engaged primarily in emotional *performances* that themselves show an interest in certain values. Smiling can be like that.

(3) Modes, relatedly, that *disclose* values we were unaware we had; that is, experiencing emotion or expressing emotion reveals an interest and value that we didn't fully recognize ourselves as having, or at least, we underappreciated that fact.

(4) Modes that *create or instate* new values and don't just track or discern antecedent ones; emotional engagement is a way that an individual *comes to care about something* and *invests* resources in it. It is a way of bootstrapping interest and value and attachment.

(5) Modes, most familiarly, perhaps, that *motivate and mobilize* us into action or mental activity; so, we act *out of* compassion or *out of* vengeful anger. The emotions, as the Stoics put it, are kinds of "impulses" (*hormai*). Or as Aristotle says, they involve desires (*orexeis*).

For a discussion of this last point, see Sherman (1977b, pp.39–50). For the Stoics on emotions as impulses (*hormai*), see Brennan (2005, ch. 7).

Page 128 **"epistemic landscape":** As Peter Goldie puts it, emotions have an epistemic tendency to build "an epistemic landscape" that coheres with an evaluation that that emotion has. In Michael Brady's terms, emotions have a "capture and consume" mode of directing attention and cognitive resources. See Brady (2007) and Goldie (2004, p. 99).

Page 129 **Summerfield Hayes, fictional:** In Dennis McFarland's remarkable Civil War novel, *Nostalgia* (2013).

Page 130 **U.S. detention center at Guantanamo:** For a recent discussion marking the 10th anniversary of Gitmo, see Kim Lawton and Nancy Sherman, "Guantanamo Ethics," *PBS*, September 6, 2013, at: http://www.pbs.org/wnet/religionandethics/2013/09/06/september-6-2013-guantanamo-ethics/20043/. I visited Gitmo in fall 2005, by invitation of the U.S. Defense Department, to investigate issues of mental and physical health of detainees in the wake of hunger strikes. For my reactions at the time, see Nancy Sherman, "Mind Games at Gitmo," *LA Times*, December 12, 2005, at: http://articles.latimes.com/2005/dec/12/opinion/oe-sherman12. For more on the issue, see Sherman (2010, chs. 5–6).

Chapter 6: HOPE AFTER WAR

Page 133 **Defiant Requiem:** For information on the *Defiant Requiem,* see http://www.murrysidlin.com/_home/DR_Performance_History_and_ Videos.html and http://www.defiantrequiemfilm.com. I attended a showing at the Washington Jewish Community Center, May 6, 2013, after which Murry Sidlin spoke. Terezin was a transit camp for Czechoslovakian Jews. Of some 140,000 Jews who passed through, 90,000 were deported to near certain death in concentration camps and killing centers. Some 33,000 died in Terezin itself. For information on Terezin, see "Theresienstadt," *Holocaust Encyclopedia,* The United States Holocaust Memorial Museum, June 10, 2013, at: http://www.ushmm.org/wlc/en/article.php?ModuleId=10005424.

Page 134 **Singing to be saved:** That survivor, Alice Herz-Sommer, a distinguished pianist before the war, recently died at age 110. Of the concerts at Terezin, she said, "This music was... our food.... Through making music, we were kept alive." She knew of music's sustaining power. Shortly after the Nazi occupation of Czechoslovakia in 1939, she began a serious study of Chopin's Études. "They are very difficult," she told a reporter at the *Sydney Morning Herald* in 2010. "I thought if I learned to play them, they would save my life." Her young son survived the camp as well, and became an eminent cellist—Raphael Sommer. Margalit Fox, "Alice Herz-Sommer, Who Found Peace in Chopin Amid Holocaust, Dies at 110," *New York Times,* February 27, 2014, at: http://www.nytimes.com/2014/02/28/world/ europe/alice-herz-sommer-pianist-who-survived-holocaust-dies-at-110. html?_r=0.

Page 134 **another aspect of their hope:** In thinking about hope, I am indebted to conversations with Adrienne Martin, especially with regard to Martin (2013) and her notion of normative hope, or hope in persons. For other work on hope that has influenced my thought in this chapter, see Walker (2006), Lear (2006), and Pettit (2004).

Page 135 **It is natural, then...:** Aristotle (1984, *Nicomachean Ethics,* I.10, 1099b33–1100a3, translation altered slightly, changing "being congratulated" to "being deemed"). Aristotle explicitly touches on hope in this passage, as in "by reason of the hopes"—*dia tēn elpida.*

Page 135 **each other's reactive uptakes and "updates":** I thank Trip Glazer for this term.

Page 135 **interpersonal engagement from childhood:** For patterns of attunement and misattunement between child and caregiver, see Stern (1985).

Page 135 **"entrust to chance...:** Aristotle (1984, *Nicomachean Ethics,* 1099b22).

Page 136 **requisite for realizing a flourishing and happy life:** Aristotle (1984, *Nicomachean Ethics,* 1099b18). Again, I am indebted to Adrienne Martin for this notion of normative hope. See Martin (2013).

Page 136 **the Stoics will press Aristotle:** For further discussion of Stoic positions, see Sherman (2005a).

Page 136 **they will have the resources:** This is not to suggest that such line drawing is ever easy or intuitive. For notions of responsibility in the context of balancing risks in force protection and protection of noncombatants, see Luban (2014). He suggests the plausibility of a strict liability view of accepting risks (and hence, acquiring responsibility) in cases where soldiers' cause danger to noncombatant civilians.

Page 137 **an appropriate reply:** McGeer (2012, p. 303); see discussion of this in Macnamara (2012).

Page 137 **looking for an appropriate response to our call:** Darwall (2006, p. 159); Walker (2006, p. 135).

Page 137 **In general, we demand some degree...:** Strawson (1962/1993).

Page 137 **A number of philosophers have been exploring:** Coleen Macnamara (2012) and Adrienne Martin (2013) have argued, independently in recent work, that a demand analysis (of the sort developed by Watson [2004], Wallace [1996] and Darwall [2006]) doesn't do well in accommodating the broad spectrum of negative and positive reactive attitudes. (Macnamara's work focuses on gratitude, while Martin's work focuses on hope.) And, as Macnamara argues, expressed attitudes construed as demandings may not even issue in tenable demands that can be complied with in the case of a paradigmatic negative reactive attitude, such as resentment. "Demands seek compliance" (p. 901). But just what demand am I making, she asks, when I express resentment when you step on my toe? "My options for complying with your demand are rather limited. I cannot comply by refraining from the offending action, since it is already in the past.... Future compliance, of course, is possible—I can refrain from stepping on your foot in the future. But while we can agree that this would be a good thing, such forbearance is not satisfying as a complete account of the response your expression of resentment aims at. It is highly implausible that my *merely* not stomping on your foot in the future renders your expression of resentment fully successful" (p. 901).

Page 137 **the structure of reactive attitudes as a call-and-response:** For call-and-response models, see Walker (2006, p. 135) and Darwall (2006, p. 159). Macnamara's view also draws from the normative account of speech acts that

Kukla and Lance develop, and specifically, their account of vocatives, or hailings ("Yo's"). See Kukla and Lance (2009, pp. 145–46).

Page 137 **in original and important work on normative hope:** Martin (2013, ch. 5, p.130; also, pp.118–22 and 124). Martin takes her lead from an earlier article by Jonathan Bennett (2008b) who notes a constriction in demand-based accounts of reactive attitudes.

Page 137 **praised if you succeed, but not blamed if you fail:** I thank Agnes Callard for clarification here at the Practical Philosophy Workshop I gave at University of Chicago, February 7, 2014.

Page 138 **sense of purpose and belonging:** This is not to downplay the boredom in war. For an interesting discussion, see http://videos.huffingtonpost.com/the-boredom-of-war-517827695.

Page 138 **dangerous and demanding engagements:** Lalo is the husband of a former Georgetown student of mine, Donna Hernandez, whose story I tell below. I have interviewed both on many occasions, formally and informally, over a period of four years or more. I first interviewed Lalo and Donna on October 17, 2012, then again July, 24, 2013, and again Lalo on his own on October 2, 2013. Our additional ongoing conversations have taken place in snippets, over tea, coffee, a meal, in class, and on the phone over those years.

Page 138 **Navy and Marine Corps Achievement Medal:** I refer to the citations in the Secretary of the Navy issued Navy and Marine Corps Achievement Medal citation awarded to Corporal Eduardo L. ("Lalo") Panyagua on June 14, 2010.

Page 138 **unhappiness as despair:** See Buss (2004) for this notion, though she claims such unhappiness is, at root, irrational.

Page 138 **Recent spikes in suicide rates:** On this, see Margaret C. Harrell and Nancy Berglass, "Losing the Battle: The Challenge of Military Suicide," *Center for a New American Security,* October 2011, at: http://www.cnas.org/files/documents/publications/CNAS_LosingTheBattle_HarrellBerglass.pdf. For a recent report suggesting that deployment to war zones is not a major factor in the rise in military suicides (and for criticism of the report), see James Dao, "Deployment Factors Are Not Related to Rise in Military Suicides, Study Finds," *New York Times,* August 6, 2013, at: http://www.nytimes.com/2013/08/07/us/deployment-factors-found-not-related-to-military-suicide-spike.html?_r=0.

Page 138 **hope can get a foothold:** For resilience and positive thinking initiatives in the Army, see Martin Seligman's designed Army-wide resilience training program: "Comprehensive Soldier Fitness," discussed in Seligman (2011),

Seligman and Fowler (2011), and Reivich, Seligman, and McBride (2011). For critiques of Seligman's positive psychology approach, see Held (2004), Ehrenreich (2009), and Roy Eidelson, "The Dark Side of 'Comprehensive Soldier Fitness,'" *Psychology Today,* March 25, 2011, at: http://www.psychology today.com/blog/dangerous-ideas/201103/the-dark-side-comprehensive-soldier-fitness. Hopefulness on my view is not an optimistic temperament or behaviorally trained positive attitude, but an aspiring attitude with regard to worthwhile ends we set for ourselves or others (in the case of normative hope) or a desire for what we believe are uncertain outcomes where that hopefulness gives us a certain cognitive resolve to put projects and plans in place (non-normative hope).

Page 138 *substantive* **hope:** By *substantive* (non-normative) hope I mean to exclude trivial hopes, such as figure in the expression "I hope it won't rain today," or "I hope he catches his train," though I don't have good ways of drawing a hard line between these usages and weightier ones aside from context. My primary interest is in hope that mobilizes focus and practical agency, as will become clear shortly. Here, too, I recognize that there are genuine and substantive ways of hoping where a notion of agency (or agential investment) seems out of place—such as future directed hopes that do not involve effort (e.g., hoping that certain legislation passes but essentially being passive about it) or past directed hopes, where practical agency is out of place (e.g., hoping that Hitler died a miserable death). On this see, Martin (2011). Still, I am thinking of hope paradigmatically as a kind of agential investment.

Page 139 **"possibilism":** Albert Hirschman's term, discussed in Cass Sunstein, "An Original Thinker of Our Time," *New York Review of Books,* May 23, 2013, at: http://www.nybooks.com/articles/archives/2013/may/23/albert-hirschman-original-thinker/?pagination=false.

Page 139 **"the confidence of my actual belief…:** Philip Pettit (2004, p. 159).

Page 139 **Forming the hope…:** Pettit (2004, p. 160).

Page 139 **"agential investment":** For an overview and critique of agential investment views, see Martin (2011). She argues that hope is not a special form of motivation, though a common way of expressing hope is through fantasies that "can influence motivation both rationally… and nonrationally" (p. 171). So in the end, she accommodates typical cases that express the motivational character of hope. Her worry is that viewing hope as itself a special form of motivation or effortful investment is too restrictive, and cannot accommodate the sort of counterexamples where hope is genuine but *passive*, whether respect to the future or past—e.g., hoping that certain legislation passes but putting no effort into advocacy and support, or hoping that Hitler died a miserable death, where agential effort just makes no sense. On this see Martin (2011). Still, the kind of hope I am interested in here is *paradigmatically* agential and motivational, whether constitutively so or as a matter of concomitant, typical expression.

Page 139 **"for immortality"**: "Choice cannot relate to impossibles, ... but there may be a wish even for impossibles—e.g., for immortality. And wish may relate to things that could in no way be brought about by one's own efforts" (Aristotle 1984, *Nicomachean Ethics,* 111b20–25).

Page 139 **"turning away from reality"**: See Freud (1974, XIV.233; XIV.244, pp. 316–18, 324–25; and XI.50–51).

Page 139 *eudaimonia*: See Nussbaum (2001, pp. 31–33) on this view of some emotions and their connection with *eudaimonia*.

Page 139 **these kinds of hopes**: For more on the role of fantasy in hope, see Martin (2011) and Lear (2006).

Page 141 **he clearly walks**: Posted at: http://www.runnersworld.com/ runners-stories/losing-his-legs-made-him-stronger-than-ever?page=single.

Page 141 **world-class paratriathlete**: See http://www.walkingwithnewlegs. com/Andre_Kajlich.html.

Page 141 **both collaborative and individual**: Bratman (1987).

Page 142 **"epistemic landscapes"**: Goldie (2005, p. 99); Brady (2007). Also, see Hurley and Macnamara (2010) for considerations on reactive attitudes as *emotions* and not beliefs, and background to this in Sherman (1997b, p. 39).

Page 142 **she "psyches" herself**: I thank Dan Brudney for this insight and others at the discussion of my paper at University of Chicago's Practical Philosophy Workshop, February 7, 2014.

Page 142 **avoid the paralysis of idle fears**: I describe this kind of mental practice in Sherman (2005a, pp. 117, 145) in connection with Seneca and Cicero's writings.

Page 142 *radical hope*

Page 143 **Army Lieutenant Colonel Greg Gadson**: I interviewed Greg Gadson on May 9, 2011. Also, see Steve Inskeep, "Where Generations of Soldiers Healed and Moved On," *NPR Morning Edition,* August 29, 2011, at: http://www.npr.org/2011/08/29/139641794/ where-generations-of-soldiers-healed-and-moved-on.

Page 143 **contractors who make and fit prosthetics...**: And in particular, Mike Corcoran, the remarkable prostheticist who works with injured military members at Walter Reed. See http://mcopro.com/team/ mike-corcoran/

Page 143 **worldwide rights for persons with disabilities:** As in the United Nations treaty for disabled rights that the Senate recently rejected; see Ramsey Cox and Julian Pecquet, "Senate Rejects United Nations Treaty for Disabled Rights in a 68–31 Vote," *The Hill,* December 4, 2012, at: http:// thehill.com/blogs/global-affairs/un-treaties/270831-senate-rejects-un-treaty-for-disabled-rights-in-vote.

Page 144 **I would like to take up an analogy…:** On the game of ball, see Seneca (1995, *On Favours,* II.17.3–6). For related analogy based on the looping back of the mutual reciprocations of the Three Graces, see Seneca (1995, *On Favours,* 1.3.8).

Page 145 **As Seneca goes on to suggest:** For an earlier discussion of Seneca on emotional expression and performance in gift giving, see Sherman (2004, 2005b).

Page 145 **trust given to someone:** I develop these ideas in the case of trust in Sherman (2014a).

Page 145 **"disrupting the status quo":** "Roberta" is a pseudonym. Preserving "heritage and tradition" is really code, she adds, for protecting "pornography in on-line briefs and pinup posters on the wall."

Page 146 **devolves to disappointment:** There can be a "double attitude," as Adrienne Martin (2013, pp. 120–24) puts it. I thank her for conversation on this point.

Page 146 **(that made on her behalf):** Martin (2013).

Page 147 **makes this all too clear:** For a painful discussion of all too common misguided parental investments in children's "vertical" identities (that is, aspirations hearing parents pass down for their deaf children to be hearing-able or straight parents for their gay children to be straight, or non-autistic parents for their autistic children to be "normal," and so on, see Solomon (2012).

Page 147 **In other cases:** I discuss these cases in Sherman (2010, ch. 4; 2013).

Page 148 **little lasting impact:** For an insightful op ed on this, see Thomas Friedman, "Don't Just Do Something. Sit There," *New York Times,* February 25, 2014, at: http://www.nytimes.com/2014/02/26/opinion/friedman-dont-just-do-something-sit-there.html?ref=thomaslfriedman&_r=0.

Page 148 **"This is just the beginning…:** As quoted in Richard A. Oppel Jr., "Falluja's Fall Stuns Marines Who Fought There," *New York Times,* January 9, 2014, at: http://www.nytimes.com/2014/01/10/us/fallujas-fall-stuns-marines-who-fought-there.html. The article also quotes one of the Marines, Adam Banotai, in 2004, a 21-year-old squad leader in Fallujah whose unit seized control of the government center early in the campaign: "I don't think anyone had the grand illusion that Fallujah or Ramadi was going to turn into Disneyland, but none of us thought it was going to fall back to a jihadist insurgency.... It made me sick to my stomach to have that thrown in our face, everything we fought for so blatantly taken away."

Page 148 **Lou Reed's "A Walk on the Wild Side":** The Blossoms respond in Lou Reed's, "A Walk on the Wild Side"; or the call and response of Merry Clayton (or Lisa Fischer) to Mick Jagger: "Rape, murder,... It's just a shot away" in the "Gimme Shelter" track. See *Twenty Feet from Stardom* for insights into the role of backup singers, typically African American women for whom the call-response pattern is inculcated early in participation in church gospel music, at: http://twentyfeetfromstardom.com.

Page 149 **may hold each other *responsible*:** Macnamara (2011) emphasizes this point.

Page 149 **evaluative attitudes are *emotions*:** Or conversely, "emotionally significant objects and events capture and consume attention" as Michael Brady (2009, p. 423) puts it.

Page 149 **brings on shame:** For an exploration of this view of shame, see Velleman (2001).

Page 150 **The citation on his achievement medal:** The Department of the Navy issued Navy and Marine Corps Achievement Medal to Corporal Eduardo L. Panyagua, June 14, 2010.

Page 151 **primarily a performance:** For Stoic lessons on the difficulty of inner change, see Cicero's critique of Stoic doctrine in connection with his own grieving, discussed in Sherman (2005a, pp. 132, 143–49).

Page 151 **a therapist's finely expressed trust:** For an excellent discussion of trust and growing trustworthiness, see Jones (2012).

Page 151 **Aristotle invokes that image:** See Aristotle (1984, *Magna Moralia,* 1212b8–1213a24; *Nicomachean Ethics,* 1170b7; and *Eudemian Ethics,* 1245a30).

CHAPTER 7: HOMECOMING

Page 155 **Vice Admiral James Bond Stockdale:** I met and interviewed Jim Stockdale several times, and wrote about those encounters in *Stoic Warriors* (Sherman 2005a) and *The Untold War* (Sherman 2010). For Stockdale's own reflections on his philosophy, see Stockdale (1995).

Page 161 **there are no homecomings:** For more on this, in connection with the April 2014 Fort Hood shooting, see my "It's the Gun, Not the Shooter" in *Foreign Affairs,* http://www.foreignaffairs.com/articles/141097/nancy-sherman/its-the-gun-not-the-shooter.

AFTERWORDS: WHERE THEY ARE NOW

Page 165 **special wilderness camp for kids:** http://www.nytimes.com/2014/07/19/world/middleeast/isis-forces-last-iraqi-christians-to-flee-mosul.html?_r=0

Page 165 **jihadists taking sledgehammers:** See http://www.artistsinuniform.org

BIBLIOGRAPHY

Abramson, Kate (2010). A sentimentalist's defense of contempt, shame, and disdain. In Peter Goldie (Ed.), *The Oxford handbook of philosophy of emotion* (pp. 189–213). Oxford: Oxford University Press.

Améry, Jean (1980). *At the mind's limits: Contemplations by a survivor on Auschwitz and its realities* (Sidney Rosenfeld and Stella Rosenfeld, Trans.). Bloomington: Indiana University Press.

Anonymous (2000). *A woman in Berlin: Eight weeks in the conquered city.* New York: Metropolitan Books.

Aristotle (1984). *The complete works of Aristotle: The revised Oxford* (Jonathan Barnes, Ed.). Bollingen Series. Princeton, NJ: Princeton University Press.

Baffico, P., and McNamara, A. (2014). *Last mission for a reluctant patriot.* Lake Forest, IL: Approaching the Spot Publishing.

Baier, Annette (1986). Trust and antitrust. *Ethics, 96*(2), 231–60.

Bar-On, Dorit (2004). *Speaking my mind: Expression and self-knowledge.* New York: Oxford University Press.

Baron, Marcia (1995). *Kantian ethics almost without apology.* Ithaca: Cornell University Press.

Barstow, Ann Llewellyn (Ed.). (2000). *War's dirty secrets: Rape, prostitution, and other crimes against women.* Cleveland, OH: Pilgrim Press.

Benedict, Helen (2009). *The lonely soldier: The private war of women serving in Iraq.* Boston: Beacon Press.

Bennett, Jonathan (2008a). Accountability II. In M. McKenna and P. Russell (Eds.), *Free will and reactive attitudes: Perspectives on P.F. Strawson's "Freedom and Resentment"* (pp. 47–68). London: Ashgate.

Bennett, Jonathan (2008b). Accountability. In M. McKenna and P. Russell (Eds.), *Free will and reactive attitudes: Perspectives on P.F. Strawson's "Freedom and Resentment"* (pp. 4–68). London: Ashgate.

Bilmes, Linda (2013). *The financial legacy of Iraq and Afghanistan: How wartime faculty spending decisions will constrain future national security budgets.* Cambridge, MA: Harvard Kennedy School.

Black, Sandra A., et al. (2011). Prevalence and risk factors associated with suicides of Army soldiers, 2001–2009. *Military Psychology, 23*(4), 433–51.

Bowlby, John (1969/1973/1980). *Attachment and loss* (3 vols.). 1: *Attachment*; 2: *Separation: Anxiety and anger*; 3: *Loss: Sadness and depression.* London: Hogarth Press.

Brady, Michael S. (2006). Appropriate attitudes and the value problem. *American Philosophical Quarterly, 43*(1), 91–99.

Brady, Michael S. (2007). Recalcitrant emotions and visual illusions. *American Philosophical Quarterly, 44*(3), 273–84.

Brady, Michael S. (2008). Value and fitting emotions. *Journal of Value Inquiry, 42*(4), 465–75.

Brady, Michael S. (2009). The irrationality of recalcitrant emotions. *Philosophical Studies: An International Journal for Philosophy in the Analytic Tradition, 145*(3), 413–30.

Bratman, Michael (1987). *Intentions, plans, and practical reasons.* Cambridge, MA: Harvard University Press.

Brennan, Tad (2005). *The Stoic life.* Oxford: Oxford University Press.

Bryant, Richard (2011). Post-traumatic stress disorder vs. traumatic brain injury. *Dialogues in Clinical Neuroscience, 13*(3), 251.

Brudholm, Thomas (2008). *Resentment's virtue.* Philadelphia: Temple University Press.

Buber, Martin (1970). *I and Thou* (Walter Kaufmann, Trans.). New York: Scribner's.

Buss, Sarah (1999). Appearing respectful: The moral significance of manners. *Ethics, 109*(4), 795–826.

Buss, Sarah (2004). The irrationality of unhapiness and the paradox of despair. *Journal of Philosophy, 101*(4), 171–200.

Butler, Joseph (1964). *Fifteen sermons* (W. R. Matthews, Ed.). London: Bell and Sons.

Calhoun, Cheshire (1992). Changing one's heart. *Ethics: An International Journal of Social, Political, and Legal Philosophy, 103*(1), 76–96.

Carter, Phillip (2013a). *Expanding the net: Building mental health care capacity for veterans*. Washington, DC: Center for New American Security.

Carter, Phillip (2013b). *Needs assessment: Veterans in the western United States*. Washington, DC: Center for New American Security.

Caston, Victor, and Silke-Maria, Weineck (Eds.). (2015). *Our ancient wars*. Ann Arbor: University of Michigan Press.

Chandrasekaran, Rajiv (2006). *Imperial life in the emerald city: Inside Iraq's green zone*. New York: Alfred A. Knopf.

Chiarelli, Peter W (2010). *Army health promotion risk reduction suicide prevention report 2010*. Collingdale, PA: DIANE Publishing.

Chused, Judith F. (1991). The evocative power of enactments. *Journal of the American Psychoanalytic Association, 39*(3), 615–39.

Cicero (2002). *Cicero on the emotions: Tusculan Disputations 3 and 4* (M. Graver, Ed.). Chicago: University of Chicago Press.

Cooper, David (1972). Responsibility and the "system". In Peter French (Ed.), *Individual and collective responsibility: Massacre at My Lai* (pp. 81–100). Cambridge, MA: Schenkman.

Cooper, John M. (2005). The emotional life of the wise. *Southern Journal of Philosophy, 43*(S1), 176–218.

Cornum, Rhonda, and Copeland, Peter (1992). *She went to war: The Rhonda Cornum story*. Nevada, CA: Presidio.

Daly, James (1982). The name of Philoctetes: Philoctetes 670–73. *American Journal of Philology, 103*(4), 440–42.

D'Arms, Justin, and Jacobson, Daniel (2000). The moralistic fallacy: On the "appropriateness" of emotions. *Philosophy and Phenomenological Research, 61*(1), 65–90.

Darwall, Stephen (2006). *The second-person standpoint*. Cambridge, MA: Harvard University Press.

Deigh, John (1994). Cognitivism in the theory of emotions. *Ethics: An International Journal of Social, Political, and Legal Philosophy, 104*(4), 824–54.

Deigh, John (1999). All kinds of guilt. *Law and Philosophy: An International Journal for Jurisprudence and Legal Philosophy, 18*(4), 313–25.

Denning, Laura Aiuppa, Meisnere, Marc, and Warner, Kenneth E (2014). *Preventing psychological disorders in service members and their families: An assessment of programs*. Washington, DC: National Academies Press.

Deonna, Julien, and Teroni, Fabrice (2008). Shame's guilt disproved. *Critical Quarterly, 50*(4), 65–72.

Deonna, Julien, and Teroni, Fabrice (2011). Is shame a social emotion? In Anita Konzelmann Ziv, Keith Lehrer, and Hans Bernhard Schmid (Eds.),

Self-evaluation: Affective and social grounds of intentionality (pp. 193–212). Philosophical Studies Series. New York: Springer Science + Business Media.

Dubik, James (1982). Human rights, command responsibility, and Walzer's Just War theory. *Philosophy and Public Affairs, 11*(4), 354–71.

Dunigan, Molly, et al. (2013). *Out of the shadows: The health and well-being of private contractors working in conflict environments.* Santa Monica: Rand Corporation.

Ebner, N. C., and Riediger, M. (2010). FACES—a database of facial expressions in young, middle-aged, and older women and men: Development and validation. *Behavioral Research Methods, 42*(1), 351–62.

Ehrenreich, Barbara (2009). *Bright-sided: How the relentless promotion of positive thinking has undermined America.* New York: Metropolitan Books.

Eisenberg, Nancy, and Strayer, Janet (1987). Empathy and its development. Cambridge Studies in Social and Emotional Development. New York: Cambridge University Press.

Ekman, Paul (1994). All emotions are basic. In Paul and Richard J. Davidson Ekman (Eds.), *The nature of emotion* (pp. 15–19). New York: Oxford University Press.

Ekman, Paul, and Rosenberg, Erika L. (Eds.). (2005). *What the face reveals: Basic and applied studies of spontaneous expression using the Facial Action Coding System (FACS)* (2nd ed.). New York: Oxford University Press.

Emde, Robert, Gaensbauer, T. J., and Harmon, R. J. (1976). Emotional expression in infancy; a biobehavioral study. *Psychological Issues, 10*(1), 125–48.

Finkel, David (2013). *Thankyou for your service.* New York: MacMillan.

Freud, Sigmund (1974). *Standard edition of the complete psychological works of Sigmund Freud* (J. Strachey, Trans.). London: Hogarth Press.

Freud, Sigmund (1986). *The complete letters of Sigmund Freud to Wilhelm Fliess, 1887-1904,* vol. 5 (J. Masson, Ed.). Cambridge, MA: Harvard University Press.

Fromm, M. Gerard (2014). Interview with Frank Ochberg. *Psychoanalytic Psychology, 31*(2), 206–16.

Gilbert, Margaret (2002). Collective guilt and collective guilt feelings. *Journal of Ethics: An International Philosophical Review, 6*(2), 115–43.

Gill, Christopher (1980). Bow, oracle, and epiphany in Sophocles' "Philoctetes." *Greece and Rome, Second Series, 27*(2), 137–46.

Goffman, Erving (1959). *The presentation of self in everyday life.* New York: Random House.

Goffman, Erving (1967). The nature of deference and demeanor. In Erving Goffman (Ed.), *Interaction rituals: Essays on face-to face behavior* (pp. 47–96). New York: Anchor.

Goldie, Peter (2003). One's remembered past: Narrative thinking, emotion, and the external perspective. *Philosophical Papers, 32*(3), 301–19.

Goldie, Peter (2004). Emotion, feeling, and knowledge of the world. In A. Solomon (Ed.), *Thinking about feeling: Contemporary philosophers on emotions* (pp. 91–106). New York: Oxford University Press.

Goldie, Peter (2005). Imagination and the distorting power of emotion. *Journal of Consciousness Studies, 12*(8-10), 127–39.

Goldie, Peter (2007). Dramatic irony, narrative, and the external perspective. *Philosophy: Journal of the Royal Institute of Philosophy, 60* (Supp.), 69–84.

Goldie, Peter (2011). Self-forgiveness and the narrative sense of self. In Christel Fricke (Ed.), *The ethics of forgiveness: A collection of essays* (pp. 81–94). New York: Routledge.

Gordon, Linda (2013). What armies do: Women under occupation. *Dissent, 60*(4), 107–11.

Graver, Margaret (1999). Philo of Alexandria and the origins of the Stoic "propathe-iai." *Phronesis: A Journal of Ancient Philosophy, 44*(4), 300–25.

Graver, Margaret (2007). *Stoicism & emotion*. Chicago: University of Chicago Press.

Green, Mitchell (2007). *Self-expression*. New York: Oxford University Press.

Greene, Joshua (2013). *Moral tribalism: Emotion, reason, and the gap between us and them*. New York: Penguin.

Greenson, R. R. (1967). *The technique and practice of psychoanalysis*. New York: International Universities Press.

Greenspan, Patricia S. (1983). Moral dilemmas and guilt. *Philosophical Studies: An International Journal for Philosophy in the Analytic Tradition, 43*, 117–25.

Griswold, Charles L. (2007). *Forgiveness: A philosophical exploration*. New York: Cambridge University Press.

Grossman, David (1995). *On killing: The psychological cost of learning to kill in war and society*. New York: E-reads/E-rights.

Grossman, David (2010). *To the end of the land*. New York: Vintage.

Grotstein, James (1995). *Splitting and projective identification*. Northvale, NJ: Jason Aronson.

Halley, Janet (2008). Rape in Berlin: Reconsidering the criminalization of rape in the international law of armed conflict. *Melbourne Journal of International Law, 9*, 2–46.

Hardin, Russell (2004). *Trust and trustworthiness*. New York: Russel Sage Foundation.

Harrell, Margaret C., and Berglass, Nancy (2011). *Losing the battle: The challenge of military suicide*. Washington, DC: Center for a New American Security.

Held, Barbara (2004). The negative side of positive psychology. *Journal of Humanistic Psychology, 44*(1), 9–46.

Herman, Judith Lewis (1992). *Trauma and recovery*. New York: Basic Books.

Hill, Thomas (1971). Kant on imperfect duty and supererogation. *Kant-Studien, 62*, 55–76.

Hochschild, Arlie Russell (1983). *The managed heart.* Berkeley: University of California Press.

Hoge, Charles (2010). *Once a warrior always a warrior.* Guilford, CT: Globe Pequot Press.

Homer (1990). *The Iliad* (Robert Fagles, Trans.). New York: Penguin.

Hoppin, Meredith Clarke (1990). What happens in Philoctetes? In Harold Bloom (Ed.), *Sophocles* (pp. 137–60). New York: Chelsea House.

Huebner, Bryce (2011). Genuinely collective emotions. *European Journal for the Philosophy of Science, 1*(1), 89–118.

Hume, David (1739/1968). *A treatise on human nature* (Selby-Bigge, Ed.). London: Oxford University Press.

Hurley, Elisa, and Macnamara, Coleen (2010). Beyond belief: Toward a theory of reactive attitudes. *Philosophical Papers, 39*(3), 373–99.

Jack, Rachael E., et al. (2012). Facial expressions of emotion are not culturally universal. *Proceedings of the National Academy of Sciences, 109*(19), 7241–44.

James, William (2003). What is an emotion? (selections). In C. Robert Solomon (Ed.), *What is an emotion?: Classic and contemporary readings* (pp. 66–76). New York: Oxford University Press.

Jones, Karen (2004). Trust and terror. In Margaret Urban Walker and Peggy DesAutels (Eds.), *Moral psychology: Feminist ethics and social theory* (pp. 3–18). Lanham, MD: Rowman and Littlefield.

Jones, Karen (2012). Trustworthiness. *Ethics, 123*(1), 61–85.

Kahn, Paul W. (2008). *Sacred violence: Torture, terror, and sovereignty.* Ann Arbor: University of Michigan Press.

Kant, Immanuel (1964). *The doctrine of virtue, part II of the Metaphysics of Morals* (Mary J. Gregor, Trans.). Philadelphia: University of Pennsylvania Press.

Kant, Immanuel (1974). *Anthropology from a pragmatic point of view* (Mary J. Gregor, Trans.). The Hague: Nijoff.

Kasher, Asa, and Yadlin, Amos (2006). Military ethics of fighting terror: Principles. *Philosophia, 34*(1), 75–84.

Kelty, Ryan, Kleykamp, Meredith, and Segal, David R (2010). The military and the transition to adulthood. *The Future of Children, 20*(1), 181–207.

Kohut, Heinz (1971). *The analysis of self.* Madison, CT: International Universities Press.

Kohut, Heinz (1977). *The restoration of the self.* Madison, CT: International Universities Press.

Kohut, Heinz (1984). *How does analysis cure?* Chicago: University of Chicago Press.

Konstan, David (2001). Murder among friends: Violation of "Philia" in Greek tragedy. (Review of Elizabeth Belfiore's book). *American Journal of Philology, 122*(2), 240–74.

Konstan, David (2006). *The emotions of the Ancient Greeks: Studies in Aristotle and classical literature.* Toronto: University of Toronto Press.

Kukla, Rebecca, and Lance, Mark Norris (2009). *"Yo!" and "lo!": The pragmatic topography of the space of reasons.* Cambridge, MA: Harvard University Press.

Kutz, Christopher (2000). *Ethics and law for a collective age.* New York: Cambridge University Press.

Laertius, Diogenes (1972). *Lives of eminent philosophers.* Cambridge, MA: Loeb Classical Library.

Lance, Mark, and Kukla, Rebecca (2013). Leave the gun; Take the cannoli! The pragmatic topography of second-person calls. *Ethics, 123*(3), 456–78.

Lansky, Melvin R. (1992). *Fathers who fail: Shame and psychopathology in the family system.* Hillsdale, NJ: Analytic Press.

Lansky, Melvin R. (1995). Shame and the scope of psychoanalytic understanding. *American Behavioral Scientist, 38*(8), 1076–90.

Lansky, Melvin R. (2003a). Modification of the ego ideal and the problem of forgiveness in Sophocles' Philoctetes. *Psychoanalysis & Contemporary Thought, 26*(4), 463–91.

Lansky, Melvin R. (2003b). The "incompatible idea" revisited: The oft-invisible ego-ideal and shame dynamics. *American Journal of Psychoanalysis, 63*(4), 365–76.

Lansky, Melvin R. (2004). Trigger and screen: Shame dynamics and the problem of instigation in Freud's dreams. *Journal of the American Academy of Psychoanalysis and Dynamic Psychiatry, 32*(3), 441–68.

Lansky, Melvin R. (2007). Unbearable shame, splitting, and forgiveness in the resolution of vengefulness. *Journal of the American Psychoanalytic Association, 55*(2), 571–93.

Lazar, Seth (2010). The responsibility dilemma for Killing in War: A review essay. *Philosophy and Public Affairs, 38*(2), 180–232.

Lear, Jonathan (2003). *Therapeutic action: An earnest plea for irony.* London: Karnac Books.

Lear, Jonathan (2006). *Radical hope: Ethics in the face of cultural devastation.* Cambridge, MA: Harvard University Press.

Lewis, Helen B. (1971). *Shame and guilt in neurosis.* New York: International Universities Press.

Lipps, T. (1903). Einfühlung, Innere Nachahmung und Organempfindung. *Archiv für gesamte Psychologie, 1*, 465–519.

Litz, Brett T. (2014). Clinical heuristics and strategies for service members and veterans with war-related PTSD. *Psychoanalytic Psychology, 31*(2), 192.

Litz, Brett, Stein, Nathan, Delaney, Eileen, Lebowitz, Leslie, Nash, William P., et al. (2009). Moral injury and moral repair in war veterans: A preliminary model and intervention strategy. *Clinical Psychology Review, 29*(8), 695–706.

Luban, David (2014). Risk-taking and force protection. In Yitzhak Benbaji and Naomi Sussman (Eds.), *Reading Walzer* (pp. 277–301). London: Routledge.

MacKinnon, Catherine (2006). *Are women human? and other international dialogues.* Cambridge, MA: Harvard University Press.

Macnamara, Coleen (2011). Holding others responsible. *Philosophical Studies, 152*, 81–102.

Macnamara, Coleen (2012). "Screw you" & "thank you." *Philosophical Studies, 130*(2), 120–40.

Maguen, Shira, and Litz, Brett (2012). Moral injury in the context of war. <http://www.ptsd.va.gov/professional/pages/moral_injury_at_war.asp%3E, accessed March 6, 2012.

Marshall, S. L. A. (2000). *Men against fire: The problem of battle command.* Norman: University of Oklahoma Press.

Martin, Adrienne M. (2008). Hope and exploitation. *Hastings Center Report, 38*(5), 49–55.

Martin, Adrienne M. (2010). Owning up and lowering down: The power of apology. *Journal of Philosophy, 107*(10), 534–53.

Martin, Adrienne M. (2011). Hopes and dreams. *Philosophy and Phenomenological Research, 83*(1), 148–73.

Martin, Adrienne M. (2013). *How we hope.* Princeton, NJ: Princeton University Press.

McEwen, Bruce S., and Lasley, Elizabeth Norton (2002). *The end of stress as we know it.* Washington, DC: Joseph Henry Press.

McFarland, Dennis (2013). *Nostalgia.* New York: Pantheon.

McGeer, Victoria (2012). Co-reactive attitudes and the making of moral community. In C. MacKenzie and R. Langdon (Eds.), *Emotions, imagination and moral reasoning.* Macquarie Monographs in Cognitive Science. Hove, UK: Psychology Press.

McLaughlin, James. (1991). Clinical and theoretical aspects of enactment. *Journal of American Psychoanalytic Association, 39*, 595–614.

McMahan, Jeff (2009). *Killing in war.* Oxford: Oxford University Press.

McMahan, Jeff (2010). The just distribution of harm between combatants and noncombatants. *Philosophy and Public Affairs, 38*(4), 342–79.

Meineck, Peter, and Konstan, David (Eds.). (2014), *Combat trauma and the Ancient Greeks*. New York: Palgrave Macmillan.

Miller, William Ian (2003). *Faking it*. New York: Oxford University Press.

Morris, Herbert (1976). *On guilt and innocence*. Berkeley: University of California Press.

Moskos, Charles (1988). *A call to civic service: National service for country and community*. New York: Free Press.

Murphy, Jeffrie G. (1999). Shame creeps through guilt and feels like retribution. *Law and Philosophy: An International Journal for Jurisprudence and Legal Philosophy, 18*(4), 327–44.

Nash, William P., and Westphal, Richar' (2011). Trauma, loss, and moral injury: Different approaches for preven. .ı and treatment. *Armed Forces Public Health Conference* (Hampton, VA).

Nash, William P., Silva, Caroline, and Litz, Brett (2009). The historic origins of military and veteran mental health stigma and the stress injury model as a means to reduce it. *Psychiatric Annals, 39*(8), 789–94.

Nash, William P., et al. (2011). Comprehensive soldier fitness, battlemind, and the stress continuum model: Military organizational approaches to prevention. In Josef I. Ruzek et al. (Eds.), *Caring for veterans with deployment-related stress disorders* (pp. 193–214). Washington, DC: American Psychological Association.

Neff, Kristin D. (2003). Self-compassion: An alternative conceptualization of a healthy attitude toward oneself. *Self and Identity, 2*(2), 85–101.

Nietzsche, Friedrich (1994). *On the genealogy of morality* (Keith Ansell-Pearson, Ed.). New York: Cambridge University Press.

Nussbaum, Martha Craven (2001). *Upheavals of thought: The intelligence of emotions*. Cambridge: Cambridge University Press.

Pettit, Philip (1995). The cunning of trust. *Philosophy and Public Affairs, 224*(3), 202–25.

Pettit, Philip (2004). Hope and its place in mind. *Annals of the American Academy of Political and Social Science, 592*, 152–65.

Pettit, Philip (2009). *Made with words: Hobbes on language, mind, and politics*. Princeton, NJ: Princeton University Press.

Pfaff (Tony), Charles A. (2011). Resolving the *ethical challenges in an era of persistent conflict*. Professional Military Ethics Monograph Series. Carlisle, PA: Strategic Studies Institute.

Pfaff (Tony), Charles A. (2012). *Resolving the ethical challenges of irregular war* (Unpublished doctoral dissertation). Washington, DC: Georgetown University.

Pigman, G. W. (1995). Freud and the history of empathy. *International Journal of Psycho-Analysis, 76*(2), 237–56.

Plant, E. Ashby, Hyde, Janet Shibley, Keltner, Dacher, and Devine, Patricia G. (2000). The gender stereotyping of emotions. *Pyschology of Women Quarterly, 24*, 81–92.

Rawls, John (1971). *A theory of justice* (Rev. ed.). Cambridge, MA: Harvard University Press.

Reivich, Karen J., Seligman, Martin E. P., and McBride, Sharon (2011). Master resilience training in the U.S. Army. *American Psychologist, 66*(1), 25–34.

Reivich, Karen, and Shatte, Andrew (2002). *The resilience factor.* New York: Broadway Books.

Ritchie, Elspeth C. (Ed.). (2011). *Combat and operational behavioral health.* Fort Detrick, MD: Office of the Surgeon General, U.S. Army.

Roberts, Mary Louise (2013). *What soldiers do: Sex and the American GI in World War II France.* Chicago: University of Chicago Press.

Roberts, Robert Campbell (2003). *Emotions: An essay in aid of moral psychology.* Cambridge: Cambridge University Press.

Roberts, Robert Campbell (2013). Justice as an emotion dispositon. In John Deigh (Ed.), *On emotions: Philosophical essays* (pp. 14–28). New York: Oxford University Press.

Ryan, Cheyney (2009). *The chickenhawk syndrome: War, sacrifice, and personal responsibility.* London: Rowman and Littlefield.

Sandridge, Norman (2008). Feeling vulnerable, but not too vulnerable: Pity in Sophocles' Oedipus Coloneius, Ajax and Philoctetes. *Classical Journal, 103*(4), 443–48.

Schechtman, Marya (2001). Empathic access: The missing ingredient in personal identity. *Philosophical Explorations: An International Journal for the Philosophy of Mind and Action, 4*(2), 95–111.

Searle, John (2009). *Making the social world.* New York: Oxford University Press.

Segal, Charles (1995). *Sophocles' tragic world.* Cambridge, MA: Harvard University Press.

Seligman, Martin E. P. (2011). *Flourish: A visionary new understanding of happiness and well-being.* New York: Free Press.

Seligman, Martin E. P., and Fowler, Raymond D. (2011). Comprehensive soldier fitness and the future of psychology. *American Psychologist, 66*(1), 82–86.

Seneca (1989). *Epistulae morales* (Richard Gummere, Trans.). Cambridge, MA: Harvard University Press.

Seneca (1995). *Seneca: Moral and political essays.* (J. M. Cooper and J. F. Procopé, Trans.) Cambridge: Cambridge University Press.

Sepinwall, Amy (2010). *Responsibility for group transgressions* (Unpublished doctoral dissertation). Washington, DC: Georgetown University.

Shay, Jonathan (1994). *Achilles in Vietnam: Combat trauma and the undoing of character*. New York: Touchstone.

Shay, Jonathan (2002). *Odysseus in America: Combat trauma and the trials of homecoming*. New York: Scribner's.

Sherman, Nancy (1988). Common sense and uncommon virtue. *Midwest Studies in Philosophy, 13*, 97–114.

Sherman, Nancy (1992). Hamartia and virtue. In Amelie O. Rorty (Ed.), *Essays on Aristotle's Poetics* (pp. 177–96). Princeton, NJ: Princeton University Press.

Sherman, Nancy (1995). The moral perspective and psychoanalytic quest. *Journal of the American Academy of Psychoanalysis, 23*(2), 223–42.

Sherman, Nancy (1997a). Kantian virtue: Priggish or passional? In Andrew Reaths, Barbara Herman, and Christine Korsgaard (Eds.), *Reclaiming the history of ethics: Essays for John Rawls* (pp. 270–96).Cambridge: Cambridge University Press.

Sherman, Nancy (1997b). *Making a necessity of virtue: Aristotle and Kant on virtue*. Cambridge: Cambridge University Press.

Sherman, Nancy (1998a). Concrete Kantian respect. *Social Philosophy and Policy, 15*(1), 119–48.

Sherman, Nancy (1998b). Empathy and imagination. *Philosophy of Emotions, Midwest Studies in Philosophy, 22*, 82–119.

Sherman, Nancy (1998c). Empathy, respect, and humanitarian Intervention. *Ethics and International Affairs, 12*, 103–19.

Sherman, Nancy (2004). Virtue and emotional demeanor. In Anthony Manstead, Nico Frijda, and Agneta Fischer (Eds.), *Feelings and emotions: Interdisciplinary explorations* (pp. 441–54). The Amsterdam Symposium. Cambridge: Cambridge University Press.

Sherman, Nancy (2005a). *Stoic warriors: The ancient philosophy behind the military mind*. New York: Oxford University Press.

Sherman, Nancy (2005b). The look and feel of virtue. In Christopher Gill (Ed.), *Norms, virtue, and objectivity: Issues in ancient and modern ethics* (pp. 59–82). Oxford: Oxford University Press.

Sherman, Nancy (2009). The fate of a warrior culture: Nancy Sherman on Jonathan Lear's *Radical Hope. Philosophical Studies: An International Journal for Philosophy in the Analytic Tradition, 144*(1), 71–80.

Sherman, Nancy (2010). *The untold war: Inside the hearts, minds, and souls of our soldiers*. New York: Oxford University Press.

Sherman, Nancy (2013). Guilt in war. In John Deigh (Ed.), *On emotions* (pp. 179–97). New York: Oxford University Press.

Sherman, Nancy (2014a). He gave me his hand but took my bow: Trust and Trustworthiness. In Peter Meineck and David Konstan (Ed.), *Combat trauma and the Ancient Greeks* (pp. 207–24). New York: Palgrave Macmillan.

Sherman, Nancy (2014b). Self-empathy and moral repair. In Sabine Roeser and Cain Todd (Eds.), *Emotions and values* (pp. 183–98). Oxford: Oxford University Press.

Sherman, Nancy (1999). The analyst as Stoic sage.

Sherman, Nancy, and White, Heath (2003). Intellectual virtue: Emotions, luck, and the Ancients. In Michael DePaul and Linda Zagzebski (Eds.), *Intellectual virtue: Perspectives from ethics and epistemology* (pp. 34–54). Oxford: Clarendon Press.

Smith, Adam (1759/2000). *The theory of moral sentiments.* New York: Prometheus.

Smith, Angela M. (2005). Responsibility for attitudes: Activity and passivity in mental life. *Ethics, 115*(2), 236–71.

Smith, Angela M. (2007). On being responsible and holding responsible. *Journal of Ethics: An International Philosophical Review, 11*(4), 465–84.

Snyder, C. R., Lopez, Shane, and Pedrotti, Jennifer (2011). *Positive psychology: The scientific and practical explorations of human strengths* (2nd ed.). Los Angeles: Sage Publications.

Solomon, Andrew (2012). *Far from the tree: Parents, children and the search for identity.* New York: Simon and Schuster.

Sophocles (2007a). Ajax. In *Four Tragedies: Ajax, Women of Trachis, Electra, Philoctetes* (Peter Meineck and Paul Woodruff, Trans.), pp. 1-62 Indianapolis: Hackett.

Sophocles (2007b). Philoctetes. In *Four Tragedies: Ajax, Women of Trachis, Electra, Philoctetes* (Peter Meineck and Paul Woodruff, Trans.), pp. 187-253. Indianapolis: Hackett.

Sorce, James F., Emde, Robert, Campos, Joseph J. and Klinnert, Mary D. (1985). Maternal emotional signaling: Its effect on the visual cliff behavior of 1-year-olds. *Developmental Psychology, 21*(1), 195–200.

Stephens, J. Ceri (1995). The wound of Philoctetes. *Mnemosune, 48*(2), 153–68.

Stern, Daniel (1985). *The interpersonal world of the infant.* New York: Basic.

Stern, Jessica (2010). *Denial: A memoir of terror.* New York: HarperCollins.

Stockdale, James B. (1995). *Thoughts of a philosophical fighter pilot.* Stanford: Hoover Press.

Strack, F., Martin, L., and Stepper S. (1988). Inhibiting and facilitating conditions of the human smile. *Journal of Personality and Social Psychology, 54,* 768–77.

Strawson, Galen (2004). Against Narrativity. *Ratio: An International Journal of Analytic Philosophy, 17*(4), 428–52.

Strawson, P. F. (1962/1993). Freedom and resentment. In John Fischer and Mark Ravizza (Eds.), *Perspectives on moral responsibility* (pp. 45–66). Ithaca: Cornell University Press.

Tannen, Deborah (2005). *Conversational style: Talk among friends.* New York: Oxford University Press.

Taylor, Gabrielle (1985). *Pride, shame and guilt.* Oxford: Oxford University Press.

Terrio, Heidi, et al. (2009). Traumatic brain injury screening: Preliminary findings in a US Army Brigade Combat Team. *Journal of Head Trauma Rehabilitation, 24*(1), 14–23.

Titchener, Edward Bradford (1909). *Lectures on the experimental psychology of the thought-processes.* New York: Macmillan.

Tollefsen, Deborah Perron (2003). Participant reactive attitudes and collective responsibility. *Philosophical Explorations: An International Journal for the Philosophy of Mind and Action, 6* (3), 218–35.

Velleman, J. David (2001). The genesis of shame. *Philosophy and Public Affairs, 30*(1), 27–52.

Velleman, J. David (2003). Don't worry, feel guilty. *Philosophy: Journal of the Royal Institute of Philosophy, 52* (Suppl.), 235–48.

Walker, David (2010). *Narrating identity: Career soldiers anticipating exit from the British Army* (Unpublished doctoral dissertation). Durham University.

Walker, Margaret Urban (2006). *Moral repair: Reconstructing moral relations after wrongdoing.* New York: Cambridge University Press.

Wallace, R. Jay (1996). *Responsibility and the moral sentiments.* Cambridge, MA: Harvard University Press.

Walzer, Michael (1977). *Just and unjust wars: A moral argument with historical illustrations.* New York: Basic.

Watson, Gary (2004). *Agency and answerability.* New York: Oxford University Press.

Williams, Bernard (1973). *Problems of the self.* Cambridge: Cambridge University Press.

Williams, Bernard (1993). *Shame and necessity.* Berkeley: University of California Press.

Williams, Bernard (1995). *Making sense of humanity.* Cambridge: Cambridge University Press.

Wilson, J., Friedman, M., and Lindy, J. (2001). *Treating psychological trauma and PTSD.* Guilford, CT: Guilford Press.

Wolf, Susan (2010). *Meaning in life and why it matters.* Princeton, NJ: Princeton University Press.

Wollheim, Richard (1984). *The thread of life*. Cambridge MA: Harvard University Press.

Woodruff, Paul (2011). *The Ajax dilemma: Justice, fairness, and rewards*. New York: Oxford University Press.

Wright, James E. (2012). *Those who have borne the battle: A history of America's wars and those who fought them*. New York: Public Affairs.

Zohar, Noam (1993). Collective war and individualistic ethics: Against the conscription of "self-defense." *Political Theory, 21*(4), 606–22.

CREDITS

Index